MESSAGE OF THE FATHERS OF THE CHURCH
General Editor: Thomas Halton

Volume 6

MESSAGE OF THE FATHERS OF THE CHURCH

Early Christian Baptism and the Catechumenate

Italy, North Africa, and Egypt

Thomas M. Finn

A Michael Glazier Book
THE LITURGICAL PRESS
Collegeville, Minnesota

A Michael Glazier Book published by The Liturgical Press

Cover design by Lillian Brulc

1   2   3   4   5   6   7   8   9

Library of Congress Cataloging-in-Publication Data

Finn, Thomas M. (Thomas Macy), 1927–
    Early Christian baptism and the catechumenate : Italy, North
Africa, and Egypt / Thomas M. Finn.
        p.   cm. — (Message of the fathers of the church ; v. 6)
    "A Michael Glazier book."
    Includes bibliographical references and index.
    ISBN 0-8146-5346-4. — ISBN 0-8146-5318-9 (pbk.)
    1. Baptism—History—Early church, ca. 30-600.   2. Conversion-
-History of doctrines—Early church, ca. 30-600.   3. Italy—Church
history.   4. Africa, North—Church history.   5. Egypt—Church
history.   6. Christian literature, Early—History and criticism.
I. Title.   II. Series.
BV803.F54   1992
265'.13'09015—dc20   92-12401
                                                                  CIP

For Marielena—
And she loved with salvation,
and guarded with kindness,
and declared with grandeur.
Hallelujah.
Odes of Solomon, 19:11

Contents

Editor's Introduction

The *Message of the Fathers of the Church* is a companion series to The *Old Testament* and The *New Testament Message*. It was conceived and planned in the belief that Scripture and Tradition worked hand in hand in the formation of the thought, life and worship of the primitive Church. Such a series, it was felt, would be a most effective way of opening up what has become virtually a closed book to present-day readers, and might serve to stimulate a revival in interest in patristic studies in step with the recent, gratifying resurgence in scriptural studies.

The term "Fathers" is usually reserved for Christian writers marked by orthodoxy of doctrine, holiness of life, ecclesiastical approval, and antiquity. "Antiquity" is generally understood to include writers down to Gregory the Great (+604) or Isidore of Seville (+636) in the West, and John Damascene (+749) in the East. In the present series, however, greater elasticity has been encouraged, and quotations from writers not noted for orthodoxy will sometimes be included in order to illustrate the evolution of the Message on particular doctrinal matters. Likewise, writers later than the mid-eighth century will sometimes be used to illustrate the continuity of tradition on matters like sacramental theology or liturgical practice.

An earnest attempt was made to select collaborators on a broad interdisciplinary and interconfessional basis, the chief consideration being to match scholars who could handle the Fathers in their original languages with subjects in which they had already demonstrated a special interest and competence. About the only editorial directive given to the selected contributors was that the

Fathers, for the most part, should be allowed to speak for themselves and that they should speak in readable, reliable modern English. Volumes on individual themes were considered more suitable than volumes devoted to individual Fathers, each theme, hopefully, contributing an important segment to the total mosaic of the early Church, one, holy, catholic and apostolic. Each volume has an introductory essay outlining the historical and theological development of the theme, with the body of the work mainly occupied with liberal citations from the Fathers in modern English translation and a minimum of linking commentary. Short lists of Suggested Further Readings are included; but dense, scholarly footnotes were actively discouraged on the pragmatic grounds that such scholarly shorthand has other outlets and tends to lose all but the most relentlessly esoteric reader in a semi-popular series.

At the outset of his *Against Heresies* Irenaeus of Lyons warns his readers "not to expect from me any display of rhetoric, which I have never learned, or any excellence of composition, which I have never practiced, or any beauty or persuasiveness of style, to which I make no pretensions." Similarly, modest disclaimers can be found in many of the Greek and Latin Fathers, and all too often, unfortunately, they have been taken at their word by an uninterested world. In fact, however, they were often highly educated products of the best rhetorical schools of their day in the Roman Empire, and what they have to say is often as much a lesson in literary and cultural, as well as in spiritual, edification.

St. Augustine, in *The City of God* (19.7), has interesting reflections on the need for a common language in an expanding world community; without a common language a man is more at home with his dog than with a foreigner as far as intercommunication goes, even in the Roman Empire, which imposes on the nations it conquers the yoke of both law and language with a resultant abundance of interpreters. It is hoped that in the present world of continuing language barriers the contributors to this series will prove opportune interpreters of the perennial Christian message.

Thomas Halton

Acknowledgments

I owe a debt of gratitude to many and wish first to acknowledge with gratitude permissions from the following authors, journals, publishers, and serials to publish from their copyrighted texts:

Rev. Thomas L. Campbell, *Dionysius: The Pseudo-Areopagite: The Ecclesiastical Hierarchy* 2:1-3, Studies in Sacred Theology, 2nd series, 83 (originally published, Washington: The Catholic University of America Press, 1955).

The Catholic University of America Press, the Fathers of the Church Series (1946-), ed. Thomas Halton, the following volumes:

FC 1 (J. Merique, trans.): *The Shepherd of Hermas:* The Third Vision, 3; The Ninth Parable, 14.

FC 6 (T. Falls, trans.): *Justin Martyr: The First Apology,* chs. 61, 65, 67.

FC 23 (S. Wood, trans.): *Clement of Alexandria: Christ the Tutor:* Book 1, 6:5-28; Book 3, 12:101.

FC 34 (E. Hunt, trans.): *Pope Leo the Great: Epistle* 16, 68-77.

FC 38 (M. Muldowney, trans.): *Augustine: Sermon* 227.

FC 44 (R. Deferrari, trans.): *Ambrose: On the Sacraments, Homilies* 1-4.

FC 51 (R. Donna, trans.): *Cyprian, Letters* 60, 70.

FC 64 (A. Stephenson, trans.): *Cyril of Jerusalem: Catecheses* 1-3.

FC 67 (R. DeSimone, trans.): *Novatian: On the Trinity* 29.

FC 81 (R. Heine, trans.): *Origen: Homily 5, On Exodus,* 1-2.

Doubleday, a division of Bantam Doubleday Dell Publishing Group, Inc., *The Gospel According to Philip,* fragments 22, 37,

41, 47, 51, 58, 59, 60, 67, 68, 72, 78, 79, 80, 83, 84, 86, 90, 92, 94, 106, 107, from Bentley Layton, ed., *The Gnostic Scriptures: A New Translation with Annotations and Introductions* (Garden City, 1987); also *The Odes of Solomon,* 11, 19, 42, from James Charlesworth, ed., *The Old Testament Pseudepigrapha,* vol. 2 (Garden City, 1985).

Thomas Halton, "Zeno of Verona: Invitations to the Baptismal Font," from *Baptism: Ancient Liturgies and Patristic Texts,* ed. A. Hamman, trans. T. Halton (Staten Island: Alba House, 1967) 64–66.

Paulist Press, *Didache* 1–7, from J. Kleist, trans., Ancient Christian Writers 6 (New York: Paulist Press 1948); also, *Egeria: Diary of a Pilgrimage* 45–47, from ACW 38 (1970), trans. G. Gingras.

St. Paul Publications, E. Yarnold, ed., *The Awe-Inspiring Rites of Initiation* (Slough, UK, 1972), the following: John Chrysostom, *Baptismal Homily* 11; Theodore of Mopsuestia, *Baptismal Homily* 3.

Theological Studies, ed. R. J. Daly, Innocent I, *Epistle 25, to Decentius,* from G. Ellard, "How Fifth Century Rome Administered the Sacraments," TS 9 (1948) 5–11.

Without the Woodstock Theological Center Library at Georgetown University and its wealth of patristic holdings this study of early Christian baptism and the catechumenate might never have seen the light of published day. Special thanks are due to its excellent professional staff for their unfailing generosity and always timely help: Rev. Eugene M. Rooney, S.J., Sr. Alma Bingnear, S.N.D., Robert W. Bauchspies, Jr., and Mr. Paul Osmanski.

I am also deeply grateful to the general editor, Thomas Halton, professor of Greek and Latin at the Catholic University of America, for the opportunity to do the fifth and sixth volumes in the Message of the Fathers of the Church series, for his deft editorial hand, and for his invaluable bibliographical help.

In addition, I wish to acknowledge that several grants from the National Endowment for the Humanities and from the College of William and Mary, and a Joseph H. Malone Fellowship from the National Council on U.S.-Arab Relations enabled me to do preliminary studies, the fruits of which nourish the General Introduction and the chapters on Italy, North Africa, and Egypt.

Finally, I am once again pleased to acknowledge my lifelong indebtedness to the late Rev. Johannes Quasten, professor of ancient Church history and Christian archaeology at the Catholic University of America, who initiated me into the world of the Fathers of the Church and ancient Christian liturgy.

Abbreviations

ACW	*Ancient Christian Writers*
ANF	*Ante-Nicene Fathers*
BAP	*Baptism: Ancient Liturgies and Patristic Texts,* ed. A. Hamman, trans. Thomas Halton. Staten Island: Alba House, 1967
CCL	*Corpus Christianorum Series Latina*
CSCO	*Corpus Scriptorum Christianorum Orientalium*
CSEL	*Corpus Scriptorum Ecclesiasticorum Latinorum*
DBL	*Documents of the Baptismal Liturgy,* ed. E. C. Whitaker. 2nd ed., London: SPCK, 1970.
FC	*Fathers of the Church*
FP	*Florilegium Patristicum*
LCC	*Library of Christian Classics*
Mansi	Johannes D. Mansi, ed., *Sacrorum Conciliorum nova et amplissima collectio.* Paris, 1901
NCE	*New Catholic Encyclopedia*
NPNF	*Nicene and Post-Nicene Fathers*
PG	*Patrologia Graeca*
PL	*Patrologia Latina*
PO	*Patrologia Orientalis*
PS	*Patrologia Syriaca*
Quasten	Johannes Quasten, *Patrology.* 3. vols. Utrecht-Antwerp/Westminster, Md.: Spectrum/Newman, 1950 ff.; vol. 4, ed. Angelo Di Berardino, trans. Placid Solari. Westminster, Md.: Christian Classics, 1986
SC	*Sources Chrétiennes*
SCA	*Studies in Christian Antiquity*
SL	*Studia Liturgica*
SeT	*Studi e Testi*
TS	*Theological Studies*
TU	*Texte und Untersuchungen*

General Introduction

Baptism, whether ancient or modern, is the hinge upon which Christian identity turns. To understand what the rite discloses about Christian identity today, however, one must understand what it disclosed in antiquity. This book is about baptism "then," specifically, baptism in the first five Christian centuries.

Practically from the beginning Christians insisted, and the creeds taught, that there was one baptism for the forgiveness of sins, just as there was one Lord and one faith. The rite, however, presented many faces, adopted many shapes, and yielded many shades of meaning. As a result, a narrative history of baptism is neither practicable nor desirable. Not practicable, because the evidence is fragmentary, leaving large gaps. Not desirable, because when it comes to the deep matters of the human heart, in this case salvation, it is preferable to let people speak for themselves.

Yet to do so poses a special problem, because the early Christians spoke in ancient tongues (Armenian, Coptic, Greek, Latin, Syriac), lived in a remote world that encompassed many complex histories and cultures, and expressed their deepest experiences largely in the language of myth, symbol, and drama. In short, what they have to say is not easily accessible. As a result, one needs help to hear and understand them. These volumes are designed to help. What the early Christians have to say about baptism and the preparations for it is organized into Volumes 5 and 6 of this series, which represent the five major cultural areas: Volume 5: West Syria (ch. 1), East Syria (ch. 2); Volume 6: Italy (ch. 1), North Africa (ch. 2), and Egypt (ch. 3). In addition to a General Introduction, each chapter has an introductory section that depicts the establishment of Christianity in the area together with its distinctive baptismal characteristics, themes, preparations, and practices. The readings, arranged chronologically, are representative rather than comprehensive and have their own introduc-

1

tions. Preference has been given to those forms of baptismal teaching and practice that the ordinary Christian heard and followed. Prominent are the homily, hymn, and Church-order book (a pastoral book of rituals and rules). Correspondence, however, is in evidence (Italy and North Africa), as are the baptismal treatise (North Africa) and sayings-collections (East Syria and Egypt). The setting is normally a congregation assembled in church, whether small and rural or large and urban. The occasion is generally instruction, more accurately, that distinctive form of religious instruction called "catechesis," about which more later. The audience is both the faithful and those seeking baptism. Specific form, setting, and occasion are described in connection with each reading.

Accessible translations, where possible, have been used and, where necessary, adapted for the contemporary reader. Some readings have been especially translated for this book. For the reader who wishes to consult the original language, an accessible up-to-date text has been cited for each reading.

Conversion: A Ritual Journey

A striking event in ancient history is the geographical spread of early Christianity from rural Palestine eastward to the Indus Valley and westward all the way to Roman Britain in less than two centuries. Even more striking is its social survival and spread from the religion of an obscure Jewish sect to the established religion of the Roman Empire in a matter of four centuries. The details of survival and spread are discussed in the chapter introductions. In general, however, the new religion moved outward and upward in the backpacks of immigrants. It was a traveling faith, largely urban, which in four centuries moved from synagogue to marketplace to house and, finally, to imperial palace.

The key was conversion, itself a journey, or as the ancients put it, a change ("turning," *epistrephein/conversio*) from one "way of walking" to another. The destination was frequently called "salvation," and many embarked. Jews might journey from one Jewish sect to another in search of a greater righteousness; pagans, from civic religion to mystery cults in search of divinity and immortality; intellectuals from an aimless life to philosophy in search of truth. The readings contain two examples of such philosophical quests (see ch. 1, Justin; and ch. 3, Clement). Indeed, the search for salvation however conceived was a hallmark of the period, often called the "Age of Anxiety." Its anxious roots lay in the shattering changes that saw old ways in flight before the onrush of new ways, especially those represented by the rise of the Roman Empire (27 B.C.E.)—a rise followed by the incursions of the barbarians (ca. 250 C.E.).

Some conversions seemed sudden (like that of Paul of Tarsus) and had a strong emotional overlay (like that of Augustine). Most, however, were gradual, the result of time and testing. For those ancients who sought the Christian "Way," the journey had clearly marked stages: (1) a period of preparation that emphasized instruction and testing and involved personal struggle; (2) penultimate preparations for baptism also characterized by instruction, testing, and ritual struggle; (3) baptismal immersion; and (4) postbaptismal "homecoming" celebrations, which included the Eucharist. In second-century Rome the stages could occupy three years; in fifth-century North Africa they might take the better part of a lifetime or only the weeks of Lent; in first-century East and West Syria and Palestine it might be a matter of days.

Central, however, is the fact that conversion, whether Christian, Jewish, or pagan, was a complex ritual process through which the subjects passed from an old way of life to a new way. They were considered reborn, emerging from the process with a new network of relations and responsibilities, new values, and a new status in society, or as the ancients put it, a "new home and family." Anthropologists are accustomed to call the process "rites of passage" (sometimes, "rites of initiation"), which typically exhibit three phases: (1) rites signaling separation from the "old way"; (2) rites effecting transition from old to new, emphasizing a state of "liminality," or of being on the boundaries *(limina)* between old and new; and (3) rites yielding initiation into the new way of life (or reintegration into the old with a new and different status).

Catechumens and Catechumenate

The rites distinctive of the journey to Christianity developed quickly into a rich, extended, and dramatic liturgical journey. Perhaps more than any other possession of the Church, they account for early Christian survival and spread—such is the power of ritual. In addition, they reveal the fundamental meaning of the Church to early Christians as the place of salvation, more accurately, that community where one finds access to Christ the Savior. For prospective converts, incorporation into the "saving" community (Church), therefore, was the destination of the journey.

Enrollment

The rite that signaled the candidates' separation from their old way of life and launched the journey proper was called "enrollment" or "enlistment." The heart of it was a searching inquiry into their personal life, status, and occupation. From that point on, candidates admitted to the process and enrolled in the Church's "book" journeyed on the boundaries between society and Church—of both but in neither—the subjects of intense and extended catechetical instruction and exorcism.

Instruction

The importance of instruction is suggested by two ancient technical terms. As already noted, "catechesis" was the term for the kind of instruction involved. Its Greek root, *echo,* gives the early Christian sense of the term: Instructions were to be so internalized that they "echoed" not only in one's mind but in one's conduct. As a result, the candidates bore the name "catechumens," designating those under instruction for baptism. Indeed, the whole process of conversion, from enrollment to the threshold of immersion, came to be called the "catechumenate."

The syllabus of instruction was twofold. For the ordinary catechumen it was the Bible as read and commented on in church, often daily. In Origen's Caesarea (ch. 3), for instance, a catechumen in the mid-third century would have heard both the Old and New Testaments, to some extent selectively, over the course of the several years prior to baptism.

For those approved for baptism (called the "competents," the "elect," the "baptizands," or the "photizands"), the syllabus was the creed, which almost invariably was the Nicene Creed, at least from the fourth century on. Orally and article by article the catechist (usually the bishop) delivered the creed to the competents shortly before baptism (the rite came to be called *traditio symboli,* "handing over the creed"). He then commented on the articles, sometimes briefly, sometimes at length. Close to baptism, sometimes as part of the rite, the competents, having committed the creed to memory, were required to make a public profession of faith (*redditio symboli,* "returning the creed"). As evidence of the occasion's drama, Augustine of Hippo has left a record of the public profession made by Marius Victorinus, the celebrated Neoplatonic philosopher (see ch. 2, *Confessions*).

From very early times, however, instruction continued after baptism as well; the focus was the religious significance of the baptismal rites and the Eucharist. Indeed, it is largely from these postbaptismal instructions (often called "mystagogical catecheses") that we discover the early Christian meaning of baptism. As the reader will quickly learn, the theology of the early Christians was the result of symbols deeply lived. The primacy of experience is further underscored by the fact that instruction on the baptismal rites was delayed until after baptism, given usually during the Easter season. Conditioned by ancient mystery-cult practice, the Church felt that the intimate meaning of the ritual drama should be spread before and understood only by the initiated.

Exorcism

Catechesis was only half the battle, and "battle" is the correct word: The purpose of the catechumenate was literally to "re-form" the candidate. Formation rather than information was its thrust ("resocialization," as the social scientist might call it). For the early Christian was persuaded that conduct mirrored conviction. Thus, as the catechumens' convictions changed from old values to new, their conduct had also to change from old ways to new. This formative task was assigned to exorcism, because the obstacle to conversion was a literally terrifying field of forces—physical, psychological, and spiritual—which the catechists identified with graphic specificity: the gods, their cultic processions, the races, the theater, the gladiatorial extravaganzas, every conceivable vice, even the instruments of the Muse of music. Invariably the forces were the institutions of pagan, usually Greco-Roman, culture, and sometimes, especially before Constantine (311/313), when it was a capital crime to be a Christian, the naked power of Rome itself.

The unseen enemy, however, was Satan and his legions—the real obstacle to conversion. The pagan institutions were only their servants. As a result, catechesis was linked to exorcism. For the Holy Spirit to enter, as the catechists put it, the evil spirit had to be driven out. Thus, exorcist was counterpart of catechist. Indeed, by the mid-third century, the exorcist corps at Rome numbered forty-two.

Although the rites differed, the dynamics of exorcism remained fairly constant. They were at their most striking in the solemn exorcism that marked the end of the catechumenate, an ordeal called the "scrutiny." It first appears (ca. 200) in the *Apostolic Tradition* of Hippolytus (ch. 1) as a searching inquiry into the life of the catechumens in order to gauge the quality and progress of their conversion, specifically, to determine whether anything of the "evil spirit" remained. By the late fourth century in North Africa, the rite had become an intense psychological ordeal (see ch. 2, Augustine). It was public, involved a physical examination, an exsufflation (a hissing and spitting) that would lead to the charge of demeaning the emperor were it done to an imperial statue, the imposition of hands, and ringing curses. Held at the end of the vigil on the Saturday night before what is now Palm Sunday, it was presided over by the bishop, who delivered the commands, expelling Satan in the name and power of Christ and the Trinity. Not everyone passed scrutiny, but those who did were anointed on the ears and nose against the possible return of Satan and his legions. These, as already noted, were the competents, or elect, that is, chosen for baptism.

But exorcism, whether daily or in the form of a scrutiny, was an awesome experience calculated to excite lively fear in the candidates and an abhorrence of the very thought of evil. Written into the rite was the early Christian theology of sin, specifically, the fall of Adam and its consequences for his descendants: They were Satan's slaves, enlisted in his ranks and yoked to his service. Perhaps a bizarre practice by modern standards, the early Church nonetheless dramatized in rite and symbol its realistic sense of the sway that culture, habit, and life's addictions held over the individual. But written into the rite as well was the conviction that God, Christ, and the Church could collectively bring to bear on the candidates the power needed to put Satan and the demons to flight, enabling them to break out of his ranks and shed his yoke. The script for exorcism, although beyond detailed reconstruction, was biblical, largely based on the encounters between Jesus and the demons.

Renunciation and Allegiance

Thus "scrutinized," the candidates could now stand on their own two feet and in their own voices formally renounce Satan and his works. Renunciation, which signaled the end of the preliminary rites, took place on the threshold of baptism itself, sometimes, as in the case of North Africa, right after the solemn scrutiny and a week before baptism, or, as was more often the case, just outside the baptistery immediately before baptism. The rite was often coupled with a pledge of allegiance to Christ that spoke of entering his ranks and accepting his yoke. Occasionally, however, the baptismal profession of faith constituted the pledge. In either case, the rite concluded with an anointing of the entire body, apparently for protection against the further assaults of the devil, now formally denounced, and, as was the custom among athletes, in preparation for the decisive Olympic struggle with Satan in the baptismal font. Whatever the precise order, the rites of renunciation and allegiance dramatized the early Christian conviction that conversion to Christ was a long, collaborative ritual process through which catechumens gradually acquired the freedom to break the powerful hold of an old way of life and to embrace the new. That there was nothing routine or automatic about the process is underscored by the fact that some, perhaps many, did not pass scrutiny or survive the renunciation.

Baptism

The journey was almost over. As we have seen, for some it lasted a lifetime, for others, several years, for still others, especially after the Church instituted Lent in the fourth century (see vol. 5, ch. 1, Cyril and Egeria), six weeks. Whatever the duration, the goal was the baptismal font, in its earliest form a stream or river. By mid-third century the font was often a converted domestic bathing facility. Elaborate cruciform and octagonal (occasionally round) baptisteries were the norm in the fourth century and thereafter. The earliest extant baptismal document, the

Didache (vol. 5, ch. 1), speaks of baptism in "living waters," that is, flowing water. There is some indication that streams were diverted to flow through the font. However, the earliest archaeological evidence of a baptistery comes from a Roman garrison town on the Euphrates, Dura Europos, in modern Iraq. It was in a private house converted to a house-church a decade or two before 256, when the building was partially destroyed in a Parthian invasion. The earliest description of a specially built baptistery comes from Jerusalem in the mid-fourth century (see vol. 5, ch. 1, Cyril and Egeria).

Whether stream or richly ornamented building, however, the baptistery was the place of the final act of the sacred drama. Here was what the Latin-speaking Christians called *sacramentum* (sacrament), and the Greek-speaking, *mysterion* (mystery). Although borrowed from Greco-Roman culture, the terms designated those rites that gave the catechumens direct access to Christ as Savior, the heart of which was immersion in water usually consecrated for the purpose. Although liturgical customs differed strikingly, the candidates invariably were naked and immersed in the baptismal water three times in the name of the Father and of the Son and of the Holy Spirit—the medievals would term the water and the words "matter" and "form."

Time and again the question came up: Why such ordinary things as water, oil, gestures, and words for such a sacred event as salvation? Underneath differences of custom lay a widely shared conviction about what happened in the font. Enunciated by Tertullian (ch. 2), who gave the West so much of its theological vocabulary, the answer is fundamental to all early Christian sacramental thinking: "The flesh is the hinge of salvation" *(caro salutis est cardo)*. He explains: "The flesh is washed that the soul may be made spotless; the flesh is anointed that the soul may be consecrated; the flesh is signed [with the cross] that the soul too may be protected; the flesh is overshadowed by the imposition of the hand that the soul may also be illumined by the Spirit; the flesh feeds on the body and blood of Christ so that the soul may be replete with God" (*On the Resurrection of the Flesh* 8).

Symbolic Participation

Tertullian's younger contemporary Origen, however, is the first of the Fathers to address the question of how candidates gained direct access to salvation. The answer lies in the dynamics of symbol, for he says about the three days Christ spent in the tomb that "those who have been taken up into Christ by baptism have been taken up into his death and been buried with him, and will rise with him" (ch. 3, *Homilies on Exodus* 5:2). As a result, he calls baptism the "mystery of the third day." By "mystery" he means immersion in the baptismal water, through which one participates not only in Christ's death and burial but also in his resurrection. Indeed, Origen, who appears to have retrieved it from the Gnostics, is the first Church Father to bring Paul's doctrine of symbolic participation in the death and resurrection of Christ (see Rom 6:1-11) to bear on baptism. As a result, the baptismal font came to be seen as at once a tomb and a womb. Gregory of Nyssa, Origen's disciple, in his *Homily on the Baptism of Christ,* explains that the water which receives the baptismal candidate, like the earth which received Christ's body, is a tomb from which, like a womb, Christ and the newly baptized arise new-born (see vol. 5, ch. 1).

But it is another disciple of Origen, Cyril of Jerusalem, who takes the decisive step. In his baptismal instructions he explains that the recipient of baptism, through the enactment of Christ's death, burial, and resurrection in baptismal rite and symbol, participates in the redemption that these events have accomplished. In short, the rites of baptism give the baptismal candidate living access to redemption through participation in the baptismal drama, especially immersion. Although the Church Fathers distinguish between the historical events of Christ's crucifixion, death, and resurrection as once-for-all and the baptismal ritual, which reenacts them, they insist that "by sharing his sufferings in a symbolic enactment we may really and truly gain salvation" (vol. 5, ch. 1, Cyril of Jerusalem, *Baptismal Catechesis* 2:5). The key is the participatory character of the liturgical symbolism that undergirds baptismal instruction in both East and West.

Culture, however, conditioned perception. Theodore of Mopsuestia (vol. 5, ch. 1), for instance, has a different perspective. Imbued with Neoplatonism, he sees the sacraments as the link between what he calls the "two ages." The first age is the visible and ever-changing world of time, space, and human life and choice; the second, the invisible and immutable future—Paradise regained. The ages are linked invisibly by the risen Christ and visibly by the sacrament, which makes present the second age through sign and symbol enacted in the first. As Theodore sees it, the sacraments make present the second age, or future, because they participate in its reality, the core of which is resurrection. Already achieved by Christ, resurrection, even though inchoative, is Paradise regained for the Christian.

Further east, in Syriac-speaking Christianity (vol. 5, ch. 2) with its deeply Semitic culture, past and present and heaven and earth all intersect in Christ, to whom the sacrament is linked by the Holy Spirit. Everything converges: Creation, the Exodus from Egypt, crossing the Jordan, Christ's baptism, and the Christian's baptism. The Holy Spirit, who hovered over the primal deep, over the Red Sea, over the Jordan, and as the dove over Christ, is the very Spirit who hovers over the baptismal waters, sanctifying the recipient (see vol. 5, ch. 2, Ephrem). Thus, what happened to Christ in the Jordan happens also to the Christian in the baptismal font.

In the West, the emphasis is on representation (anamnesis). First used in the *Apostolic Tradition* of Hippolytus (ch. 1), this biblical term (see 1 Cor 11:23-25; Luke 20:19) is often taken to mean "in memory of" or "commemoration." The underlying sense, however, is that the liturgy of baptism (and the Eucharist) renders present the events signified, especially the hinge event upon which the entire early liturgy turns: the death and resurrection of Christ. Thus, a more adequate translation is "re-presentation." Christ's redeeming death and resurrection are "re-presented" at a later time and in a different place (without being repeated).

Whether East or West, however, the underlying conviction was about the resurrection of Christ, which, as early Christians saw it, shattered the normal boundaries of space and time. For them Christ's resurrection made him and the saving events of his life accessible in their own present through the sacramental liturgy, in this case, baptism.

The Efficacy of Baptism

As for the power of baptism, early Christians were convinced that the sacrament receives its saving power from the Christ who is risen and in glory but who died on the cross. The passion of Christ was literally the crucial event. Meditating on the spear the soldier thrust into Christ's side (see John 19:34-35), the Church Fathers both Eastern and Western see the sacraments of baptism and the Eucharist embodied in the blood and water that gush forth. John Chrysostom (vol. 5, ch.1), for instance, insists that the water came out first and then blood, since, in the order of things, baptism comes first and then the Eucharist; he then adds, "It was the soldier, then, who opened Christ's side and dug through the rampart of the holy temple, but I am the one who has found the treasure and gotten the wealth" (*Baptismal Homily* 3:16).

The catechist is not breaking new ground but only handing on a tradition at least as old as the second century (see ch. 2, Tertullian, *On Baptism* 9) and as far reaching as Jacob of Serugh (vol. 5, ch. 2, *Memra* 7, *On the Baptism of the Law,* ll. 185-191). Indeed, the Council of Florence reflects this ancient tradition when, a thousand years later, its *Decree for the Armenians* explains that the passion of Christ is the "efficient" cause of the sacramental efficacy, including the sacrament of baptism (Mansi 31:1054).

The Pattern of Baptism

Directly related to efficacy is the widespread patristic view of the pattern according to which sacraments accomplish their effects. (Subsequent ages would call it the "institution" of the sacraments.) In the Eucharist, for instance, the pattern is the Last Supper; for baptism it is Christ's own baptism. For both, the power of the sacrament issues from Christ's institution. Tertullian sets the tone for the West when he writes that Christ was fashioning baptism throughout his life, but particularly when he was baptized, walked on water, changed water into wine at Cana, washed the feet of his disciples, and finally (as we have just seen), "when he receives a wound [and] water bursts forth from his side, as the soldier's spear can tell" (ch. 2, *On Baptism* 9). Years later, Ambrose of Milan (ch. 1, *On the Sacraments* 3:4) attempts more precision when he proposes (not persuasively, as it turned out) that Jesus instituted the sacrament when he washed the feet of the disciples at the Last Supper (see John 13:12-18).

For Origen and the Eastern tradition generally, however, the focus is squarely on Christ's own baptism: What happened at the Jordan happens also in the baptismal font. Indeed, the baptismal font is often called "Jordan." Narsai, the East Syrian disciple of Theodore of Mopsuestia, sums up much patristic tradition on the subject when he writes that Christ descended into the water, bathed in it, sanctified it, and conferred on it the power of the Holy Spirit to give life and make it a "womb which begets people spiritually" (vol. 5, ch. 2, *Homily on the Epiphany*, 1. 294). Indeed, Christ entering the Jordan is the pattern to which Egyptian consecratory prayers over the baptismal font appeal (see ch. 3, Serapion; Coptic Rite).

Sacrament as Sign

Thanks largely to Augustine, sacraments came to be regarded as signs composed of "words" and "things," which cause what they signify. He holds that the spoken word is the quintessential human sign because it actualizes what it signifies, that is, it renders its referent present to the mind. As the incarnate Word of God, Christ, therefore, he argues, is the perfect sign because he embodies God. The sacraments, for Augustine, are of the same order—perfect Word—because they are signs that embody Christ to such an extent that even "if Judas baptizes, it is Christ who baptizes" (*Commentary on John* 5:18, 6:7). His contemporary, Leo the Great (ch. 1), puts the matter even more strikingly: "What was visible in Christ has passed over into the sacraments of the church" (*Sermon* 74).

Reminiscent of Tertullian, for whom, as we have seen, the flesh is the hinge of salvation, the point Augustine and Leo seek to maintain is that precisely as signs composed of words, gestures, and material elements, baptism renders accessible the saving action of Christ. As a result, there is an enduring quality established by the words joined to the material elements and celebrated by the minister. Indeed, Augustine and his predecessor Optatus (ch. 2) argue that the recipient of a sacrament receives "something" from the sacrament irrespective of the minister's moral character (i.e., whether he is a known or public sinner) or of his ecclesiastical status (heretic or schismatic). As a result and contrary to North African tradition (see Cyprian, ch. 2), they hold that even when a schismatic (one separated from the Church) or a heretic (one of erroneous belief) baptizes, the sacrament is valid.

Augustine goes even further, arguing that baptism imprints a "mark" ("seal" and "character" are his other terms) on the recipients quite irrespective of their "worthiness" or dispositions, in virtue of which the "benefit" or "grace" of the sacrament revives (see ch. 2, *On Baptism* 10–13). Quite apart, then, from the minister's situation or the recipient's dispositions, Christ offers salvation, or, as the two North Africans also put it, the sacrament is valid. In arguing thus, Optatus and Augustine establish for their medieval successors the distinction between the validity of a properly celebrated sacrament and its fruitfulness: Validity depends on the act of Christ embodied in the sign rather than on the moral character or ecclesiastical situation of the minister; fruitfulness depends on the dispositions of the recipient. Coupled with the patristic doctrine of symbolic participation discussed above, their approach sets the foundation for the medieval teaching that in their very celebration sacraments effect what they signify *(ex opere operato)*.

The Minister

In his incisive way (as we have just seen) Augustine asserts that even if Judas baptizes, it is really Christ who baptizes. Nonetheless, the usual ecclesiastical minister of the sacrament is the bishop. As Chrysostom puts the matter, he is the "visible high priest," whereas the "unseen great High Priest is Christ" (vol. 5, ch. 1, *Baptismal Homily* 11:12). But we learn from Tertullian that presbyters, deacons, and laymen can baptize (see ch. 2, *On Baptism* 17). Ultimately, however, the minister is the Trinity. In commenting on the passive and impersonal baptismal formula used in Syrian Christianity ("N. is baptized in the name . . ."), for instance, both Chrysostom and his friend Theodore of Mopsuestia insist that the sacrament summons Father, Son, and Spirit in their consubstantiality to baptize. Both are convinced (as are the North Africans, Optatus and Augustine) that the visible minister is only instrumental in the hands of the Trinity. As much as the two friends might excoriate a bishop or other minister of baptism for immoral character, moral condition, they hold, cannot impede God's action. Nonetheless, they require orthodox faith in the Trinity for validity. Chrysostom, for instance, argues against the validity of Arian baptism by asserting that unless the minister professes true (Nicene) Trinitarian faith neither remission of sin nor filial adoption is granted (see vol. 5, ch. 1, *Baptismal Homily* 2:26). His conviction was widespread in the fourth-century

East, though not in the West, where the issue was settled by the Council of Arles (314), namely, that neither schism nor heresy could render an otherwise properly celebrated baptism invalid. Medieval theology would clarify the ministerial issue by insisting that the minister need only intend to do what the Church intends done (Council of Florence, *Decree for the Armenians,* Mansi 31:1054).

Faith and Baptism

From the outset faith entered into the very constitution of baptism, not precisely the divine gift by which one believed—that was presupposed, because the norm was adult baptism. Rather, the faith in question was the creed. In one form or another it was elicited from the candidates as they stood in the baptismal pool. In fact, in second-century Rome the creed constituted the form according to which baptism was administered and required the candidates' explicit assent of faith (see ch. 1, *Apostolic Tradition* 20).

At different times different customs obtained. In fourth-century Syria, as we have already seen, the creed was given to the candidates approved for baptism orally, article by article, at the beginning of Lent; they returned it by public profession just before baptism. In North Africa the custom was for the candidate to profess the creed in the presence of the assembled congregation the Sunday before (Easter) baptism and to repeat profession at baptism. Whatever the custom, an explicit act of creedal faith was an integral part of baptism; indeed, many, including Augustine (*Letter to Bonanus* 98:9), call baptism the "sacrament of faith." The Council of Orange (529), looking back over the long journey to the baptismal font, calls the first stirrings, which prompted one to start out on the journey, the "beginnings of faith" (cann. 5, 7, 8, and conclusion; Mansi 8:718).

The inner disposition of the recipient, however, was not thereby downplayed. We have already seen in detail (see above, on catechesis, exorcism) the intense screening process characteristic of the catechumenate. Yet not everyone who passed scrutiny was truly converted. About the unconverted, Gregory of Nyssa (vol. 5, ch. 1) warns, "Though it may be a bold thing to say, yet I will say it and will not shrink; in these cases the water is but water, for the gift of the Holy Spirit in no way appears in him who is thus baptismally born" (*Great Catechetical Oration* 40).

A note of caution. Early Christian baptism had clearly in view adults; yet infants and children (and the incapacitated) were not thereby excluded. In the *Apostolic Tradition* of Hippolytus, for instance, an important rubric enjoins the baptism of children, including infants, ahead of everyone else (see ch. 1). Although the North African Tertullian rejects infant baptism (ch. 2, *On Baptism* 18), Cyprian, bishop of Carthage, who considers Tertullian his "master," urges his people not even to wait the customary eight days after birth to baptize their children (ch. 2, *Letter* 74). Origen (ch. 3) gives the reason. "The church has received from the apostles the custom of administering baptism even to infants," he writes, "for those who have been entrusted with the secrets of the divine mysteries [the apostles] knew very well that all are tainted with the stain of original sin, which must be washed off by water and the spirit" (*Commentary on Romans* 5:9).

Although early Christian baptismal liturgies had primarily in view the adult, they reached out also to embrace infant and incapacitated alike. For that faith that entered into the very constitution of baptism was the faith of the Church. Where circumstance dictated, the Church's faith could supply for the faith of the individual, and, in any case, early Christians did not think that God was hemmed in by the sacraments.

Postbaptismal Rites

What prevents a narrative history of the sacrament of baptism is the sometimes striking variation of rite and custom in time and cultural area. Nowhere is this more apparent than in the rites that followed baptism. For instance, the earliest Church order, the *Didache* (vol. 5, ch. 1), leaves the postbaptismal record blank, whereas the late second-century Roman liturgy paints the portrait of the naked newly baptized coming up out of the font to be greeted by a presbyter and a rich variety of rites.

According to the *Apostolic Tradition* of Hippolytus (ch. 1), first they were anointed with oil in the name of Christ. When dried and dressed, they entered the church, there to be met by the bishop, who imposed his hands and prayed about baptismal remission of sins, rebirth, and grace. He embraced each and then poured blessed oil on their heads, signed them on the forehead, and embraced them with a kiss. The newly baptized then prayed together with the congregation, were welcomed with the kiss of peace, and celebrated their first Eucharist, at which they received a cup of milk mixed with honey and a cup of water (in addition to the bread and wine). This "first Communion" included a homily in which the bishop explained to the newly baptized the meaning of the rites they had just celebrated.

In a comparatively short space of time but in different places with differing customs, the postbaptismal liturgy became a drama in its own right. Although the following picture is a composite, it is nonetheless fairly representative by the late fourth century. As the newly baptized came up out of the baptismal pool, they prayed the Lord's Prayer, sent prayers of intercession heavenward, vested in white garments, received lighted candles, and sometimes were crowned with garlands. They processed to the Eucharist, often chanting Psalm 22 (23), interpreted to extol baptism and the Eucharist (see below, on baptismal typology): "The Lord is my shepherd, I shall not want; he makes me lie down in green pastures. He leads me beside still waters; he restores my soul. . . ."

An entire week of daily Eucharistic celebrations followed in which the newly baptized occupied center stage. A striking feature was instruction in the meaning of the baptismal rites, several sets of which are included in the readings.

The rites reveal the depth and timbre of early Christian thinking about the effects of baptism. The nakedness of the newly baptized as they emerged from the font emphasized rebirth, an image of baptism at least as old as the letters of Paul and John's Gospel. They could pray the Lord's Prayer (Our Father) because they were now new-born and sinless children in that family of which God was Father. Their intercessory prayers were especially valued because they could now speak boldly to their Father, an intimacy claimed particularly by the children of the family. The white garment, the counterpart of the "tunics of shame" they had stripped off (Paul's "old" or "sinful man") before entering the font, dramatized the conviction that they "had put on Christ," that is, possessed the grace of resurrection and immortality. The baptismal candle stressed the sacrament as enlightenment—a theme that first appears in the Letter to the Hebrews (see 6:4) and develops many associations in the early centuries, prominent among them the baptismal gift of faith and the interior renovation accomplished by the grace of baptism. Among others, the *Ordo of Constantinople* (vol. 5, ch. 1) recapitulates the themes by then (ca. 420) deeply traditional:

> As one in need, you lift your hands to heaven. In this you may know how poor you are whom the Master receives, how he enriches your nakedness with his grace, how with the chrism he puts on you the odor of good deeds [a reference to the full anointing before baptism], how with the oil, he makes you shine brilliantly, how you lay aside your corruption in the grave of the bath, how the Spirit raises you up to a new life, how he clothes your body with shining garments, how the lamps you hold in your hands symbolize the illumination of the soul.

Where the work of baptism was crowned by coronation—doubtless drawn from marriage customs—the rite emphasized an ancient theme: baptism as marriage between Christ and the newly baptized. Reflecting an ancient tradition, for instance, John Chrysostom says to the newly enrolled before him: "Come let me talk to you as I would to a bride about to be led to the holy nuptial chamber. . . . But let no one who hears these words of mine fall into a crass or carnal interpretation. I am talking of the soul and its salvation" (vol. 5, ch. 1, *Baptismal Homily* 1:3-4; see also vol. 5, ch. 2, Jacob of Serugh, *Memra* 7, ll. 29-36).

Generally, the members of the congregation tendered the newly baptized a familial embrace. In so doing they signified that baptism initiated the newly baptized into the family, which had not only God as Father but Christ as elder brother, the Holy Spirit as its bond, and the baptized as brothers and sisters—in short, the Church. Although beyond the scope of this book, the Eucharist (see vol. 7 of the series), as the meal of their new family (the Church), awaited.

An early and widespread Eucharistic custom was to give the newly baptized (in addition to the bread and wine) a cup of baptismal water and one of milk and honey mixed. The water symbolized the penetration of baptism to their inmost being, and the milk and honey, their entry into the Promised Land of gifts and grace, together, as we shall see, with their return to Paradise.

About the bread and wine, the newly baptized could now be nourished by that "other" sacrament that gushed from the pierced side of Christ, the Eucharist—for the two sacraments combined to bring the Church into being. Again, Chrysostom: "I said that there was a symbol of baptism and the mysteries [the Eucharist] in that blood and water. It is from both of these that the church is sprung. . . . It is from his side, therefore, that Christ formed his church, just as he formed Eve from the side of Adam" (vol. 5, ch. 1, *Baptismal Homily* 3:17).

Anointing and the Holy Spirit

The crucial act in the baptismal rites was "the washing." Yet anointing was almost as important; its significance was closely allied to immersion. The reason reflects the bedrock Christian conviction that Jesus was the "Messiah" or "Anointed One" and that the Christian, as incorporated into Christ, is similarly an anointed one—a "christ." It was a conviction rich in history and custom.

Background

From bathing to cult, almost every aspect of life in the Greco-Roman world involved the use of oil, especially anointing, or smearing with scented oil (chrism). The Bible reflects Greco-Roman practice, terminology, and world-view, but with this difference: Biblical literature shows a marked tendency to emphasize sacred anointing. The biblical terminology provides a rich background for early Christian thought and practice. The root word "to anoint" (Hebrew, *masah;* Greek, *chriein*) gave the name "messianic" to an ancient tradition in Israel.

Although Israel itself was God's anointed, kings, priests, and prophets were typically the anointed ones and, as such, the bearers of God's spirit. After the Babylonian Exile (587–533 B.C.E.), the history of God's people, though it had its bright spots, was largely the history of subjugation to foreigners: Persians, Greeks, and Romans. Understandably, a certain preoccupation with the future came to the fore (ca. 200 B.C.E.). Grounded in the ancient traditions, people began to look for God to intervene as he had in the past to save his people. This expectation often centered around an "anointed one"—a David, a Moses, an Elijah, an Enoch—as God's agent to usher in a better future. In short, an "anointed one," a *messiah/christos*. Messianism was especially characteristic of the Jewish sectarian groups that abounded in the first century of our common era.

Early Christianity

Against this background and the expectations to which it gave rise, early Christians saw Jesus as the Anointed One—at once king, priest, and prophet—sent to fulfill the hope for a new age and redemption. Jesus' baptism at the hands of John came quickly to the fore as the privileged moment when he was revealed as the Anointed One, that is, anointed with the Holy Spirit and attested by the Father as his well-loved Son (see Mark 1:11; Matt 3:16-17; Luke 3:21-23).

When Christ's baptism emerged as the pattern for Christian baptism, the details of the Jordan scene called for ritual attention. In time, anointing became part of the baptismal rite to signify the "christening" of the candidates—they had become "christs," according to Tertullian (see ch. 2, *On Baptism* 7). Like their Master, the newly baptized emerged from the font as God's royal, priestly, and prophetic sons and daughters (see 1 Pet 2:9) and the bearers of the Spirit.

Anointing also yielded one of the earliest terms for baptism, the "seal." Although the term denoted a mark of ownership and protection (sheep of the flock, etc.), it pointed beyond itself to another mark, circumcision, which was also called the "seal," that is, the mark of God's covenant with Abraham. As the mark of the new covenant, baptism was the new or "second" circumcision (see ch. 3, Origen, *Homily on St. Luke* 14; see also vol. 5, ch. 2, Aphrahat). There is reason to believe that "seal" was transferred from baptism itself to anointing, because widespread custom called for the baptismal candidates to have the sign of the cross traced on their foreheads, very often with oil. The cross was the distinctively Christian mark of ownership—sign of the new covenant in Christ's blood, as circumcision was the sign of the old covenant. The washing and the anointing were linked well before the end of the second century, possibly as early as the end of the first.

Two Traditions

Although anointing in the baptismal rites differed from place to place, two dominant patterns developed early, the Western and the Syrian. At Rome, for instance, there were two separate anointings: One took place just before baptism and the other, just after. The first sought to exorcize, heal, and strengthen the candidate for combat with Satan; the second, performed with consecrated and scented oil (chrism), was associated with the gift of the Holy Spirit (see ch. 1, *Apostolic Tradition;* Ambrose). Both anointings covered the whole body, but the latter was done in two stages: (1) When the newly baptized emerged from the water, a presbyter anointed their bodies with chrism; (2) after they had dried, dressed, and entered the church, the bishop imposed hands on them, poured chrism on their heads, and signed their foreheads with the sign of the cross. Eventually the full anointing after baptism would disappear, and only the anointing and signing of the forehead would survive. Cyril of Jerusalem provides the earliest explanation of its meaning: "Christ was anointed with a mystical oil of gladness; that is, with the Holy Spirit, called the 'oil of gladness' because he is the cause of spiritual gladness; so you, being anointed with ointment, have become partakers and fellows of Christ" (vol. 5, ch. 1, *Baptismal Catechesis* 3:2).

The second pattern is Syrian (both Greek- and Syriac-speaking) and knew only an anointing before baptism. Also given in two stages, the first consisted of anointing the forehead in the sign of the cross; the second was a full anointing from head to foot. Both anointings sought to put the candidate under Christ's protection and to exorcize, heal, and strengthen. In Greek-speaking Syria this prebaptismal anointing had no connection with the Holy Spirit. In Syriac-speaking Syria, however, there was a more kaleidoscopic view. Ephrem (vol. 5, ch. 2), for instance, sees many splendors in the prebaptismal anointing, especially the radiance of the Holy Spirit: "The oil is the dear friend of the Holy Spirit, it serves him, following him like a disciple. With it the Spirit signed priests and anointed kings; for with the oil the Holy Spirit imprints his mark on his sheep. Like a signet ring whose impression is left on wax, so the hidden seal of the Spirit is imprinted by oil on the bodies of those who are anointed in baptism; thus they are marked in the baptismal mystery" (*Hymns on Virginity* 6).

The importance of the disparate Syrian and Western patterns of anointing is twofold: The Syrian emphasized the fact that baptism itself is the privileged moment of transformation through the descent of the Holy Spirit, while the Western focused attention on the continuing work of the Holy Spirit in baptismal rebirth and life after baptism. Ambrose of Milan, for instance, associates postbaptismal anointing with the outpouring of the seven gifts of the Spirit, which perfect baptism and empower the newly baptized to live a Christian life (see ch. 1, *On the Sacraments* 3:8–10). At almost the same time, John Chrysostom in Syrian Antioch exhorts his candidates to recognize that the Holy Spirit in his fullness descends at the moment of immersion (see vol. 5, ch. 1, *Baptismal Homily* 2:25).

A Shift in the West: Confirmation

No one disputed that the Holy Spirit was the treasured gift of baptism. Gradually in the West, however, changing custom drove a wedge between baptism and the postbaptismal anointing (coming to be called "consignation"). By the fifth century, for instance, the rite was regularly separated from baptism and reserved to the bishop (see ch. 1, Innocent, John the Deacon). Given the pressure from the conversion of the Western barbarian tribes and coupled with the rise of infant baptism as normal practice, it proved to be only a matter of time before the separable rite became a separate sacrament.

The development was largely set by mid-ninth century when the Benedictine abbot Rabanus Maurus (d. 856), doubtless shaped by the tradition handed on by Ambrose and, to some extent, by the "strengthening" significance inherent in anointing, proposed its theology, namely, that the rite confers that distinctive gift by which the Holy Spirit (already received in baptism) strengthens the gifts of baptism (*On the Institution of Clerics* 1:28–30). In short, as the West came to see it, the work of baptism was "confirmed" by the special outpouring of the Spirit signified by the anointing, which strengthens one to overcome the difficulties of living in Christ—a sacrament of confirmation. In his celebrated theological textbook, *On the Sentences,* Peter Lombard (ca. 1150), for instance, numbers confirmation among the seven sacraments, concluding that its distinctive grace is the "gift of the Holy Spirit for strength, whereas in baptism the Spirit is given for the remission of sin" (book 4, distinction 7:3).

A Shift in the East: Chrismation

The first mention of a postbaptismal anointing in the unalloyed Syrian tradition, albeit West Syrian, is in the baptismal homilies of Theodore of Mopsuestia (ca. 420). He writes that when the bishop sealed the newly baptized on the forehead in the name of the Father and of the Son and of the Holy Spirit, "this sign shows you that, when the Father, the Son and the Holy Spirit were named, the Holy Spirit came upon you" (*Baptismal Homily* 3:27).

In East Syria (vol. 5, ch. 2) a postbaptismal anointing first clearly appears during the early sixth century in two contemporaries of Jacob of Serugh, Philoxenus of Mabbug (d. 523) and Severus of Antioch (d. 538). When outlining the baptismal liturgy, the former simply mentions a postbaptismal "imprinting," which the latter identifies as a symbol of the Holy Spirit.

Whether the shift to a postbaptismal anointing in the Syrian traditions, sometimes called "chrismation," signifies a gift distinct from the baptismal gift of the Holy Spirit is not clear. Looking at the ancient Syrian tradition as a whole, however, it is not a question of either/or: The Holy Spirit in his fullness is given through the water *and* the oil. Beyond the scope of this work is a discussion of the complex history of the postbaptismal anointing and its significance for the Churches that stand in continuity with the Syrian tradition.

The Bible and the Baptismal Liturgy

As we have already seen, a single principle binds together like a golden thread all the disparate traditions about baptism: The flesh is the hinge of salvation. The thread that binds together the disparate baptismal theologies is biblical. The genius of the early Christian catechists lies in their unique ability to unite Bible and liturgy by drawing the theology of the rites from key events narrated in the Bible.

The biblical events important for the meaning of baptism have water as their focus. Those in the Hebrew Bible that stand out are Creation (Gen 1–3), the Flood (Gen 7–8), crossing the Red Sea (Exod 14), crossing the Jordan (Josh 3), and Elisha, Naaman, and the Jordan (2 Kgs 5). Two events in the New Testament that have special importance, as we have seen in detail, are Christ's baptism in the Jordan (Mark 1:9-11; Matt 3; Luke 3:1-21) and his pierced side from which water and blood flowed (John 19:34).

Some catechists, like those of the Antioch school (see vol. 5, ch. 1), were restrictive in their use of the applicable biblical events. Others, like the Alexandrians (see ch. 3, especially Origen), were expansive and explored the events with the lenses of allegory. Still others, especially the Syriac-speaking commentators, were allusive and worked as if by the free association of biblical ideas.

Yet undergirding their several attempts to link biblical event and liturgical rite was the deep conviction that God intervenes in the movements, achievements, and crises in human affairs to save humankind. More pertinent, they were convinced that the history of salvation narrated in the Bible is one long and continuous sweep of saving events from Creation to Christ, such that the earlier event signals and anticipates the later event, which fulfills it. To adapt Tertullian's sacramental principle: Key biblical events are the hinge (like the flesh) upon which the history of salvation turns.

Called "typological thinking," the dynamics of this early Christian approach to the Bible are complex. For instance, the primeval waters of the Book of Genesis over which the spirit of God moves and from which light and life spring; the flood waters bearing Noah's ark; the waters of the Red Sea through which the Israelites pass to a new way of life; the waters of the Jordan through which Joshua leads the Israelites to a second circumcision and the better life of the Promised Land—in typological Christian thinking each of these points beyond itself to the waters of the Jordan, in which John the Baptist immerses Jesus, who summons all to a new and better life in the kingdom of God. In turn, Jesus' baptism points ahead to his death and resurrection. The God who intervenes to create, to save Noah and his precious cargo, to bring the fugitive Hebrews dry-shod through the Red Sea, to lead the people of Israel across the Jordan, is the very God who intervenes at the Jordan through John the Baptist to bring to fruition in Jesus the salvation prepared from the beginning of time.

Thus linked to the key events of the past, the baptism of Jesus in the Jordan fulfills and redefines the historic significance of each of the earlier events. Conversely, each of the earlier events, a saving event in its own right, prepares for, anticipates, and reveals something of the historic significance of Jesus' baptism, which in turn illuminates the death that he himself calls a baptism (see Mark 10:38-39). To early Christians the key biblical events, like a rich Oriental tapestry, are woven into the fabric of biblical history as patterns that lead to a central figure and then lead away to the sacramental events that lie beyond the biblical border.

Although the catechists vary the term with "figure," "shadow," and "image," they call the earlier (Old Testament) event, which points to the New Testament event as its fulfillment, a "type." The New Testament fulfillment is the "antitype," "reality," "substance," or "truth." Thus, for instance, the Exodus from Egypt is the type and the baptism of Jesus, the antitype. Cyril of Jerusalem (vol. 5, ch. 1), whose baptismal catecheses have been classics for a millennium and a half, sees the significance of the rite of the renunciation of Satan through the lenses of the Exodus account (12–14). After recounting its highlights, he writes:

> Pass, pray, from the old to the new, from the figure [lit. "type"] to the reality. There Moses sent by God to Egypt; here Christ sent from the Father into the world. Moses' mission was to lead out from Egypt a persecuted people; Christ's to rescue all the people of the world who were under the tyranny of sin. There the blood of a lamb was the charm against the destroyer; here, the blood of the unspotted Lamb, Jesus Christ, is appointed your inviolable sanctuary against demons. Pharaoh pursued that people of old right into the sea; this outrageous spirit, the impudent author of all evil, followed you, each one, up to the very verge of the saving streams [of the baptistery]. That other tyrant is engulfed and drowned in the Red Sea; this one is destroyed in the saving water (*Baptismal Catechesis* 1:3).

Typology such as this, however, was not an early Christian invention, for the catechists found biblical warrant. Paul, for instance, developed a powerful typological lesson for his turbulent Corinthian Christians from the experience of the Israelites in the Sinai Desert (see 1 Cor 10:1-6). Origen (ch. 3) comments: "Writing to the Corinthians he says in a certain passage, 'For we know that our fathers were all under the cloud, and were all baptized in Moses in the cloud and in the sea. . . .' Do you see how much Paul's teaching differs from the literal meaning? What the Jews supposed to be a crossing of the sea, Paul calls a baptism; what they supposed to be a cloud, Paul asserts is the Holy Spirit'' (*Homilies on Exodus* 5:2). Although Origen here considers the Jewish interpreters of his time ''literalists,'' typological thinking had its origin among Jewish scholars, as Paul is witness. Indeed, for them the bath that formed part of the rite of proselyte conversion was an extension of the waters of the Red Sea, and they had long understood the Passover Seder, which both Paul and Origen saw as a type of the Eucharist, as a new Exodus.

Against this background, the early Christian catechists saw the liturgy, in this case the baptismal liturgy, as the ongoing biblical history of salvation narrated—more accurately, enacted—in myth, symbol, and ritual drama. Although the events of the old dispensation were linked indissolubly to those of the new, both were linked to the sacraments, which rendered accessible the God who saves. In his incisive way, Augustine, for instance, counsels that the counterpart of the biblical miracles is to be found in the sacraments of baptism and Eucharist (see ch. 2, *On Baptism* 3:21). In the allusive way of the East Syrians, Jacob of Serugh (vol. 5, ch. 2) links the Exodus through the Red Sea, John the Baptist at the Jordan, and Christ's gift of baptism:

> Thus you should understand that there are three different categories of baptism for those who have been baptized as we have described:
> One is of the Law, another is of John, while this third one was opened up by the Son of God.
> The baptisms in the Law are a shadow,
> while the baptism of John is of repentance,
> whereas the baptism of the Son of God gives birth to the ''first born,''
> providing sons to be brothers to the Only-Begotten.
> Moses in the wilderness depicted the image of baptism,
> John opened it up, so that it might be for repentance,
> then Christ came and kindled it with the Holy Spirit and Fire,
> so that it might be giving birth to new and immortal children.
> The great Moses with his baptism marked out
> the baptism wherein the whole world is to receive forgiveness;
> John cleansed off the filth of his own people in baptism

in order to sanctify them and so they might then see the Son
of God.

Christ came and opened up baptism on his cross

so that it might be, in the place of Eve, a "mother of living
beings" for the world;

water and blood, for the fashioning of spiritual children,

flowed forth and so baptism became the mother of life (*Memra*,
7:159–190).

Nowhere in early Christian literature, however, is early Christian theology of baptism better recapitulated than in the typology of Paradise. The first Adam, whose disobedience drove him from the "garden of delights," gave place to the Second Adam, Christ, whose death, as the Good Thief was to discover (see Luke 23:43), opened Paradise anew. The gates once opened, baptism was the way of return. The Jordan, which, as some thought flowed from Paradise, in fact flows back into Paradise whence it came; so also its surrogate, the font. In one of the earliest and most remarkable of the Syriac baptismal poems, the *Odes of Solomon* (vol. 5, ch. 2), the odist limns:

And [the Most High, my God] took me to his Paradise,
wherein is the wealth of the Lord's pleasure.

(I contemplated blooming and fruit-bearing trees,
and self-grown was their crown.

Their branches were flourishing
and their fruits were shining;
their roots [were] from an immortal land.

And a river of gladness was irrigating them,
and the region round about them in the land of eternal life.)

Then I adored the Lord because of his magnificence.

And I said, blessed, O Lord, are they
who are planted in your land,
and who have a place in your Paradise,

And who grow in the growth of your trees,
and have passed from darkness into light (*Ode* 11).

An ancient theme, it also endured. As if instructed by the odist, Gregory of Nyssa (vol. 5, ch. 1), the architect of the Eastern Christian mystical tradition, could lead his congregation two centuries later in the following prayer from the conclusion of his *Homily on the Baptism of Christ* (Epiphany):

> For you truly, O Lord, are the pure and eternal fount of goodness, who did justly turn away from us, and in loving kindness did have mercy upon us. You did hate, and were reconciled; you did curse, and did bless; you did banish us from Paradise, and did recall us; you did strip off the fig-tree leaves, an unseemly covering, and put upon us a costly garment; you did open the prison, and release the condemned; you did sprinkle us with clean water, and cleanse us from our filthiness. No longer shall Adam be confounded when called by you, nor hide himself, convicted by his conscience, cowering in the thicket of Paradise. Nor shall the flaming sword encircle Paradise around, and make the entrance inaccessible to those that draw near; but all is turned to joy for us that were the heirs of sin: Paradise, yes, heaven itself may be trodden by man: and the creation, in the world and above the world, that once was at variance with itself, is knit together in friendship.

For early Christians the religious meaning of baptism embedded in the rites and symbols of the liturgy was disclosed by the types and antitypes, which, tutored by an ancient tradition, they drew from the Bible.

Chapter 1

Italy

Roman Influence

Rome was a magnet for immigrants and visitors, and Christians were no exception to the force of its attraction. They were already well established in the city when Paul wrote his Letter to the Romans (50 C.E.). By the end of the century (96 C.E.), a prominent Roman Christian named Clement (he worked, it seems, in the Roman equivalent of the State Department) intervened by letter in the name of the Roman Church to bring some of the unruly members of the Church at Corinth to a better mind about authority in the Church there. Shortly after the turn of the century, the Antiochene bishop Ignatius hailed the Roman Church as "presiding in love" (*To the Romans,* preface), at least in part because of its highly developed welfare system and its concern to come to the aid of Christian communities wherever they were. Some sixty years later the Eastern-born bishop of Lyons (France), Irenaeus, extolled the Church at Rome as a font and touchstone of authentic apostolic teaching. In addition, he appealed to its antiquity and foundation by Peter and Paul, summoning other Churches to agree with it because of its strong leadership (*Against the Heresies* 3:3,2). About the same time, another Eastern bishop, Abercius (below), etched in stone an account of his journey to the Church at Rome to see the gold-vested "queen" and the "people bearing the splendid [baptismal] seal" (*Epitaph,* ll. 7–9).

Soon Bishop Victor (189–198) would intervene in the East to settle the controversy about Easter (namely, whether it should be celebrated on Good Friday or on Easter Sunday); the Roman baptismal liturgy would shortly acquire wide influence (see below, *Apostolic Tradition*); soon thereafter, Bishop Stephen (254–257) would reprimand Cyprian of Carthage and the North Africans (ch. 2) for insisting on the rebaptism of heretics; and in the next century, Ambrose of Milan (below), the leading Churchman of the West, would publicly acknowledge a tradition of deference to the Church at Rome. In short, Roman Christianity assumed prominence in the Mediterranean Christian world, especially in the West; by the end of the fourth century this prominence would be the foundation of what came to be called the "Roman primacy" (see below, Papal Correspondence). In the process, Roman baptismal liturgy and teaching achieved corresponding prominence, first throughout Italy, and then north (France, Germany), west (Spain), and, to some extent, in the east (see vol. 5, ch. 1, *Apostolic Constitutions*). Further, with respect to North Africa, there is reason to believe that the first Latin-speaking Christians emigrated to Rome from Roman Africa's major city, Carthage; in addition, the city's bishop, Cyprian (ca. 258; ch. 2), is witness to the strong but often tense ties between African and Roman Christianity. Finally, the bonds between Egyptian Christians and those at Rome and in the Italian peninsula surfaced early and exhibited great vitality over the years. Ambrose of Milan's approach to baptism, for instance, owes much to Origen (ch. 3), and the Egyptian Church orders revise and update Hippolytus' *Apostolic Tradition* (see ch. 3, *Canons of Hippolytus*).

The Christian Predicament

Christian spread to Rome and the West, however, did not come easily. The earliest Christians in Rome were Jewish "Nazarenes," or followers of "the Way" (see vol. 5, ch. 1, *Didache*) from Palestine. They lived their religious lives, it seems, within the synagogues of Rome until the year 49, when trouble between Christian and non-Christian Jews caused the Roman authorities to expel the former and some, at least, of the latter. Although an imperial decree permitted their return in 54, the returnees found that Gentiles dominated the Christian community, which had moved from synagogues to houses. Although the house-groups exhibited a variety of mix between Jew and Gentile as well as a wide range of attitudes toward Jewish practice, Roman Christianity's Jewish heritage remained ever present.

But there were other troubles. Within a decade of the return Emperor Nero (54–68) singled the Christians out as scapegoats in the burning of Rome (64) and executed many with untoward savagery, according to the Roman historian Tacitus (55–120). Part of the problem was that Christians were, and long remained, foreigners (largely Syrian). As such they became easy targets for social hostility, which erupted against them time and time again, both at Rome and elsewhere in the empire.

Unfortunately, their social predicament was soon compounded by a legal predicament. Like their Jewish brethren, Christians refused to worship any god but their own. Although Rome tolerated this exclusivism in Jews because they had both antiquity and the status of client nation in the empire, Roman magistrates did not accord Christians the same consideration once it was clear that they were not Jews. By the early second century, simply to bear the name Christian constituted a capital offense. In mid-second-century Rome, for instance, the Roman Christian teacher Justin (see below) was executed together with six of his converts and catechumens for no other crime than Christian profession.

Until the Constantinian peace brought Christianity legal toleration (311/313) and, subsequently, establishment as the religion of state (381/391), this social and legal hostility glowered like a storm cloud on the Christian horizon. It signaled that the Christians of Rome and elsewhere were a people who lived on the margins of society and very likely were seditious. As one early Christian put it: "Christians share everything as citizens and endure everything as foreigners. Every foreign land is their fatherland, yet for them every fatherland is a foreign land" (*Letter to Diognetus* 5:5–6).

Early Christian marginality was extremely important for the development of the baptismal liturgy, especially at Rome, where Christians dwelled in the eye of the storm, so to speak. Anthropologists have coined the term "liminal" (from *limina,* "boundaries") for groups that live, as the early Christians did, on the fringes of society; they point out that this condition of liminality is the fertile source of rituals and symbols, not to mention myths, philosophical systems, and works of art. It is no accident, therefore, that Hippolytus (below) records a richly articulated and dramatic ritual of preparation for and initiation into the body of Roman Christians. Indeed, what emerges is an extended exorcismal drama that functioned to neutralize and counter the social and legal jeopardy in which Roman Christians found themselves. The fact that the Roman community survived the hostility of populace and police alike in the first two centuries to flourish in the third century and thereafter is testimony enough to the power of ritual in general and, specifically, to the power of the baptismal ritual.

Christian "Schools"

In addition to the characteristics of prominence and liminality, the Roman Christians had a strong "school" tradition. A striking feature of the Greco-Roman world was its mode of doing philosophy. Well before Christianity, philosophy had become a way of teaching people how to live virtuously in the world rather than just to think about it. Groups formed whose members devoted themselves to a way of both teaching and living. In short, they formed the philosophical schools so popular around the Mediterranean—popular because they offered a compelling and credible way of life as well as a way of understanding a difficult and hostile world.

By mid-second century the celebrated physician Galen (d. 199) conceded that Christians whom he had come to know in Rome were a philosophical school—albeit second or third rate in his view. Justin is representative of this "school" characteristic of Roman Christianity. He described his quest for salvation as a philosopher's quest (ch. 3, Clement), took pride in the fact that he wore the philosopher's coat, and formed a school that met at the house of a certain Martin close to the Tiburtine baths. As already noted, he was executed with six of his students.

Indeed, Roman Christianity at that time seemed almost to be organized in schools. Toward the end of the century it numbered at least ten different and often opposing schools. The rise of the determined bishop, Victor (d. 198), of the "Catholic" school, however, brought a concerted unity to the community, and under Victor the striking baptismal liturgy recorded by Hippolytus (below), subsequently so influential, took definitive shape. In short, the Catholic school prevailed, probably because it could establish its claim to authenticity by means of the doctrine of apostolic tradition and succession proposed by Irenaeus (see above).

An added note: At about the same time, Catholic or Orthodox Christianity was in the ascendant elsewhere in the Mediterranean Christian world. Other forms—Gnostic, Marcionite, Montanist, and others—came to be labeled "sectarian" (heretical) or "heterodox" (as opposed to Orthodox or Catholic) or "schismatic" (ch. 2, Optatus and Augustine).

The Readings

The selections cover the second to the seventh centuries, range over Italy, and are drawn from works of prophecy (Hermas), defense of the faith (Justin Martyr), inscription (Abercius), Church order (Hippolytus), treatise (Novatian), Paschal homily (Zeno), postbaptismal instruction (Ambrose), papal correspondence (Innocent and Leo), letter of instruction (John the Deacon), and two sacramentaries (Leonine and Gelasian). With the exception of Novatian, Ambrose, and, to some extent, Zeno, the works concern themselves with liturgical practice and pastoral questions about baptism. The architects of the rites are Hippolytus and the compilers of the sacramentaries. The architect of Italian baptismal theology is Ambrose, who, like his contemporaries Cyril, Chrysostom, and Theodore (vol. 5, ch. 1), draws the religious significance out of the rites themselves.

A valuable study of the early Christians at Rome is George La Piana, "The Roman Church at the End of the Second Century," *Harvard Theological Review* 18 (1925) 201–277.

The Shepherd of Hermas

The *Shepherd of Hermas* contains the earliest Western baptismal text. The work itself defies categorization, save to say that its mood is apocalyptic and its form, a series of five visions, twelve mandates (moral instructions), and ten parables (allegories). The "Shepherd" of the title is the Angel of Repentance, who appears in the fifth vision and remains as the author's primary interpreter. "Hermas" is the author, about whom (together with his work) there is dispute. The internal evidence, coupled with early tradition, makes of him a Hellenized Jewish Christian sold early into slavery and resold in Rome. There he was manumitted, pursued a variety of livelihoods, and functioned as a teacher in one of the city's more apocalyptic congregations. He compiled the work over the years; the final version dates from the middle of the second century (the Ninth Parable, which constitutes the second reading, seems to have been the latest addition).

The problem that suffuses the work is Christian preoccupation with business and other material concerns, especially among members of his congregation. As Hermas sees it, the preoccupation has brought them to compromise with the disordered ethics and values of the city at large. (Even his children, we learn, led disorderly lives, apostatized during persecution, and betrayed their parents.) Hermas' response is straightforward: (1) people's inner contradictions come from a divided (*dipsychia,* "two-souled") heart; (2) the only avenue is repentance; and (3) those who repent will be saved and those who do not will not. Further, the time is at hand, for the end, even if delayed, is imminent.

Against this background of apocalyptic urgency, repentance is the key. Some in Rome were teaching that there was no forgiveness for sins committed after baptism. The Shepherd, however, assures Hermas that although there is no second baptism, there is a second chance (though only one), what the author calls a "prescribed repentance." Nonetheless, baptism is the first and fundamental chance, "the remission" (Mandate 4:3).

Remission or repentance—either—is urgent. In the time left to the world, a mystical tower, founded on water, is under construction. In the first reading, an aged woman interpreter (she later appears young, joyous, and beautiful) identifies the tower as the Church. In the second reading (the Shepherd is the interpreter) we are told of the necessity of the water (baptism) for the tower. In the process we learn, as in Syria, of the "harrowing of hell" (already hinted at in 1 Pet 3:19): The apostles and teachers have to descend into the underworld to bring baptism to the righteous of pre-Christian times. What happens to them in baptism happens to all. They put off death, receive life, and are fitted into the Church like stones in the tower.

The baptismal liturgy that stands behind Hermas is almost certainly that described by Justin in the next selection. As in Syrian Christianity, baptism is the "seal," here linked with the "name of the Son of God," denoting his ownership of the baptized in whose protective power they now stand.

The text is that of Robert Joly, ed., SC 53 (1958); the translation, that of Joseph M. F. Marique, FC 1 (1947) 245–246, 335–336. A valuable study of the social setting of the Church at Rome as it is recoverable in Hermas is Carolyn A. Osiek, *Rich and Poor in the Shepherd of Hermas* (Washington: Catholic Biblical Association, 1983).

Third Vision
3. First Revelations About the Tower

11:1. After showing me this, she wished to rush away. I said to her: "Lady, what good is it to see and not to know what this means?" "Insistent fellow!" she said. "You do wish to know about the tower." "Yes," I said, "in order that I may tell my brothers, lady, and they may have greater joy and upon this message may know the Lord in great glory." 2. She said: "Many will listen and some will rejoice for having listened, but some, too, will weep. But, even the latter, if they listen and repent, will also rejoice. Let me tell you now the parables of the tower. I shall reveal everything to you. And do not importune me any more about the revelation, since these revelations are at an end. They have been fulfilled. Yet you will not cease asking for revelations, shameless as you are. 3. The tower which you see being built, that is I, the Church, who has appeared to you now and formerly. So, ask me whatever you wish about the tower and I shall reveal it to you, that you may rejoice along with the saints." 4. I said to her: "Lady, since, on one occasion, you considered me worthy of the whole revelation, make it." She said: "Whatever can possibly be revealed to you will be revealed. Only let your heart be directed to God and so not doubt whatever you see." 5. Then I asked her: "Why, lady, is the tower built on waters?" "Yes," she said, "as I told you before, you do enquire persistently. With your enquiries you are finding the truth. The reason why the tower is built on water is this: Your life has been saved by water and will be so saved. The tower has been put on a foundation by the omnipotent and glorious Word of the name and it is held together by the Lord's invisible power."

Ninth Parable

14. [Even the prophets and apostles must receive baptism.]

15:1. "Sir, tell me another thing," I said. "What is it?" he said. "Why," I said, "did the stones that had borne these spirits go up from the abyss, and why were they put into the building?" 2. "They had to ascend," he said, "by means of water in order to be made living. Otherwise, if they had not shed the death of their former life, they could not enter the kingdom of God. 3. Those, also, who were deceased so received the seal of the Son of God and entered the kingdom of God. For, a man is dead before he receives the name of the Son of God, but, when he receives the seal, he puts off death and receives life. 4. The seal, therefore, is water. The dead go down into the water and come out of it living. Therefore, this seal was proclaimed to them and they put it to use to enter the kingdom of God." 5. "Then, why, sir," I said, "did the forty stones come out of the abyss with them, if they already had the seal?" "Because," he said, "the apostles and teachers who preach the name of the Son of God, after having been laid to rest in power and faith in the Son of God, preach also to those who have been laid to rest before them. To the latter they themselves passed on the seal they proclaimed. 6. So, they went down with them into the water and came up again. But, the apostles and teachers, though they were alive, went down and returned alive. But those who had been laid to rest before them went down dead and came up alive. 7. With the help of the apostles and teachers they were made to live and came to the knowledge of the name of the Son of God. For the same reason they returned in their company and were fitted into the building of the tower along with them, built into it without having been trimmed. They went to their rest in justice and great purity. They merely did not have the seal. Now you have the solution of this matter also." "Yes, sir," I said.

Justin Martyr

The first Western Christian to describe the actual rite of baptism and its significance is Justin Martyr. Born in Flavia Neapolis in Samaria (Nablus near Shechem) of wealthy pagan parents at the turn of the first century, his early years comprised a philosophical quest among the dominant philosophical schools of the day. The quest ended when an old Jewish Christian teacher converted him to Christianity, which he embraced as the "perfect" philosophy about 130. He taught as a traveling philosopher (he even wore the traditional philosopher's mantle) in a number of cities, among them Ephesus and Rome, where he won important disciples, including Tatian, the Syrian from Nisibis (ca. 150), and Irenaeus, who would become the bishop of Lyons (ca. 178). During his second stay in Rome (150–165) Justin, as already noted, established his school at the house of Martin near the Tiburtine baths, where he was eventually arrested with six of his disciples (three of whom were catechumens) by the Roman authorities. After a trial before the prefect of the city, Rusticus, they were executed on the grounds of professing Christianity, by then reckoned as an unlawful cultic association (ca. 165).

Like many of his philosophical colleagues, Justin embraced controversy in both writing and the philosophical arena—he records an acrimonious debate with the Cynic philosopher Crescens in Rome, a dialogue with the Jew Trypho in Ephesus, and an encounter with the heretic Marcion, probably in Rome. His most celebrated work of controversy is the *First Apology* (ca. 148), an expository defense of Christian belief and practice addressed to Emperor Antoninus Pius (138–161), his philosopher son, Verissimus, and the philosopher Lucius. Justin devotes the bulk of the work (chs. 1–60) to a plea for justice to Christians, to their depiction as good citizens and a boon to the state, and to an argument for the superiority of Christianity over other Greco-Roman religions, as well as for its being the true heir of ancient Israel. In chapters 61–67, from which the reading is drawn, he describes Christian religious life, at least its distinctive traits, and concludes with a final plea for justice, adding several documentary appendices (chs. 68–71).

Although Justin may have left out some details, the main lines of the baptismal rites are clear: (1) an indeterminate period of instruction (there is an indication that the syllabus was a Trinitarian baptismal creed in use at Rome, together with biblical commentary and the exposition of moral precepts and virtues); (2) some sort of testing, which included a profession of faith; (3) a brief period of communal prayer and fasting; (4) immersion (probably triple—there was a tradition that Peter baptized in the River Tiber (see ch. 2, Tertullian) in the name of the Father and of the

Son and of the Holy Spirit; and (5) the baptismal Eucharist. There is reason to believe that Justin explained the meaning of the baptismal rites to his catechumens more or less the way he explains them to his addressees. About baptism, he holds that the practice is rooted in God, who exists in three persons and who claims the baptized as his own, and that baptism bestows on them both knowledge that God has forgiven them and new insight (enlightenment) into the content of Christian faith.

Justin's description of the daily religious life of Roman Christians is included because it is the earliest extant description of the Church as a discrete living community. He regarded himself as an authentic ecclesiastical teacher, handing on the tradition of the Roman Church, by which he meant the main body of Roman Christians under an official he calls "the ruler of the brethren" (he does not use the term "bishop"), as distinct from splinter groups. In addition to repentance, forgiveness, new birth, and enlightenment (Justin is the first datable Christian writer to use enlightenment in connection with baptism), he regards entry into the Christian community as a major accomplishment of baptism. The newly baptized now had an extended family that would stand by them at every turn. The execution of Justin and his companions indicates the jeopardy in which Christians stood and how important such support was.

The text is that of Prudentius Maran, ed., *Apologia I Pro Christianis,* PG 6; the translation, that of Thomas B. Falls, FC 6 (1948). For helpful studies, see Cullen I. K. Story, "Justin's Apology I. 62–64: Its Importance for the Author's Treatment of Christian Baptism," *Vigiliae Christianae* 16 (1962) 172–178, and L. W. Barnard, *Justin Martyr: His Life and Thought* (Cambridge, England: The University Press, 1967), especially 126–150.

First Apology
Chapter 61

Lest we be judged unfair in this exposition, we will not fail to explain how we consecrated ourselves to God when we were regenerated through Christ. Those who are convinced and believe what we say and teach is the truth, and pledge themselves to be able to live accordingly, are taught in prayer and fasting to ask God to forgive their past sins, while we pray and fast with them. Then we lead them to a place where there is water, and they are regenerated in the same manner in which we ourselves were regenerated. In the name of God, the Father and Lord of all, and of our Savior, Jesus Christ, and of the Holy Spirit, they then receive the washing with water. For Christ said: "Unless you be born again, you shall not enter into the kingdom of heaven" (John 3:3). Now, it is clear to everyone how impossible it is for those who have been born once to enter their mothers' wombs again. Isaiah the Prophet explained, as we already stated, how those who have sinned and then repented shall be freed of their sins. These are his words: "Wash yourselves, be clean, banish sin from your souls; learn to do well: judge for the fatherless and defend the widow; and then come and let us reason together, says the Lord. And if your sins be as scarlet, I will make them white as wool; and if they be red as crimson, I will make them white as snow. But if you wlll not hear me, the sword shall devour you: for the mouth of the Lord has spoken it" (Isa 1:16-20). And this is the reason, taught to us by the apostles, why we baptize the way we do. We were totally unaware of our first birth, and were born of necessity from fluid seed through the mutual union of our parents, and were trained in wicked and sinful customs. In order that we do not continue as children of necessity and ignorance, but of deliberate choice and knowledge, and in order to obtain in the water the forgiveness of past sins, there is invoked over the one who wishes to be regenerated, and who is repentant of his sins, the name of God, the Father and Lord of all; he who leads the person to be baptized to the laver calls him by this name only. For, no one is permitted to utter the name of the ineffable God, and if anyone ventures to affirm that his name can be pronounced, such a person is hopelessly mad. This washing is called illumination, since they who learn these things become illuminated intellectually. Furthermore, the illuminated one is also baptized in the name of Jesus Christ, who was crucified under Pontius Pilate, and in the name of the Holy Spirit, who predicted through the prophets everything concerning Jesus.

Chapter 65

After thus baptizing the one who has believed and given his assent, we escort him to the place where are assembled those whom we call brethren, to offer up sincere prayers in common for ourselves, for the baptized person, and for all other persons wherever they may be, in order that, since we have found the truth, we may be deemed fit through our actions to be esteemed as good citizens and observers of the law, and thus attain eternal salvation. At the conclusion of prayers we greet one another with a kiss. Then, bread and a chalice containing wine mixed with water are presented to the one presiding over the brethren. He takes them and offers praise and glory to the Father of all, through the name of the Son and of the Holy Spirit, and he recites lengthy prayers of thanksgiving to God in the name of those to whom he granted such favors. At the end of these prayers and thanksgiving, all present express their approval by saying "Amen." This Hebrew word, "Amen," means "So be it." And when he who presides has celebrated the Eucharist, they whom we call deacons permit each one present to partake of the Eucharistic bread, and wine and water; and they carry it also to the absentees.

Chapter 66

We call this food the Eucharist, of which only he can partake who has acknowledged the truth of our teachings, who has been cleansed by baptism for the remission of his sins and for his regeneration, and who regulates his life upon the principles laid down by Christ. Not as ordinary bread or as ordinary drink do we partake of them, but just as, through the word of God, our Savior Jesus Christ became incarnate and took upon himself flesh and blood for our salvation, so, we have been taught, the food which has been made the Eucharist by the prayer of his word [see words of institution below] and which nourishes our flesh and blood by assimilation, is both the flesh and blood of that Jesus who was made flesh. The apostles in their memoirs, which are called Gospels, have handed down what Jesus ordered them to do; that he took bread and, after giving thanks, said: "Do this in remembrance of me; this is my body." In like manner, he took also the chalice, gave thanks, and said: "This is my blood" (see Luke 22:19; Matt 26:26-27; 1 Cor 11:23-32), and to them only did he give it. The evil demons, in imitation of this, ordered the same thing to be performed in the Mithraic mysteries. For, as you know or may easily learn, bread and a cup of water, together with certain incantations, are used in their mystic initiation rites.

Chapter 67

Henceforward, we constantly remind one another of these things. The rich among us come to the aid of the poor, and we always stay together. For all the favors we enjoy we bless the Creator of all, through his Son Jesus Christ and through the Holy Spirit. On the day which is called Sunday we have a common assembly of all who live in the cities or in the outlying districts, and the memoirs of the apostles or the writings of the prophets are read, as long as there is time. Then, when the reader has finished, the president of the assembly verbally admonishes and invites all to imitate such examples of virtue. Then we all stand up together and offer up our prayers, and, as we said before, after we finish our prayers, bread and wine and water are presented. He who presides likewise offers up prayers and thanksgivings, to the best of his ability, and the people express their approval by saying "Amen." The Eucharistic elements are distributed and consumed by those present, and to those who are absent they are sent through the deacons. The wealthy, if they wish, contribute whatever they desire, and the collection is placed in the custody of the president. [With it] he helps the orphans and widows, those who are needy because of sickness or any other reason, and the captives and strangers in our midst; in short, he takes care of all those in need. Sunday, indeed, is the day on which we all hold our common assembly because it is the first day on which God, transforming the darkness and [prime] matter, created the world; and our Savior Jesus Christ arose from the dead on the same day. For they crucified him on the day before that of Saturn, and on the day after, which is Sunday, he appeared to his apostles and disciples, and taught them the things which we have passed on to you also for consideration.

Abercius

"The queen of all ancient Christian inscriptions is the epitaph of Abercius." So speaks one of the towering figures in early Christian studies. Abercius was the aging bishop of Hieropolis, a small city in Phrygia (central Turkey), toward the end of the second century. The key event in his life was a trip to Rome and back through East Syria, which he records in this inscription, found a century ago by the Scot archaeologist William Ramsay.

Abercius' epitaph constitutes the earliest epigraphical reference to the Church at Rome. Already depicted by Hermas and Justin, it is here described by an Eastern visitor in images borrowed from the Apocalypse (Rev 12:1-9). The identifying mark of the Christians there (and everywhere) is the people bearing the "splendid" seal of baptism (l. 9), and the focus is communities widely dispersed yet closely bound together, the most resplendent of which is the Church at Rome ("the queen with the golden robe . . ."). Abercius' own "seal," along with the letters of introduction (a collection of Paul's letters), gave him access to the hospitality of communities large and small across the Mediterranean Basin. Christ is at once the chaste shepherd and the fish (see ch. 2, Tertullian); Mary is the virgin; and Mary catching the fish from the stream is the incarnation—an interplay of baptismal images that appear also in Tertullian. The images are Eucharistic as well. Indeed, the epitaph is the oldest stone monument that mentions the Eucharist.

The text is contained in Johannes Quasten, ed., FP 7 (1935); the translation is Quasten 1:172 (the source of the above quote).

Epitaph

1. The citizen of an eminent city, I made this (tomb)
2. In my lifetime, that I may have here a resting-place for my body.
3. Abercius by name, I am a disciple of the chaste shepherd,
4. Who feeds his flocks of sheep on mountains and plains,
5. Who has great eyes that look on all sides.
6. He taught me . . . faithful writings.
7. He sent me to Rome, to behold a kingdom
8. And to see a queen with golden robe and golden shoes.
9. There I saw a people bearing the splendid seal.
10. And I saw the plain of Syria and all the cities, even Nisibis,
11. Having crossed the Euphrates. And everywhere I had associates
12. Having Paul as a companion, everywhere faith led the way
13. And set before me for food the fish from the spring
14. Mighty and pure, whom a spotless Virgin caught,
15. And gave this to friends to eat, always
16. Having sweet wine and giving the mixed cup with bread.
17. These words, I, Abercius, standing by, ordered to be inscribed.
18. In truth, I was in the course of my seventy-second year.
19. Let him who understands and believes this pray for Abercius.
20. But no man shall place another tomb upon mine.

21. If one do so, he shall pay to the treasury of the Romans two thousand pieces of gold,
22. And to my beloved fatherland Hieropolis, one thousand pieces of gold.

The Apostolic Tradition *of Hippolytus*

Discovered early this century embedded as a foundation document in several ancient Egyptian and Syrian Church orders, the *Apostolic Tradition* is Western Christianity's oldest extant liturgical document. As such, it is invaluable for light shed on the religious life of the early Roman Christian community. Scholarly consensus attributes it to Hippolytus, the Roman presbyter (170?-253), dates it at the turn of the second century, and considers it to reflect Roman liturgical practice (with some emending by the author) from the time of the Roman bishop Victor I (189-198)—a generation after Justin.

The work consists of forty-three brief, prescriptive chapters. The first fourteen deal with the constitution of the Church and contain the earliest rites of ordination; the last twenty-two, with community practices. The middle chapters (15-21) describe in detail the process of becoming a Christian.

A good deal of consolidation had taken place in the Church at Rome since Justin's time, largely under the influence of Bishop Victor. The community was still comparatively small, made up of house-churches, and was living on the fringes of the city's religious, political, and social world. However, it had drawn in its boundaries, primarily because of the intensified social and legal jeopardy, noted above. As a result, baptism had become a complex rite of passage intended to select, to form, and to initiate only the demonstrably committed. The period of instruction had expanded from brief and indeterminate to three years devoted to intensive oral instruction coupled with daily exorcism; at the outset was a searching inquiry into a candidate's mode of life. Before anyone was admitted to baptism, a second inquiry, or scrutiny (see below, Ambrose, John the Deacon; also see ch. 2, Augustine), was made to gauge whether one's life showed signs of true conversion. From that point on an exorcismal drama ensued, which sought to break the power Satan (in the person of the goddess

Roma) and his cultural legions held over those approaching baptism. The climax was solemn baptism at dawn (most likely on Easter), which initiated one new born into an extended family with powerful family bonds. The resultant safety net was of such resilience that Roman Christians survived to flourish in spite of the escalating social and legal hostility that marked the first half of the third century.

The baptismal liturgy described in the *Apostolic Tradition,* the substance of which doubtless characterized baptism in and around Rome for an extended period, exerted great influence, especially in Egypt and West Syria. Although the original text has long been lost, the work has been reconstituted from versions in Latin, Arabic, Ethiopic, and two Coptic dialects, as well as from several adaptations such as the *Apostolic Constitutions* (vol. 5, ch. 1) and the *Canons of Hippolytus* (ch. 3).

A word about the author. If, as seems certain, he was Hippolytus, he was a man of prominence in the Church at Rome as a theologian and controversialist already in the time of Bishop Victor. He clashed with several of Victor's successors about both belief and practice, which led him eventually to separate from the Church (which he began to call Callistus' "school" after the then bishop, 217–222) and to establish his own group as the true Church. An underlying problem seems to have been his view of the Church, namely, that it is a community of saints, reminiscent of the view espoused by the teachers Hermas mentioned (see above), who allowed no further forgiveness after baptism, and Novatian (see below).

Part of the problem surfaces in ch. 16 where it deals with concubinage. Roman law forbade marriage *(matrimonium)* between the freeborn and the slaveborn. Such a relationship, however stable, was regarded as concubinage *(contubernium).* The law had direct and lasting effect on Christians, because many were slaves. When it was a question of a Christian woman who was a slave, domestic stability prompted the Church to confer legitimacy on the relationship. Callistus extended the same recognition to slaveborn men who were "married" to freeborn women. Hippolytus charged Callistus with condoning adultery and regarded Callistus' action as an innovation that ran counter to the tradition, as well as an open invitation to laxity in a Church intended to be without spot or wrinkle. At this point he seems to have made formal his separation from Callistus' school. Eventually, Hippolytus was arrested for his Christianity and exiled to the silver mines in Sardinia, where he died about 235, apparently in company with the current Roman bishop, Pontanius (230–235). In any case, Hippolytus was posthumously rehabilitated in the Church at Rome as a martyr, and his followers presumably reconciled.

The rites had important social function, which lay in their structure: They comprise an extended and complex rite of passage from a hostile society with powerful institutions of social control (Rome) to a new community within that society (the Church), characterized by what one social analyst has called a "shared sense of humanity, equality, and soul." The religious significance lay in the rites themselves. The catechumens stood on the fringes of the Church, neither in nor out. The power of their old way of life, lived under Satan's rule, had to be broken gradually by re¨- gious instruction coupled with exorcism, normally over a three-year period. The gauge for conversion was conduct: Did the catechumens obey the commandments and perform the works of mercy? Even then, they had to be tested in the ordeal of solemn exorcism. And only then were they judged ready enough to renounce Satan and his (Roman) legions on their own, after which, stripped of their old allegiance and immersed in the baptismal pool, they professed their new allegiance to the Trinity, to the Church, and to the resurrected life. Thus reborn, they were embraced by their new family and nourished by the symbols of their new life: Eucharistic bread and wine, baptismal water, and the milk and honey of the Promised Land.

Earlier in the *Apostolic Tradition* (4:10–12) we learn the source of the rite's effectiveness: anamnesis (re-presentation). As discussed in the General Introduction ("Symbolic Participation"), baptism and the Eucharist, as symbolic dramas, rendered present and accessible to those about to be baptized the death and resurrection by which Christ accomplished the salvation of humankind, including the destruction of Satan's power—however and wherever embodied.

The reconstituted Latin text is that of Bernard Botte, ed., *La tradition apostolique: Essai de reconstitution* (Münster: Aschendorf, 1963), which he has also used in the second revised edition of his more accessible *La tradition apostolique: après les anciennes versions,* SC 11bis (1984). Where Botte offers two versions of the text, the translation is informed by his French translation, because it represents his preferred reading. An alternate English translation and an invaluable introduction is provided in Gregory Dix, ed., *The Treatise on the Apostolic Tradition of Hippolytus,* rev. ed. by Henry Chadwick (London: SPCK, 1968). See also T. M. Finn, "The Ritual Process and Survival in Second-Century Rome," *Ritual Studies* 3 (1989) 69–89; G. C. Cumming, ed., *Essays on Hippolytus* (Bramcote Notts: Grove Books, 1978) and his *Hippolytus: A Text for Students* (Brancote Notts: Grove Books, 1976); and T. M. Finn, "The *Apostolic Tradition* of Hippolytus: The Document and the Religious and Social World of Early Christianity," *Aufsteig und Niedergang der Römischen Welt* 2, 27, forthcoming in 1993.

The *Apostolic Tradition* of Hippolytus

15. On Newcomers to the Faith

PROSELYTE
BAPTISM   >

Those who present themselves for the first time for instruction [lit., to hear the word] shall first of all be brought to the teachers before the congregation arrives. They shall be asked about the reason for coming to the faith, and those who have
SOMEONE TO
VOUCH FOR ...
NOT A SPY?   > brought them [i.e., their sponsors] will testify about whether they are ready for instruction [lit., capable of hearing the word]. They shall be asked about the kind of life they lead: whether he [*sic*] has a wife or whether he is a slave. And if any is the slave of one of the faithful, whether he has his master's approval for taking instruction. If his master does not testify that he is a good man, let him be rejected. If his master is a pagan, teach him to please his master lest scandal arise. If, however, one [of the candidates] have a wife, or a wife, a husband, let them be taught to be content, husband with wife and wife with husband. If, however, someone does not have a wife, let him be taught not to fornicate but to take a wife according to the law, or to remain single [lit., as he is]. Should someone be pos-
ILL   > sessed of a demon, he is not to be instructed in the teaching until he is pure.

16. On Jobs and Professions

Moreover, inquiry shall be made about the jobs and occupations of those who seek to be instructed. If anyone runs a house of prostitution, let him cease or be sent away. If anyone is a sculptor or paints let him be taught not to make idols: let him either cease or repent. If anyone is an actor or is engaged in theatrical presentations, let him cease or be rejected. As for him who teaches children, it is best that he cease; if he has no [other] craft, let him be allowed to continue. Likewise, the charioteer who competes in the games and those who take part in them, let them cease or be rejected. The gladiator, or one who trains gladiators to fight, or one who engages in the arena hunt, or an official in the gladiatorial enterprise, let him cease or be rejected. He who is a priest of idols, or an idol attendant, let him cease or be rejected.

An enlisted man [lit., a soldier under orders] shall not kill anyone. If he is ordered to, he shall not carry out the order, nor shall he take the [military oath]. He who has the power to execute [lit., of the sword] or the city magistrate who wears the purple, let him cease or be rejected. A catechumen, or one of the faithful who wants to become a soldier, let them be rejected, because they have shown contempt for God.

The prostitute, or the profligate, or the eunuch, or one who does unspeakable things, let them be rejected; they are impure.

A magician is not to be brought to the inquiry. The maker of charms, or the astrologer, or the diviner, or the interpreter of dreams, or the charlatan, or the fringe-cutter, or the phylactery-maker, let them either cease or be rejected.

Someone who is a concubine, if she is a slave and if she brings up her children and remains faithfully attached to one man, let her hear the word; otherwise let her be sent away. The man who has a concubine, let him cease and take a wife according to the law; if, however, he refuses, let him be rejected.

If we have omitted anything, the occupations [in question] will instruct you; for all of us have the Spirit of God.

17. Concerning the Period of Instruction

Catechumens will be under instruction from a period of three years. If someone is zealous and applies himself well to the work of the catechumenate [lit., to the thing], not the period of time but [evidence of] conversion alone shall be judged.

18. Concerning the Prayer of Those Under Instruction

When the teacher has finished his instruction, the catechumens will pray among themselves, apart from the faithful; the women, whether catechumens or faithful, will stand and pray together in a specially designated place [lit., some place] in the church. When [the catechumens] have finished praying, however, they will not give the kiss of peace, because their mouths are not holy. The faithful, nonetheless, greet each other, men, the men, women, the women; the men, however, will not greet the women, moreover, let the women cover their heads with a mantle, and not just with a kind of linen, for [such] is not a veil.

19. Concerning the Imposition of the Hand

After a prayer, when the teacher has imposed his hand over the catechumens, let him pray and dismiss them. Whether he is a cleric or layman, let him do so. If a catechumen is arrested on account of the name of the Lord [i.e., because he is a Christian], let him not be of divided heart [lit., of double heart] about the testimony; should violence come to him and he is killed, although his sins are not yet forgiven [i.e., he is not yet baptized], he will [nonetheless be] justified. For he has received baptism in his own blood.

20. Concerning Those to Be Baptized

When those to be baptized are chosen [ELECTED], let the life of each be examined: whether they have lived with integrity while they were catechumens, whether they visited the sick, whether they did every [sort of] good work. When those who accompanied them testify about him [*sic*], "He has thus acted," let them hear the gospel. From the moment when they are set apart, let the hand be imposed over them daily, while they are exorcised. When the day of their baptism approaches, the bishop will exorcise each one of them to learn whether he is pure. If someone is not good or not pure, he will set them aside, because [such a one] has not heard the instructions with faith. For it is not possible that the alien [i.e., Satan] hide himself forever.

Immediate Preparations

Let those to be baptized be instructed to bathe on Thursday [lit., the fifth day of the week]. If a woman, however, is in her period, let her be put aside and baptized another day. [PREPARATION DAY]

Let those to receive baptism fast on the eve of the Sabbath [Friday] and on the Sabbath [as well]; and on the Sabbath let them be assembled in a place the bishop designates. Let him command them all to pray and kneel. And, imposing his hand over them, let him command every alien spirit to flee from them and not to return again to them. When he has finished exorcising them, let him exhale on their faces, and when he has signed their forehead, ears and noses [with the cross], let him raise them to a standing position. They will [then] pass the entire night in vigil, hearing [Scripture] reading and instruction [thereon].

Let those about to be baptized bring nothing with them except what each brings for the Eucharist. For is fitting from that very hour that he who has been made worthy offer the oblation.

21. Concerning the Giving of Holy Baptism

At cockcrow, first let prayer be offered over the water; let the water flow or be poured into the font. Let it be done this way, unless there be some necessity. If, however, the necessity is permanent and urgent, use such water as you find.

Renunciation of Satan

[Those about to be baptized] shall take off [their] clothes. First baptize the children. Let those who can, speak for themselves. But those unable to speak for themselves, let their parents or someone from their family speak for them. Then, baptize the men and finally the women, after they have let down their hair and put away [any] gold jewelry they are wearing. And let none take any alien object [amulet] down into the water [with him].

At the appointed time for baptism, let the bishop give thanks over the oil, which he puts in a vial and calls the oil of thanksgiving. He then takes some other oil, which he exorcises and calls the oil of exorcism. A deacon then carries the oil of exorcism and stations himself at the left hand of the presbyter; another deacon takes the oil of thanksgiving and stands at the presbyter's right. Taking each candidate for baptism, let the presbyter command him to renounce saying, "I renounce you, Satan, and all your service and all your works." And when each one has renounced [Satan], let [the presbyter] anoint him with the oil of exorcism, saying to him: "May every spirit depart from you." And in this way let him [the anointing presbyter] hand the naked candidate to the bishop or to the presbyter who stands close to the water, in order to baptize him.

Immersion

Let the deacon descend with the candidate this way. When he who is to be baptized descends into the water, the one who baptizes imposes his hand on him and asks: "Do you believe in the Father Almighty?'' [In the Sahidic, Ethiopic, and Arabic versions there follows a post-Nicene baptismal creed.]

And for his part, let him who is being baptized say: ''I believe.'' And again he who is doing the baptizing, let him impose his hand on his head. Then, let him say: ''Do you believe in Christ Jesus the Son of God, who was born from the Holy Spirit and from the Virgin Mary, was crucified under Pontius Pilate, died, [was buried], rose on the third day from the dead, ascended into the heavens, and sits at the right hand of the Father; and who will come to judge the living and the dead?'' When he has said, ''I believe,'' let him [the one baptizing] say, ''Do you believe in the Holy Spirit and in the holy church and in the resurrection of the flesh?'' Let him who is being baptized say: ''I believe''; so a third time let him be baptized.

Chrismation, Prayer, the Kiss of Peace

Afterwards, when [the newly baptized] has emerged [from the font], let him be anointed with oil which has been consecrated [i.e., the oil of thanksgiving] by a presbyter saying: ''I anoint you with holy oil in the name of Jesus Christ.'' When each [newly baptized] has dried, let them dress and then enter the church.

With his hand imposed [over] them, let the bishop say the following prayer, ''Lord God, you who have made them worthy to receive the remission of sins through the bath of regeneration by the Holy Spirit, send into them your grace that they may serve you according to your will; for to you is glory, to the Father and the Son with the Holy Spirit, both now and for the ages of the ages. Amen.''

Then, as he pours consecrated oil from his hand and imposes his hand on [the newly baptized's] head, let [the bishop] say: ''I anoint you with holy oil in the Lord Father almighty and Christ Jesus and the Holy Spirit.'' And as he signs him on the forehead, let him offer the kiss and say: ''The Lord be with you.'' Then let him who is signed say: ''And with your spirit.'' The bishop will do thus to each. Then [the newly baptized] shall pray together with the congregation, for they do not pray with the faithful unless all these [rites] have been completed. And when they have prayed, they shall offer the kiss of peace.

The Eucharist

Next let the offering be presented to the bishop by the deacons and he will give thanks over the bread as a representation—

which the Greeks call "antitype"—of the body of Christ; and over the cup mixed with wine as an antitype—which the Greeks call "likeness"—of the blood which was poured out for all those who believe in him; and over the mixture of milk and honey in fulfillment of the promise made to the fathers when [God] spoke about a land flowing [with] milk and honey, and for which Christ also gave his flesh through which those who believe are nourished, making the bitterness of the heart sweet by the sweetness of his word; and over water presented in the offering as a sign of the [baptismal] bath, that the inner man, that is, the soul, may obtain the same effects as the body. The bishop will explain all these things to those who receive them.

When [the bishop] has broken the bread and as he offers each the kiss of peace, he will say: "The bread of heaven in Christ Jesus." Each one who receives will respond: "Amen." If there are not enough presbyters, let deacons take the cups and stand with deference in the proper order: the first is to be he who holds the water, the second, the milk, and the third, the wine.

Those who receive will taste of each of the three cups, as he who offers says, "In God the Father Almighty." He who receives then says: "And in the Lord Jesus Christ" [and the recipient will say, "Amen."] "And in the Holy Spirit and the holy church." And he will say: "Amen." This is to be done for each recipient. Moreover, when everything is over, let each hasten to do good work[s].

Novatian

For Western Christians the third century was scarred with controversies, none more poignant than the one already joined in Hermas and Hippolytus, namely, whether to reconcile to the Church Christians who had fallen away during persecution (the lapsed). There were three responses: (1) for grave sins committed after baptism, especially apostasy, no reconciliation; (2) for grave sins after baptism, including apostasy, reconciliation, but only after an extended period of penance (or on one's deathbed); and (3) for all grave sins reconciliation is both possible and readily available. The Decian persecution (249-250) and its renewal under Valerian (253-260) sharpened the issue for Italy and North Africa, because many did lapse in Rome and Carthage (modern Tunis; see ch. 2). Not surprisingly, the lapsed argued for leniency, and they garnered support from an unexpected quarter—from those called "Confessors" because they remained steadfast to the point of torture and imprisonment. At the other extreme, heirs of people like Hippolytus and the opponents of Hermas argued for the strict view—no reconciliation. But Catholics eventually opted for the moderate view—penance followed by reconciliation.

Another poignant issue related to the problem of the lapsed was whether to rebaptize heretics. Those who said yes argued that the authentic Church is composed of those possessed of the Holy Spirit, who is given in baptism. Thus, they argued, heretical groups, because they have separated from the authentic Church, do not confer valid baptism—once separated from the Spirit, they cannot give what they do not have. Therefore, when their members seek to return to the Church, they must be baptized anew. The spokesman was a Roman presbyter named Novatian, whose disciples spread to North Africa, Syria, Asia Minor, and Spain. The founder himself, according to a recent tomb discovery in Rome, appears to have been martyred about 258. Novatianist Christians are known to have existed as late as the eighth century.

Novatian's most famous work, *On the Trinity,* is written in highly cultivated Latin, probably before he broke with the Church. Following the outline of the Roman baptismal creed, he treats of the Holy Spirit last, to whom he ascribes the full effects of baptism: It is the Holy Spirit who effects from water the second birth and all its consequent effects (29:16 ff.). The vision of the Church as the pure and Spirit-filled Church of prophets and martyrs dominates his baptismal teaching.

The text is from G. F. Diercks, ed., *Novatiani Opera,* CCL 4 (1972) 70–72. The translation is that of Russell J. DeSimone, FC 67 (1972) 101–104; the liturgy to which he alludes is almost certainly that of the *Apostolic Tradition.* For an account of Novatian, see Quasten, 2:212–233.

On the Trinity: The Holy Spirit
Chapter 29

11. He [the Holy Spirit] it is who came upon the Lord as a dove after he had been baptized, and abode in him. In Christ alone he dwells fully and entirely, not wanting in any measure or part; but in all his overflowing abundance dispensed and set forth, so that other men might receive from Christ a first out-

pouring, as it were, of his graces. For the fountainhead of the entire Holy Spirit abides in Christ, that from him might be drawn streams of grace and wondrous deeds because the Holy Spirit dwells affluently in Christ.

12. In fact, Isaiah prophesied this when he said: "And the spirit of wisdom and of understanding rests upon him, the spirit of counsel and might, the spirit of knowledge and piety, and the spirit of fear of the Lord shall fill him" [Isa 11:2].

13. He reiterated the very same thing in another passage in the person of the Lord himself: "The Spirit of the Lord is upon me, because he has anointed me; to bring good news to the poor he has sent me" [Isa 61:1].

14. Likewise David says: "Therefore God, your God, has anointed you with the oil of gladness above your fellow kings" [Ps 44(45):8].

15. The apostle Paul says of him: "For he who does not have the Spirit of Christ, he does not belong to Christ" [Rom 8:9]; and, "Where the Spirit of the Lord is, there is freedom" [2 Cor 3:17].

16. He it is who effects from water a second birth, the seed, as it were, of a divine generation. He is also the consecrator of a heavenly birth, "the pledge" of a promised "inheritance" [Eph 1:14], a kind of written bond, so to speak, of eternal salvation. He it is who makes us the temple of God and makes us his dwelling place. He importunes the divine ears "on our behalf with ineffable groanings" [Rom 8:26], thereby discharging his duties as advocate and rendering his services in our defense. He has been given to dwell in our bodies and to bring about our sanctification. He brings our bodies, by this operation of his in us, to eternity and to the resurrection of immortality, inasmuch as he accustoms them to be mingled in himself with celestial power and to be associated with the divine eternity of his Holy Spirit.

17. For in him and through him, our bodies are trained to advance to immortality, learning to bridle themselves with moderation according to his commands.

18. For it is he who lusts against the flesh because the flesh is contrary to him [see Gal 5:17].

19. It is he who checks insatiable desires, breaks unbridled lust, quenches illicit passions, overcomes fiery assaults, averts

drunkenness, resists avarice, drives away wanton revelries, binds together noble loves, strengthens good affections, does away with factions, explains the Rule of Truth [i.e., the creed], refutes heretics, banishes the impious and guards the gospels.

20. Of him the apostle likewise writes: "Now we have received not the spirit of the world, but the Spirit that is from God" [1 Cor 2:12].

21. Of him he exults when he says: "But I think that I also have the Spirit of God" [1 Cor 7:40].

22. Of him he says: "And the spirit of the prophets is under the control of the prophets" [1 Cor 14:32].

23. Of him he states: "Now the Spirit expressly says that in after times some will depart from the faith, giving heed to deceitful spirits and doctrines of devils, speaking lies hypocritically, and having their conscience seared" [1 Tim 4:1-2].

24. Grounded in this Spirit, "No one" ever "says 'Anathema' to Jesus" [1 Cor 12:3]; no one has denied that Christ is the Son of God, nor has rejected God the creator; no one utters any words against the Scriptures: no one lays down alien and sacrilegious ordinances; no one makes contradictory laws.

25. Whoever "shall have blasphemed" against him, "does not have forgiveness, either in this world or in the world to come" [Matt 12:32; Mark 3:29; Luke 12:10].

26. It is he who in the apostles renders testimony to Christ, in the martyrs manifests the unwavering faith of religion, in virgins encloses the admirable continence of sealed chastity. In the rest of men, he keeps the laws of the Lord's teaching uncorrupted and untainted. He destroys heretics, corrects those in error, reproves unbelievers, reveals impostors, and also corrects the wicked. He keeps the church uncorrupted and inviolate in the holiness of perpetual virginity and truth.

Zeno of Verona

Except for a dispute between Rome and Carthage when Cyprian was the bishop of Carthage (248–258, ch. 2), Rome was silent on matters baptismal until Pope Innocent I wrote to Decentius of Gubbio about postbaptismal anointing (416; see below). Indeed, there was silence on the whole Italian peninsula until the late fourth century. It was broken first in Verona, a city of centuries-old commercial and military importance three hundred miles north of Rome and one hundred miles east of Milan. Remarkably, its first-century amphitheater is still in use, and recently two fourth-century Christian basilicas have been excavated beneath the cathedral. Although Christianity in the city dates from the third century, its first bishop of record was Lucillus (ca. 343). The one who broke the silence was Zeno, thought to be its eighth bishop, who died in 379 or 380. There is reason to believe that he was of African origin. Little, however, can be said of his life with any certainty beyond the fact that Ambrose of Milan (below) knew him, and that Zeno looked to Ambrose and the Milanese Church for leadership.

The legacy of his homilies (collected in two books of sixty and thirty-two homilies respectively), however, discloses a well-educated pastor of some eloquence yet self-deprecating, who showed a marked preference for the Hebrew Bible and for the paschal liturgy. Reminiscent of Abercius' *Epitaph* (above) and Tertullian (ch. 2), the iconography consistently shows him with a fishing rod in his hand and a fish on his line, both strong baptismal images. Unfortunately, only about thirty of his homilies are developed in any substantial way; most are little more than summaries. Such is the case with the seven *Invitations to the Baptismal Font* here given, although they may have been part of one complete homily addressed to those about to be baptized. His preferred image of baptism is rebirth, and of the baptismal font, the womb, or as he puts it in the last invitation, the "genital font" *(fons genitalis)*. Related to this emphasis on baptismal fertility is his emphasis on Mary as the image of the Church.

One can see fleeting glimpses of the Verona baptismal liturgy in the *Invitations* (and elsewhere in the homilies); given the influence of Ambrose and Milan, however, the rites could scarcely have differed from those of Milan, to which we turn next. The text is *Zenonis Veronensis Tractatus,* ed. B. Lofstedt, CCL 22 (1971) 83, 123, 202; the translation, that of Thomas Halton, BAP (1967) 64–66.

Invitations to the Baptismal Font
Invitation 1

Brethren, exult with joy in Christ. Borne on the wings of your every yearning, receive the gifts of heaven. For now the saving warmth of the eternal font invites you. Now your Mother adopts you to make you her child. You are to be born not by the ordinary rules of childbirth—mothers groaning in the pains of labor and bringing you into the miseries of this world, weeping, sullied, and wrapped in sullied swaddling clothes—but exulting in joy, children of heaven, children free from sin, to be bountifully nourished, not in the foul-smelling cradles, but at the altar rails in the midst of sweet perfumes. Through our Lord Jesus Christ.

Invitation 2

Brethren, without delay and with more speed than words, enter the heavenly gates. Do not believe that in immersing yourselves in the pool of regeneration, the source of eternal life, that a grace is conferred on you that is an accepter of persons. Your regeneration is brought about by your judgment alone, in the knowledge that you have that nobility of soul which is measured by the greatness of your faith. Therefore, with faith and fortitude, put off that old man with his foul-smelling rags, all you who presently are to take part in the procession, regenerated and clothed in white garments, having been enriched with the gifts of the Holy Spirit.

Invitation 3

Brethren, why do you hesitate? Thanks to your faith, the wave of rebirth has already begotten you. It is bringing you forth through the sacraments. Hasten with all speed to the center of your desire. Lo, a solemn hymn is being chanted. Lo, the sweet wail of the new-born is heard. Lo, the most illustrious brood of the begotten proceeds from the one womb. A new thing, that each one is born spiritually. Run, then, forward to the mother who experiences no pains of labor although she cannot count the number of those to whom she gives birth. Enter, then. Enter! Happily you are going to drink the new milk together.

Invitation 4

Why do you delay? Though differing in age, sex, and state in life, you are soon going to be joined in unity. Fly to the fountain, to the sweet womb of your virgin mother. It is where you belong, thanks to your divine nobility and your faith. Realize that your future happiness will be proportioned to your faith. O admirable and most holy benevolence of God, that birth takes place without maternal labor, that our spiritual birth is free from tears. This regeneration, this resurrection, this eternal life, our mother has given to all. She incorporates us in one body after assembling us from every race and from every nation.

Invitation 5

Brethren, exult. Your own faith has given you birth. You have fled the snares of this world, its sin, its wounds, its death. You have invoked the assistance of your Father in majesty. Fly, then, not with swiftness of foot, but on wings of thought, to the water of the saving font. Immerse yourselves with confidence. Fortunately, by the death of your old man, you are destined to be victorious.

Invitation 6

Hasten, brethren, hasten to the bath that will purify you thoroughly. The living water, tempered by the Holy Spirit and fire, most sweet, now invites you with its tender murmur. Already the attendant of the bath is girded, expecting your arrival, ready to give the necessary anointing and drying, and a golden denarius sealed with triple effigy. Therefore, rejoice. For you will plunge naked into the font but you will soon emerge clothed with a heavenly garment, dressed in white. And he who does not soil his baptismal robe will possess the kingdom of heaven. Amen.

Invitation 7

Brethren, you burn with thirst deep and ardent. The sweet murmur of the flowing nectar invites you. Fly without delay to the milk of this genital font. Drink with confidence while you may. Be bathed in the waves of the river flowing over you. Fill your vessels with all urgency and with much devotion, so that you will always have enough water, remembering this before all else that you can never spill a drop or come to fetch it again.

Ambrose of Milan

The youngest son of the Praetorian prefect of Gaul, Ambrose was born in 339 at Trier (Germany), the residence of emperors and the political capital of the empire west of the Alps. When his father died the family moved to Rome, where Ambrose trained for a career in public service and eventually attained the rank of consular governor of Amelia Liguria, the northern Italian province whose capital was Milan. Within three years (373) his career took an unexpected turn: By popular acclamation, though still a catechumen, he became bishop of Milan. Quickly baptized and then consecrated, Ambrose embarked on an episcopal life that was at once active, pastoral, and political. He soon became the leading Churchman in the West and remained so until his death in 397.

As Milan's bishop, Ambrose played a major part in the conversion of the man who would succeed him as ecclesiastical leader of the West, Augustine (ch. 2). Indeed, Augustine says of Ambrose the preacher that he hung on Ambrose's words, through which truth "slipped in," leading him from the seen to the unseen (*Confessions* 5:13–14; 6:3–4).

Among Ambrose's homilies are three sets that explicitly deal with baptism and its liturgy. The first, *Explanation of the Creed,* constitutes a brief commentary on the baptismal creed delivered about 385, shortly before Easter. It was occasioned by the widespread liturgical custom of confiding the creed, article by article, to those soon to be baptized *(traditio symboli).* They were to internalize and recite it from memory on the Sunday before Easter *(redditio symboli).* The second, *On the Sacraments,* and the third, *On the Mysteries,* are two versions of his Easter-week homilies on the baptismal rites and their meaning (see vol. 5, ch. 1, Cyril and Theodore). The former is a stenographic record of the postbaptismal homilies, which may echo the very words Augustine heard when he was among the newly baptized during Easter week in 387. The latter is a similar record of postbaptismal homilies (perhaps the same), but edited for publication, doubtless by Ambrose himself. Both works date from the decade 380–390, most likely from the middle of the decade. The reading comprises the first three homilies from *On the Sacraments,* which are devoted to the baptismal rites. The fourth and much of the fifth concern the Eucharist. The remainder of the fifth homily and the entire sixth consist of a commentary on the Lord's Prayer, which appears in the Easter-week instructions for the first time and presupposes a prebaptismal rite for the petition-by-petition handing over of the Lord's Prayer *(traditio orationis dominici).*

A note is in order about two postbaptismal rites at Milan, especially because Ambrose points out with vigor that the Milanese liturgy follows that of Rome closely (*On the Sacraments* 3:5). He speaks of only one major difference: Following the injunction in John 13:4-11 (Jesus washes the disciples' feet), the newly baptized have their feet washed when they come out of the baptismal pool (3:4-7). In fact, Ambrose's homilies provide something of a fourth-century window on baptism in Rome as well as in Milan and elsewhere in Italy (see above, Zeno) and to some extent in North Africa. In addition, they witness to the fact that much of baptism in the *Apostolic Tradition* of Hippolytus has survived. Nonetheless, Lent has replaced the three-year catechumenate (see vol. 5, ch. 1, Egeria), and as the following outline suggests, there has been much revision and development in the baptismal drama first scripted by Hippolytus.

Baptismal Preparation

1. Enrollment. The candidates "put their names in" on the Epiphany. Reminiscent of Jesus' healing of the blind man in John 9:7, the rite involved smearing the eyes with mud to signify the "eye-opening" work to come in the Lenten catechumenate (3:11–12).

2. Daily instruction and frequent exorcism. Primarily moral, the instructions highlighted the Abraham story in Genesis 12–25 (*On Abraham* 1).

3. Delivery of the creed *(traditio symboli)*. As noted, the creed, together with a brief explanation, was given orally to the candidates, doubtless on the Sunday two weeks before Easter.

4. Scrutiny (*Explanation of the Creed* 1; see below, John the Deacon; also see ch. 2, Augustine). A solemn exorcism, involving even physical examination, the rite was a psychological ordeal that sought to test whether any impurity of mind or body remained in the candidates. The scrutiny was held in close association with the recitation of the creed, probably in vigil on Saturday night before Holy Week.

5. Recitation of the creed *(redditio symboli)*. Each of the candidates professed the creed before the congregation on the Sunday before Easter; Augustine gives an account of Marius Victorinus' profession (*Confessions* 8:3–5) at Rome (ca. 360). At some time later in the day, the *traditio* of the Lord's Prayer very likely took place.

Baptism

6. The opening *(aperitio)*. Recalling the incident in Mark 7:34 where Christ opens a blind man's eyes with a mixture of saliva and clay, the rite took place just outside the baptistery at the end of the Easter Vigil and involved touching the candidates' ears and nostrils to invigorate "faith and piety" (1:2-3).

7. First anointing (1:4). The rite involved rubbing the entire body with olive oil, which according to Ambrose constituted an exorcism and a strengthening of the candidate for the struggle with the devil to follow (see General Introduction, "Anointing and the Holy Spirit").

8. Renunciation (1:5). Facing West, the candidates then renounced the devil and his works, which Ambrose considers the world and its pleasures.

9. Allegiance (1:6). Facing East, the candidate spoke unrecorded words that announced allegiance to Christ.

10. Entry into the baptistery (1:9). Ambrose uses the procession to comment on the traditional biblical "types" of baptism (1:10-2:13).

11. Exorcism and consecration of the baptismal water (2:14-15). To signify that the passion of Christ is the source of baptism's effectiveness, the bishop, as he prayed over the water, traced the sign of the cross on the waters (he may also have plunged his staff in).

12. Immersion (2:20-23). The candidates were immersed three times in the waters, each being asked the baptismal creed in the form of three questions, the first about God the Father, the second about God the Son, and the third about God the Holy Spirit in the Church and about resurrection. The response was "I believe."

13. Anointing the head (2:24-3:1). Reminiscent of Israel's practice of anointing priests and kings, chrism was poured on the heads of the candidates as they emerged from the font.

14. Foot washing (3:4-7). Recalling the account of Jesus washing the feet of the disciples at the Last Supper (John 13:2-11), the bishop washed the feet of the newly baptized.

15. White garment (4:5-6; 5:14). To symbolize their baptismal transformation, the candidates were vested in white.

16. Consignation (3:8-10). As a special sign associated with the sevenfold gift of the Holy Spirit and perfection, the newly bap-

tized were signed with oil (most likely, chrism) in the sign of the cross.

17. The kiss. In his correspondence (*Epistle* 41:14–15), Ambrose mentions that a liturgical embrace was given the newly baptized as new born of the Christian family (see vol. 5, ch. 1, Chrysostom).

18. Milk and honey (5:15–17). As part of the Eucharist, the candidates were given a cup of mixed milk and honey.

Some final observations. Ambrose, who introduced responsorial singing in the West, indicates that the newly baptized chanted Psalm 22 (23) in procession from the baptistery to the basilica for the Eucharist (*On the Sacraments* 5:13). In the bishop's hands, it recapitulates a series of types about baptism and the Eucharist:

> How often have you heard Psalm 22 and not understood it! See how it is applicable to the heavenly sacraments: "The Lord feeds me and I shall want nothing; he has set me in a place of pasture; he has brought me upon the water of refreshment; he has converted my soul. He has led me on the paths of justice for his own name's sake. For though I should walk in the midst of the shadow of death, I will fear no evils, for you are with me. Your rod is power, the staff suffering, that is, the eternal divinity of Christ, but also corporeal suffering; the one created, the other redeemed. You have prepared a table before me against them that afflict me. You have anointed my head with oil; and my chalice which inebriates me how goodly it is!"

In the third homily (6, 8–10) Ambrose singles out the final post-baptismal anointing of the head (consignation) as the baptismal rite that signifies par excellence the gift of the Holy Spirit. He calls it the "effecting of perfection" (3:8).

Within a few years this anointing was reserved to the bishop alone, introducing a growing separation between baptism and the final anointing (see below, Papal Correspondence) and the implication that the anointing conferred the Spirit in a special way. Also, Ambrose is the first catechist to use the Song of Songs in a baptismal commentary (5:5–17): He uses its images as an allegory of the newly baptized and the sacraments of initiation.

Finally, Ambrose was profoundly influenced by the Alexandrian (ch. 3) school of biblical and liturgical interpretation, especially by the work of Origen, Didymus the Blind (ca. 313–398), and Cyril.

The text is that of B. Botte, ed., SC 25bis (1961); the translation, Roy J. Deferrari, FC 44 (1963). For valuable studies see Botte, SC 25, introduction; Edward J. Yarnold, "The Ceremonies of Initiation in the 'De Sacramentis' and 'De Mysteriis' of St. Ambrose," *Studia Patristica* 10, TU 107 (1970) 453–463; Orrin T. Wheeler, "Baptism According to St. Ambrose" (Ph.D. diss., Woodstock College, 1958).

On the Sacraments 1

1. I approach a sermon on the sacraments which you have received, whose scope should not have been presented to you before. For in the Christian man faith is first. Thus, even in Rome they are called "the faithful" who have been baptized, and our father Abraham was justified by faith, not by works. So you have received baptism, you have believed. Surely it is unfitting that I consider anything else; for you would not have been called to grace if Christ had not judged you worthy of his grace.

2. What have we done on the Sabbath? "The opening," of course. These mysteries of "the opening" were celebrated when the priest touched your ears and nostrils. What does this signify? In the gospel, our Lord Jesus Christ, when the deaf and dumb man was presented to him, touched his ears and his mouth: the ears, because he was deaf; the mouth, because he was dumb. And he said: "Effetha" [Mark 7:34]. This is a Hebrew word, which in Latin means *adaperire* [to open]. Therefore, the priest has touched your ears, that your ears may be opened to the sermon and exhortation of the priest.

3. But you say to me: "Why the nostrils?" In the one case, because he was dumb, he [Christ] touched the mouth in order that, since he was unable to speak the heavenly sacraments, he [the man] might receive the power of speech from Christ; and in the other case, because the person was a man! In this case, because women are being baptized, and there is not the same purity on the part of the servant as with the Lord—for, since one pardons sins, and sins are forgiven for the other, what comparison can there be?—thus, because of the grace of the work and of the favor, the bishop does not touch the mouth but the nostrils. Why the nostrils? In order that you may receive the good odor of eternal piety, that you may say: "We are the good

odor of Christ" [2 Cor 2:15], just as the holy apostle said, and that there may be in you the full fragrance of faith and devotion.

4. We have come to the font; you have entered; you have been anointed. Consider whom you have seen, what you have said; consider; repeat carefully. A Levite [deacon] meets you; a priest meets you; you are anointed as an athlete of Christ, as if to contend in the contest of this world. You have professed the struggles of your contest. He who contends has what he hopes for; where there is a struggle, there is a crown. You contend in the world, but you are crowned by Christ. And for the struggles of the world you are crowned, for, although the reward is in heaven, the merit for the reward is established here.

5. When you were asked: "Do you renounce the devil and his works?"—what did you reply? "I do renounce." "Do you renounce the world and its pleasures?"—what did you reply? "I do renounce." Be mindful of your words, and never let the sequence of your bond be broken. If you give a man surety, you are held responsible, so that you may receive his money; you are held bound, and the lender binds you if you resist. If you refuse, you go to a judge and there you will be convicted by your own bond.

6. Consider where you promised, or to whom you promised. You saw the Levite, but he is the minister of Christ. You saw him minister before the altar. Therefore, your surety is held, not on earth, but in heaven. Consider where you receive the heavenly sacraments. If the body of Christ is here, here, too, are the angels established. "Wherever the body shall be, there shall the eagles also be" [Matt 24:28], you have read in the gospel. Wherever the body shall be, there shall the eagles also be, who are accustomed to fly so as to escape the earthly and to seek the heavenly. Why do I say this? Because men, too, are angels, whoever announce Christ and seem to be received into the place of angels.

7. How? Observe: John the Baptist was born of a man and a woman. Yet give heed, because he himself also is an angel: "Behold, I send my angel before your face, who shall prepare your way before you" [Matt 11:10]. Observe again. Malachias the Prophet says: "For the lips of the priest shall keep knowledge and they shall seek the law at his mouth: because he is the angel of the Lord of hosts" [Mal 2:7]. These words are spoken for this reason, that we may proclaim the glory of the priesthood, not that something may be arrogated to personal merits.

8. So you have renounced the universe; you have renounced the world; be solicitous. He who owes money always considers his bond. And you who owe Christ faith keep faith, which is much more precious than money; for faith is an eternal patrimony, money a temporal one. And do you, therefore, always remember what you have promised; you will be more cautious. If you keep your promise, you will also keep your bond.

9. Then you approached nearer; you saw the font; you also saw the priest above the font. I cannot doubt that that could not have fallen upon your mind, which fell upon that Syrian Naaman, for, although he was cleansed, yet he doubted first [4 Kgs 5:1]. Why? I shall tell; observe:

10. You entered; you saw water; you saw the priest; you saw the Levite. Lest, perchance, someone say: "Is this all?"—yes, this is all, truly all, where there is all innocence, where there is all piety, all grace, all sanctification. You have seen what you were able to see with the eyes of your body, with human perception; you have not seen those things which are effected but those which are seen. Those which are not seen are much greater than those which are seen. "For the things which are seen are temporal, but the things which are not seen are eternal."

11. Therefore, let us say first—hold the bond of my words and exact it—"We marvel at the mysteries of the Jews, which were handed down to our fathers, first the age of the sacraments, then the sanctity of those who vouch for them." This I assure you, that the sacraments of the Christians are more divine and earlier than those of the Jews.

12. What superiority is there over the people of the Jews having passed through the sea [Exod 14:1-15; John 6:49], that meanwhile we may speak of baptism? Yet the Jews who passed through, all died in the desert. But he who passes through this font, that is from the earthly to the heavenly—for there is a passage here, thus Easter, that is, "his passage" [Exod 12:10], the passage from sin to life, from fault to grace, from defilement to sanctification—he who passes through this font does not die but rises.

13. Naaman then was leprous [see 4 Kgs 5:1-14]. A girl said to his wife: "If my master wishes to be made clean, let him go to the land of Israel, and there he will find him who can rid him of leprosy." She told her mistress, and the wife told her husband, Naaman the king of Syria, who sent him, as one most acceptable to himself, to the king of Israel. The king of

Israel heard that he had been sent to him to be cleansed of leprosy, and rent his garment. Then Eliseus the Prophet commands
him: "Why is it that you have rent your garment, as if there
were no powerful God to cleanse the leper? Send him to me."
He sent him. When he approaches, the prophet says: "Come,
go down to the Jordan, dip and you will be cured."

14. He began to ponder with himself and say: "Is this all?
I have come from Syria to the land of Judaea and I am told:
'Come to the Jordan and dip and you will be cured,' as if the
rivers in my own country were not better." His servants said
to him: "Lord, why do you not do the word of the prophet?
Rather, do it and try." Then he went to the Jordan, dipped,
and, arose cured.

15. What, then, does this mean? You have seen water: not
all water cures, but the water which has the grace of Christ cures.
One is an element, the other a consecration; one an opus, the
other an operation. Opus belongs to water; operation belongs
to the Holy Spirit. Water does not cure unless the Holy Spirit
descends and consecrates that water, as you have read that, when
our Lord Jesus Christ gave the form of baptism, he came to
John, and John said to him: "I ought to be baptized by you;
and do you come to me?" Christ replied to him: "Suffer it now:
for so it becomes us to fulfill all justice" [Matt 3:14-15]. Behold that all justice is established in baptism.

16. Therefore, why did Christ descend, except that that flesh
of yours might be cleansed, the flesh which he took over from
our condition? For no washing away of his sins was necessary
for Christ, "who did no sin" [1 Pet 2:22], but it was necessary
for us who remain subject to sin. Therefore, if baptism is for
our sakes, the form has been established for us, the form of
our faith has been set forth.

17. Christ descended; John stood by, who baptized, and behold! the Holy Spirit descended as a dove. [See the accounts
in Matt 3; Mark 1; Luke 3.] Not a dove descended, but "as
a dove." Remember what I said: "Christ took on flesh, not
'as flesh,' but that true flesh of yours; Christ truly took on flesh.
But the Holy Spirit in the likeness of a dove, not as a real dove,
but in the likeness of a dove descended from heaven." So John
saw and believed [John 1:34; 20:8].

18. Christ descended; the Holy Spirit also descended. Why
did Christ descend first, the Holy Spirit afterwards, when the
form and practice of baptism includes this: that the font be con-

secrated first, then that he descend who is to be baptized. For, when the priest first enters, he performs the exorcism according to the creation of water; afterwards he delivers an invocation and prayer, that the font may be sanctified and that the presence of the eternal Trinity may be at hand. But Christ descended first, and the Spirit followed. For what reason? Not that the Lord Jesus himself might seem to be in need of the mystery of sanctification, but that he himself might sanctify, that the Spirit also might sanctify.

19. So Christ descended into the water, and the Holy Spirit descended as a dove; God the Father also spoke from heaven: You have the presence of the Trinity.

20. Moreover, the Apostle says that in the Red Sea there was a figure of this baptism, in these words: "All our fathers were baptized in the cloud and in the sea" [1 Cor 10:1-2], and he added: "Now all these things happened to them in figure" [1 Cor 10:11], but to us in reality. Then Moses held the staff [Exod 14:9–15:21]. The people of the Jews were shut in. The Egyptian approached with armed men. On one side the Hebrews were shut in by the sea. They were unable to cross the sea or to turn back against the enemy. They began to murmur.

21. Behold, let it not provoke you that they were heard. Although the Lord heard, yet they are not without fault who murmured. It is your duty, when you are restrained, to believe that you will go forth, not to murmur: to invoke, to question, not to express a complaint.

22. Moses held a staff and led the people of the Hebrews by night in a pillar of light, by day in a pillar of a cloud. What is light but truth, since it gives forth an open and clear brightness? What is a column of light but the Lord Christ, who has dispelled the shadows of infidelity, has infused the light of truth and grace into human inclinations? But surely the column of a cloud is the Holy Spirit. The people were in the sea and the column of light went ahead, then the column of a cloud followed like the shadow of the Holy Spirit. You see that by the Holy Spirit and by the water he displayed a figure of baptism.

23. In the flood [Gen 6:12; 9:17], also, already at that time there was a figure of baptism, and still, of course, there were no mysteries among the Jews. If, then, the form of this baptism preceded, you see that the mysteries of the Christians are older than were those of the Jews.

24. But, meanwhile, in consideration of the weakness of my voice and reasons of time, let it suffice today to have tasted the mysteries even from the sacred font. On tomorrow, if the Lord grants the power of speaking or the opportunity, I shall go into the matter more fully. There is need of your sanctity [they had just been baptized] having ears prepared and minds more ready so as to be able to grasp what we can gather from the series of Scriptures and shall go into, that you may have the grace of the Father and of the Son and of the Holy Spirit, to which Trinity is the everlasting kingdom from the ages and now and always, and forever and ever. Amen.

On the Sacraments 2

1. Yesterday we began to discuss that in the flood, also, a figure of baptism had preceded. What is the flood except where the just is reserved for the seminary of justice, and where sin dies? So the Lord, seeing that the sins of men were flourishing, reserved the just man alone with his progeny, but ordered the water to go out even above the mountains. And thus in that flood all corruption of the flesh perished; only the stock and the kind of the just remained. Is not this a flood, which baptism is, in which all sins are washed away, only the mind and grace of the just are raised up again?

2. The apostle [Eph 4:5] proclaims many kinds of baptism, but *one baptism*. Why? There are the baptisms of the Gentiles, but they are not baptism. They are baths, but they cannot be baptisms. The flesh is bathed; fault is not washed away; rather, in that bath fault is contracted. There were baptisms among the Jews, some superfluous, others in figure. And the figure itself was of benefit to us, since it is an indication of the truth.

3. What was read yesterday? It said: "An angel of the Lord went down at a certain time into the pond, and, as often as the angel went down, the water was moved. And he that went down first into the pond, after the motion of the water, was made whole of whatsoever infirmity he lay under" [John 5:4]. This signifies the figure of our Lord Jesus Christ about to come.

4. Why "angel"?—for he himself is the angel of great counsel; "at a certain time," which was saved for the last hour, that at the very setting he might overtake the day and defer the setting. So, "as often as the angel went down, the water was moved." Perchance you say: "Why now is it not moved?" Give

heed why: "Signs for the incredulous, faith for those who believe" [1 Cor 14:22].

5. "He that went down first was made whole of every infirmity." Why is "first"? In time or in honor? Understand both! If in time, "he that went down first" was made whole beforehand, that is, of the people of the Jews rather than of the people of nations. If in honor, "he that went down first," that is, who had fear of God, zeal for justice, grace, charity, affection for chastity, he himself rather was made whole. Yet at that time one was saved; at that time, I say, in a figure "he that went down first" alone was cured. How much greater is the grace of the church in which all are saved, whoever go down!

6. But see the mystery: Our Lord Jesus Christ comes to the pond. Many sick were lying there. And easily were many sick lying there, where only one was cured. Then he said to the paralytic: "Go down." He said: "I have no man" [John 5:3]. Behold where you are baptized, whence the baptism is, if not from the cross of Christ, from the death of Christ. There is all the mystery, because he suffered for you. In him you are redeemed; in him you are saved.

7. He says: "I have no man." That is: "Because by a man came death and by a man the resurrection" [1 Cor 15:21], he was not able to go down, he was not able to be saved, who did not believe that our Lord Jesus Christ had taken on flesh from a virgin. But this man who was awaiting the mediator of God and men, the man Jesus, expecting him of whom it was said: "And the Lord will send a man who will make them whole" [Isa 19:4], said: "I have no man," and so he deserved to come to good health, because he believed in him coming. Yet he would have been better and more perfect if he had believed that he had already come whom he hoped would come.

8. Now, behold the incidents one by one. We said that a figure had preceded on the Jordan, when the leprous Naaman was cleansed. That girl of the captives, who is she but one who had the likeness of the church and represented a figure? For the people of the nations was captive; I do not mean captivity established under some enemy, but I mean that captivity which is greater, when the Devil with his own dominates with cruel power and subjects the captive necks of sinners to himself.

9. So you have one baptism, another in the flood; you have a third kind, when the fathers were baptized in the Red Sea; you have a fourth kind in the pond, when the water was moved.

Now I ask you whether you should believe that you have the presence of the Trinity at this baptism, with which Christ baptizes in the church.

10. Thus the same Lord Jesus in his gospel says to the apostles: "Go, baptize the nations in the name of the Father, and of the Son, and of the Holy Spirit" [Matt 28:19]. These are the words of the Savior.

11. Tell me, O man, Elias [3 Kgs 18:36] invoked fire from heaven, and fire went down; Eliseus [4 Kgs 6:5] invoked the name of the Lord, and from the water the head of the axe, which had been submerged, came up. Behold, another kind of baptism. Why? Because every man before baptism is pressed like the head of the axe and submerged; when he has been baptized, not as the head of an axe but as a lighter kind of productive wood, he is raised. Thus, here also is another figure. It was an axe with which pieces of wood were cut. The handle fell from the axe, that is, the head was submerged. The son of the Prophet did not know what he was doing, but this alone he knew, that he besought Eliseus the Prophet and asked for a remedy. Then Eliseus threw a piece of wood, and the head of the axe was raised. So do you see that in the cross of Christ the infirmity of all men is raised?

12. Another example—although we do not keep an order; for who can grasp all the accomplishments of Christ, as the apostles have related?—When Moses [Exod 15:22-25] had come into the desert and the people were thirsty and the people had come to the fountain of Mara and wished to drink, because, when he first took a swallow, he tasted a bitterness and began to be unable to drink, on this account Moses cast a stick into the fountain and the water, which was bitter before, began to grow sweet.

13. What does this signify except that every creature subject to corruption is water bitter for all? Although sweet for a time, a creature who cannot cast off sin is bitter. When you drink, you will thirst; when you take the sweetness of the drink, again you taste the bitterness. So the water is bitter, but when it has received the cross of Christ, when the heavenly sacrament, it begins to be sweet and pleasant, and worthily sweet, in which fault is withdrawn. So, if in a figure baptisms have such great power, how much more power does baptism have in reality?

14. Now, then, let us take thought. A priest comes; he says a prayer at the font; he invokes the name of the Father, the

presence of the Son and of the Holy Spirit; he uses heavenly words. The words are heavenly, because they are Christ's, that we baptize "in the name of the Father and of the Son and of the Holy Spirit" [Matt 28:19]. If, then, at the words of men, at the invocation of a holy man, the Trinity was present, how much more is the Trinity present there where eternal words operate? Do you wish to know that the Spirit came down? You have heard that he came down as a dove. Why as a dove? That the unbelievers might be called to faith. In the beginning there ought to have been a sign; in later generations there ought to be perfection.

15. Accept another example: After the death of our Lord Jesus Christ the apostles were in one place and they were praying on the day of Pentecost, and suddenly there came a great sound, as of a mighty wind coming, and there appeared cloven tongues as it were of fire [Acts 2:1-3]. What does this signify except the coming down of the Holy Spirit? He wished to show himself to the unbelievers even corporeally, that is, corporeally by a sign, spiritually by a sacrament. So the testimony of his coming is manifest, but upon us the privilege of faith is now conferred, because in the beginning signs were made for the unbelievers [1 Cor 14:22]; now in the fullness of the church, not by a sign, but by faith must we gather the truth.

16. Now let us examine what it is that is called baptism! You came to the font; you went down into it; you gave heed to the highest priest; you saw the Levites [deacons] and the priest at the font. What is baptism?

17. In the beginning our Lord God made man so that, if he had not tasted sin, he would not have died the death. He contracted sin; he was made subject to death; he was ejected from paradise. But the Lord, who wished his benefits to endure and to abolish all the snares of the serpent, also to abolish everything that caused harm, first, however, passed sentence on man: "Dust you are and into dust you shall return [Gen 2:7, 15:17; 3:6-24], and he made man subject to death. It was a divine sentence; it could not be resolved by a human condition. A remedy was given: that man should die and rise again. Why? That that also, which before had ceded to a place of damnation, might cede to a place of benefit. What is this except death? Do you ask how? Because death intervening makes an end to sin. For when we die, surely we have ceased to sin. The satisfaction of the sentence seemed to be that man, who had been made to live, if he had not sinned, began to die. But that the per-

petual grace of God might persevere, man died, but Christ found resurrection, that is, to restore the heavenly benefit which had been lost by the deceit of the serpent. Both, then, are for our good, for death is the end of sins and resurrection is the reformation of nature.

18. However, lest in this world the deceit and snares of the Devil might prevail, baptism was found. Hear what Scripture—rather, the Son of God—says about this baptism, that the Pharisees, who did not wish to be baptized by John's baptism, "despised the council of God" [Luke 7:30]. Then baptism is the council of God. How great is grace, where there is the council of God!

19. Listen then: For, that in this world, also, the grip of the Devil might be loosened, there was discovered how man alive might die and alive might rise again. What is "alive"? That is: the living life of the body, when it came to the font, and dipped into the font. What is water but of earth? So it satisfies the heavenly sentence without the stupor of death. Because you dip, that sentence is resolved: "You are dust and into dust you shall return" [Gen 3:19]. When the sentence has been fulfilled, there is opportunity for heavenly benefit and remedy. So water is of earth, but the potentials of our life did not permit that we be covered with earth and rise again from earth. Then earth does not wash, but water washes. Therefore, the font is as a sepulcher.

20. You were asked: "Do you believe in God the Father almighty?" You said: "I do believe," and you dipped, that is: you were buried. Again you were asked: "Do you believe in our Lord Jesus Christ and in his cross?" You said: "I do believe," and you dipped. So you were also buried together with Christ. For who is buried with Christ rises again with Christ. A third time you were asked: "Do you believe also in the Holy Spirit?" You said: "I do believe," you dipped a third time, so that the threefold confession absolved the multiple lapse of the higher life.

21. Finally, to furnish you an example, the holy apostle Peter, after he seemed to have lapsed by the weakness of his human condition [see John 18:25-27], who had before denied, afterwards, that he might wipe out and resolve the lapse, is asked a third time if he loved Christ. Then he said: "You know that I love you" [John 21:15-18]. He said it a third time, that he might be absolved a third time.

22. Thus, then, the Father dismisses sin; thus the Son dismisses it; thus, too, the Holy Spirit. But do not marvel that we are baptized in one name, that is, "in the name of the Father, and of the Son, and of the Holy Spirit" [Matt 28:19], because he said one name, in which is one substance, one divinity, one majesty. This is the name of which it is said: "Whereby we must be saved" [Acts 4:12]. In this name you all have been saved; you have returned to the grace of life.

23. So the apostle exclaims, as you heard in the reading of the gospel today [see Rom 6:1-14], that whoever is baptized is baptized in the death of Jesus. What is "in the death"? That, just as Christ died, so you also taste of death; just as Christ died to sin and lives for God, so you, too, died to the former allurements of sins through the sacrament of baptism and rose again through the grace of Christ. So death is, but not in the reality of corporal death but in likeness. For when you dip, you take on the likeness of death and burial, you receive the sacrament of that cross, because Christ hung on the cross and his body was transfixed with nails. You then are crucified with him; you cling to Christ, you cling to the nails of our Lord Jesus Christ, lest the Devil be able to take you from him. Let the nail of Christ hold you, whom the weakness of human condition recalls.

24. So you dipped; you came to the priest. What did he say to you? He said: "God the Father Almighty, who regenerated you by water and the Holy Spirit and forgave you your sins, himself will anoint you for life everlasting." See, for what you were anointed, he said: "For life everlasting." Do not prefer this life to that life. For example, if some enemy rises up, if he wishes to take away your faith, if he threatens death, that someone may prevaricate, beware what you choose. Do not choose that in which you are not anointed, but choose that in which you are anointed, so that you prefer eternal life to temporal life.

On the Sacraments 3

1. Yesterday we discussed the font, whose likeness is as a kind of sepulcher into which, believing in the Father and Son and Holy Spirit, we are received and dipped and rise, that is, are resuscitated. Moreover, you receive myrrh, that is, ointment upon the head. Why upon the head? Because "the eyes of a wise man are in his head" [Eccl 2:14], Solomon says. For wis-

dom without grace grows cold, but when wisdom has received grace, then its work begins to be perfect. This is called regeneration.

2. What is regeneration? You have it in the Acts of the Apostles, for that line which is mentioned in the second psalm, "You are my Son, this day have I begotten you" [Acts 13:33], seems to refer to the resurrection. For the holy apostle Peter [Ps 2:7], in the Acts of the Apostles thus interpreted [see Acts 13:15-41; 2:14-36], that at that time, when the Son rose from the dead, the voice of the Father resounded: "You are my Son, this day have I begotten you." Therefore, he is also called "the first-born from the dead" [Col 1:18]. So, what is resurrection other than we rise from death to life? Thus, then, even in baptism, since it is a likeness of death, undoubtedly, when you dip and rise again, it becomes a likeness of resurrection. Thus, according to the interpretation of the apostle [Rom 6:3-11], just as that resurrection was a regeneration, so that resurrection from the font is a regeneration.

3. But why do you say that you dip in water? For this reason do you roam about; for this reason does uncertainty hold you? Indeed, we read: "Let the earth bring forth fruit from itself, and the earth bring forth yielding fruit" [Gen 1:11-12]. Similarly, too, you have read about water, "Let the waters bring forth creatures having life" [Gen 1:20-21], and creatures having life were born. They indeed were in the beginning of creation, but for you it was reserved for water to regenerate you unto grace, just as water generated other creatures unto life. Imitate the fish, which indeed has obtained less grace, yet should be an object of wonder to you. It is in the sea and is upon the waters; it is in the sea and swims upon the floods. A tempest rages in the sea, storms shriek, but the fish swims; it is not submerged, because it is accustomed to swim. So even for you this world is a sea. It has diverse floods, heavy waters, severe storms. And do you be a fish, that the water of the world may not submerge you. Moreover, beautifully does the Father say to the Son: "This day I have begotten you" [Ps 2:7]. That is "When you redeemed the people, when you called them to the kingdom of heaven, when you fulfilled my will, you proved that you were my son" [Exod 15:13].

4. You came up from the font. What followed? You heard the reading. The girded priest—for, although the presbyters also do this, the highest priest, girded, I say, washed your feet. What

mystery is this? Surely, you have heard [John 13:4-11] that the Lord, after he had washed the feet of the other disciples, went to Peter, and Peter said to him: "Do you wash my feet?" That is: "Do you, Lord, wash the feet of a servant; do you without stain wash my feet; do you, the author of the heavens, wash my feet?" You have this also elsewhere [Matt 3:14]: He went to John and John said to him: "I ought to be baptized by you, and come you to me?" [1 Pet 2:22]. I am a sinner, and have you come to a sinner, that you who have not sinned may put aside your sins? Behold all justice [Matt 3:15], behold humility, behold grace, behold sanctification. He said: "If I do not wash your feet, you shall have no part with me" [John 13:8].

5. We are not unaware of the fact that the church in Rome does not have this custom, whose character and form we follow in all things. Yet it does not have the custom of washing the feet. So note: perhaps on account of the multitude this practice declined. Yet there are some who say and try to allege in excuse that this is not to be done in the mystery, nor in baptism, nor in regeneration, but the feet are to be washed as for a guest. But one belongs to humility, the other to sanctification. Finally, be aware that the mystery is also sanctification: "If I wash not your feet, you shall have no part with me." So I say this, not that I may rebuke others, but that I may commend my own ceremonies. In all things I desire to follow the church in Rome, yet we, too, have human feeling; what is preserved more rightly elsewhere we, too, preserve more rightly.

6. We follow the apostle Peter himself; we cling to his devotion. What does the church in Rome reply to this? Surely for us the very author of this assertion is the apostle Peter, who was the priest of the church in Rome, Peter himself, when he said: "Lord, not only my feet, but also my hands and my head" [John 13:9]. Behold faith: That he first pleaded an excuse belonged to humility; that he afterwards offered himself belonged to devotion and faith.

7. The Lord answered him, because he had said "hands and head": "He that is washed, does not need to wash again, but to wash his feet alone" [John 13:10]. Why this? Because in baptism all fault is washed away. So fault withdraws. But since Adam was overthrown by the Devil, and venom was poured out upon his feet, accordingly you wash the feet, that in this part, in which the serpent lay in wait, greater aid of sanctification may be added, so that afterwards he cannot overthrow you.

Therefore, you wash the feet, that you may wash away the poisons of the serpent. It is also of benefit for humility, that we may not be ashamed in the mystery of what we disdain in obedience.

PRAYER
INVOKING

8. There follows a spiritual sign which you heard read today, because after the font there remains the effecting of perfection, when at the invocation of the priest the Holy Spirit is poured forth, "the spirit of wisdom, and of understanding, the spirit of counsel, and of virtue, the spirit of knowledge, and of godliness, the spirit of holy fear" [Isa 11:2-3], as it were, seven virtues of the Spirit.

9. All virtues, of course, pertain to the Spirit, but these are, as it were, cardinal; as it were, principal. For what is so principal as godliness? What so principal as knowledge of God? What so principal as virtue? What so principal as counsel of God? What so principal as fear of God? Just as fear of this world is infirmity, so fear of God is great fortitude.

10. There are seven virtues, when you are signed. For, as the holy apostle says [1 Cor 12:4-11], because the wisdom of our Lord is manifold, he says, and the wisdom of God is manifold [Eph 3:10], so is the Holy Spirit manifold, who has diverse and various virtues. Therefore, he is called the "God of hosts" [Ps 79:5, 8, etc.], which can be applied to the Father and the Son and the Holy Spirit. But this belongs to another discussion, to another time.

11. After this what follows? You are able to come to the altar. Since you have come, you are able to see what you did not see before. This is a mystery that you have read in the gospel [John 9:1-7]; if, however, you have not read it—certainly you have heard it: A blind man presented himself to the Savior to be cured, and he who had cured others only by a word and speech, and by his power restored the sight of eyes, yet in the book of the gospel which is written according to John, who truly before the rest saw great mysteries and pointed them out and declared them, wished to prefigure this mystery in him. Surely, all the evangelists were holy, all the apostles; all were holy except the betrayer. Yet St. John, who was the last to write his gospel, as if a friend required and chosen by Christ, poured forth the eternal mysteries by a kind of greater trumpet. Whatever he has said is a mystery. Another [Matt 9:27-30; Luke 18:35-43; Mark 8:22-25] said that the blind man was cured. Matthew said it, Luke said it, Mark said it. What does John alone

say?—"He took clay and spread it upon his eyes and said to him: Go to Siloe. And rising he went and washed and he came seeing" [John 9:7].

12. Do you also consider the eyes of your heart. You saw the things that are corporeal with corporeal eyes, but the things that are of the sacraments you were not yet able to see with the eyes of the heart. So, when you gave your name, he took mud and besmeared it over your eyes. What does this signify? That you confessed your sin, that you examined your conscience, that you performed penance for your sins, that is, that you recognize the lot of human generation. For, even if he who comes to baptism does not confess sin, nevertheless by this very fact he fulfills the confession of all sins, in that he seeks to be baptized so as to be justified, that is so as to pass from fault to grace.

13. Do not think it a matter of indifference. There are some—I know for certain that there was someone who said it—when we said to him: "In this age you ought rather to be baptized," he said: "Why am I baptized? I have no sin; I have not contracted sin, have I?" This one did not have the mud, because Christ had not besmeared him, that is, he had not opened his eyes; for no man is without sin.

14 . He who takes refuge in the baptism of Christ recognizes himself as human. So, too, he placed mud upon you, that is, modesty, prudence, consideration of your frailty, and said to you: "Go to Siloe." "Which," he says, "is interpreted sent." That is: Go to that font, at which the cross of Christ the Lord is preached; go to that font, at which Christ redeemed the errors of all.

15. You went, you washed, you came to the altar, you began to see what you had not seen before. That is: Through the font of the Lord and the preaching of the Lord's passion, your eyes were then opened. You who seemed before to have been blind in heart began to see the light of the sacraments.

So, most beloved brethren, we have come all the way to the altar, to the richer discussion. And thus, since this is a matter of time, we cannot begin the whole disputation, since the discussion is more comprehensive. What has been said today is enough. Tomorrow, if it pleases the Lord, we will discuss the sacraments themselves [i.e., the Eucharistic Rites].

Baptism in Papal Correspondence:
Innocent I and Leo the Great

A long silence stands between Rome's two great early Church orders, the *Apostolic Tradition* and the *Gelasian Sacramentary* (early 600s, below). It was broken indirectly by Zeno and Ambrose and directly by Novatian (above); three Popes, Stephen (see ch. 2, Cyprian), Innocent I (402–417), and Leo I, called "the Great" (440–461), and a Roman deacon (below, John, ca. 500). For the Western Church the entire period from Ambrose on was one of social and political turmoil: In 410 the Goths overran Italy and took Rome; in 452 the Huns invested the city; in 478 Theodoric the Goth deposed the last of the Roman emperors.

It was also a period of doctrinal controversy about the respective roles of God and man in salvation (Pelagianism); whether Christ is composed of two persons, the divine Son and the man Jesus; and the integrity of Christ's divine and human natures (see vol. 5, ch. 1, Theodore; also see vol. 5, ch. 2, Narsai).

Generally speaking, Western bishops stood out in the turmoil as mediators between barbarians and Romans and stood fast in the religious controversies as champions of orthodoxy. Nowhere is this more the case than in Rome and in the persons of Innocent and Leo, both of whom, in the process, consolidated the primacy of the bishop of Rome. As a result of their extensive concerns and widespread activity, papal sermons and correspondence became increasingly important. Indeed, although a number of Innocent's letters have been preserved, Leo is the first Pope whose letters and sermons became the object of archival collection, a sort of forerunner of the collection and codification of civil and canon law.

Innocent I

The first reading is Innocent's letter to Bishop Decentius of Engubium (Gubbio in Umbria, Italy). Decentius had addressed eleven questions to Innocent on subjects ranging from conformity with Roman custom and practice to whether Saturday should be a day of fasting. Four questions related directly or indirectly to baptism. The first (no. 6) asked whether a liturgical minister other than the bishop could perform the postbaptismal anointing of the head. The answer is extremely important for understanding baptism in the West. Already Ambrose had emphasized the special connection between this "spiritual signing" and the "perfecting gift" of the Holy Spirit. Here Innocent (he calls it "consignation") reserves the anointing for the bishop alone, because only he has the "plenitude" of the priesthood. In this separation lies the origin of the sacrament of confirmation (see General Introduction, "Anointing and the Holy Spirit"). The second (no. 9) inquired about the proper minister for reconciling the Christian who sinned seriously after baptism; the third (no. 10) about when reconciliation was to take place (Holy Thursday); and the fourth (no. 11) about anointing the sick with chrism blessed by the bishop at baptism. Solemn baptism had become the focus of reconciliation, rebirth, and consecration of the oil for the sick.

The text of *Epistle 25, to Decentius,* is in PL 20, 551-561; the translation is that of Gerald Ellard, "How Fifth-Century Rome Administered Sacraments," TS 9 (1948) 5-11, who also gives a background study.

Epistle 25, to Decentius

6. Now as to the anointing of neophytes [in confirmation], it is clear that this cannot be done by any save the bishop. For even if the presbyters are priests of the second order, they still do not possess the plenitude of priestly office. Not only the custom of the church shows that only the fullness of the priesthood can confirm, or can impart the sacred Paraclete, but even that passage of the Acts of the Apostles [8:14-18], which asserts that Peter and John were sent to bestow the Holy Spirit on those already baptized. It is permitted priests, when they baptize, either apart from the bishop or in his presence, to anoint the newly-baptized with chrism [provided this has been consecrated by the bishop: see below, *Gelesian Sacramentary*], but it is not allowed to priests to anoint the forehead with the same holy oil, this being the exclusive prerogative of the bishop in imparting the Holy Spirit. But as to the words [i.e., the "form"] of confirmation these I may not speak, lest I seem rather to betray them than to reply to your question.

9. As to the baptized who through some vice or sin are overcome by Satan, your charity enquires whether they may be anointed by priest or deacon. This, unless the bishop order it,

is not allowed. For hands are to be imposed [in absolution] only insofar as the bishop shall have authorized it. That this be done, it belongs to the bishop to order that [absolving] hands be imposed by either priest or other clerics. Otherwise could it not well happen that the afflicted person, in being brought at great inconvenience a long way to the bishop, could experience such a turn that he could neither be brought to the bishop, nor carried back home to his own [i.e., in emergency]?

10. As to those performing public penance, either on account of serious transgressions, or for more venial sins, if no sickness intervenes, the custom of the Roman church shows that they are to be reconciled on the Thursday before Easter. Moreover, it is the part of the bishop to judge as to the gravity of the offenses, to weigh the accusation of the penitent, to appraise the corrective of his weeping and his tears, and to order him to be absolved, when he has seen an appropriate satisfaction. But if one shall have fallen sick, and his life is despaired of, he is to be absolved even before the Paschal time, lest he depart this world without Communion.

11. Since in this connection also your charity wished to consult us, our own son, the Deacon Celestine, has himself written us that your charity poses that passage written by the blessed James the apostle: "Is one of you sick? Let him send for the presbyters of the church, and let them pray over him, anointing him with oil in the Lord's name. Prayer offered in faith will restore the sick man, and the Lord will give him relief: but if he be guilty of sins, they will be pardoned" [Jas 5:14, 15]. Now there is no doubt that this can and ought to be understood of the sick faithful, who have been sealed with the holy oil of chrism, blessed by a bishop; not priests only, but all the faithful can use the holy oil in their own and their dear ones' necessities. Moreover the question here added strikes us as superfluous, to question as to the bishop's power in what is allowed the presbyters. For the apostle spoke expressly of presbyters, because bishops, engaged in other occupations, cannot go to all who lie sick. But if the bishop either can visit some such sick person, or sees fit to do so, and to bless him and anoint him with chrism, this he surely may do, he who himself consecrates the chrism. It [last anointing] may not be given to those who are performing public penance, because it belongs to the "sacraments." For how should one of the "sacraments" be considered "fit" for those to whom the others are denied?

Leo the Great

The second reading is Pope Leo's letter to the Sicilian bishops about the proper days for solemn baptism. Some 140 of the collected letters are considered genuine, and they fall roughly into four groups: doctrinal, *responsa* (answers to inquiries about Church custom), corrective, and executive (acknowledgment and the like). His most celebrated letter is doctrinal, *The Tome,* preserved in the Acts of the Council of Chalcedon (it is *Epistle* 28 in modern collections). Written to Bishop Favian of Constantinople and dated June 13, 449, the letter argues what Leo regards as the proper understanding of the incarnation, namely, that the divine and human natures in Christ preserve their distinctiveness because they "both meet in the one person" of the Son (see vol. 5, chs. 1 and 2; also see ch. 3 in this vol.). The letter at hand was penned two years earlier and is primarily rescriptive. Although he speaks out against the Sicilian custom of Epiphany baptism, he discusses in detail the reasons for paschal baptism, providing a valuable summary of a long tradition. The text is in PL 54, 695–704; the translation is that of Edmund Hunt, FC 34, (1957) 68–77. See the recent study of Thomas J. Talley, *The Origins of the Liturgical Year* (New York: Pueblo, 1986).

Epistle 16, to the Sicilian Bishops

[Citing Christ's command that Peter feed the sheep (John 21:15-17), Leo first grounds his intervention in the mandate of his office as Peter's successor. He then reminds the bishops both that they hold the episcopal office from the "See of the blessed apostle Peter" and that they have confused the mysteries of Christmas and Easter by celebrating baptism on the Epiphany. Hallowed by long custom, he argues, the former festival solemnizes Christ's early years, from conception and birth to baptism. Leo then turns to the tradition of paschaltide baptism.]

Although, then, what pertains to Christ's lowliness and what pertains to his glory come together in one and the same person, and although whatever divine power and human weakness exist in him all tend to effect our redemption, it is especially in the death of the Crucified and in his resurrection from the dead that the power of baptism establishes a new creature out of the old. That is, both the death and the life of Christ operate in those being reborn, as the apostle says: "Do you not know that all we who have been baptized in Christ have been baptized into his death? For we were buried with him by means of baptism into death, in order that, just as Christ has risen from the dead through the glory of the Father, so we also may walk in newness of life. For if we have been united with him in the likeness of death, we shall be so in the likeness of his resurrection also" [Rom 6:3-5]. And there are other things which the teacher of the Gentiles treated more fully in recommending the sacrament of baptism. Hence it is apparent from the spirit of this teaching that, for baptizing the sons of men and adopting them as sons of God, that day and that season were chosen on which the actions performed on the members might be, through symbolism and mystical rite, in harmony with what was done in the head itself. For, in the rite of baptism death comes from the slaying of sin, and the triple immersion imitates the three days of burial, and the rising out of the water is like his rising from the tomb. Hence, the very nature of the rite shows that ordinarily the right day for the reception of this grace is the one on which both the power of the gift and the form of the rite had their origin. What follows helps very much to confirm this point. The Lord Jesus Christ himself, after he arose from the dead, gave to his disciples (and in them he instructed all those who are in charge of churches) the rite and the power of baptizing, saying: "Go, therefore, and make disciples of all nations, baptizing them in the name of the Father, and of the Son, and of the Holy Spirit" [Matt 28:19]. Of course, he could have instructed them about this even before his passion, except that he especially wanted it understood that the grace of rebirth began with his resurrection. Actually, the feast of Pentecost, which is hallowed by the coming of the Holy Spirit and is attached to the feast of Easter as an appendage, is also used for this rite of baptism. Although other feasts are celebrated on different days, this feast of Pentecost always occurs on that day of the week made famous by the Lord's resurrection. It somehow extends the hand of helping grace and invites those who were excluded from the Easter day by a troublesome sickness or a long journey or difficulties in sailing, so that those hindered by any necessities whatever may gain the effect they desire as a gift of the Holy Spirit. [Leo, then, gives biblical warrant for the custom of baptism at Pentecost—the promise of "another Advocate" who will teach them all things (John 16:13-26). He continues:]

Now we give a sufficiently apt example as proof that we are not defending this idea on our own authority but are holding to it on apostolic authority. We are following the example of the blessed apostle Peter, who, on that very day when the promised coming of the Holy Spirit filled the entire group of believers, consecrated in the waters of baptism three thousand persons whom his preaching had converted. This is taught by the reliable account of holy Scripture, of which the Acts of the Apostles are a part, where it says: "Now on hearing this they were pierced to the heart and said to Peter and the rest of the apostles, 'Brethren, what shall we do?' But Peter said to them, 'Repent and be baptized every one of you in the name of Jesus Christ for the forgiveness of your sins; and you will receive the gift of the Holy Spirit. For to you is the promise and to your children and to all who are far off, even to all whom the Lord our God calls.' And with very many other words he bore witness, and exhorted them, saying, 'Save yourselves from this perverse generation.' Now they who received his word were baptized, and there were added that day about three thousand souls" [Acts 2:37-41].

Therefore, since it is obviously quite clear that these two times about which we spoke are the right ones for baptizing the elect in the church, we warn your Charities not to add any other days for this observance. For, although there are also other feast days on which great reverence is due to the honor of God, for the principal and greatest sacrament we must hold to an exception, for which there are reasons and mystical significance. We are, however, at liberty to assist those in danger by administering baptism at any time. Thus we put off the free vows of those who are well and live in peaceful security to those two connected and related feasts, but not so as to deny at any time to anyone this single source of salvation when there is danger of death, critical times of siege, trials from persecution or fear of shipwreck.

Someone, however, may possibly feel that the feast of the Epiphany, which must be celebrated with the honor due to its rank, also possesses the privilege of baptism, since certain men think that on that same day the Lord approached St. John to be baptized. The man who thinks this should realize that the grace of that baptism by John and the reason for it were of a different order and did not share in that same power whereby regeneration is brought, through the Holy Spirit, to those about whom it is said: "Who were born not of the blood, nor of the will of the flesh, nor of the will of man, but of God" [John 1:13]. The Lord did not need to have any sin forgiven, nor was he seeking a way of rebirth. He simply wished to be baptized (as he wanted to be circumcised and to have a victim offered as a purification for himself) in order that he who had been born of a woman, as the apostle says, might also be under the Law, which he had not come to destroy but to fulfill and, by fulfilling, to consummate it. As the blessed apostle proclaims, saying: "For Christ is the consummation of the Law for justice for everyone who believes" [Rom 10:4]. Christ devised the sacrament of his own baptism in himself because, "in all things having the first place" [Col 1:8], he showed that he was himself the source of it. And he ratified the power of regeneration at the time when there flowed forth from his side the blood of redemption and the water of baptism [John 19:34]. Hence, just as the Old Testament was a witness to the New and the "Law was given through Moses, grace and truth came through Jesus Christ" [John 1:17], just as diverse sacrifices prefigured the one victim and the killing of many lambs ended with the immolation of him about whom it is said, "Behold the Lamb of God, who takes away the sins of the world" [John 1:29]—so also John, not Christ but his forerunner, not the bridegroom but the friend of the bridegroom, was so faithful and a man who sought not his own but the things of Christ that he professed himself unworthy to loose the sandals on Christ's feet. For he indeed baptized with water for penitence, but Christ would baptize "with the Holy Spirit and with fire" [Matt 3:11], Christ who with his twofold power would restore life and destroy sins. Consequently, dearest brothers, because of these real proofs, so many and so weighty, which remove all doubt, you see clearly that only two periods, namely Easter and Pentecost, are to be used for baptizing the elect. And according to apostolic regulation, they are to be investigated with exorcism, made holy by fasting, and instructed by frequent discourses. We lay it to your Charities' charge not to deviate at all in future from customs initiated by the apostles. For hereafter, no one can be excused if he believes that apostolic regulations can be neglected in any way.

[Leo concludes by reminding the bishops of the custom of semi-annual meetings and of the September 29 meeting.]

Issued on the twenty-first of October in the consulship of the most illustrious Calepius and Ardaburis [447].

John the Deacon

Except as author and recipient of the following letter, neither John the Deacon nor Senarius is known. Evidence in the letter shows that it was written in the early sixth century (ca. 500). Among other questions, Senarius had asked about the catechumenate and especially about the "scrutinies." John's reply provides a firsthand view of Roman baptism at the end of the fourth century, as well as a brief commentary on the baptismal liturgy.

Infant baptism, already a tradition in Hippolytus (above), was on the way to becoming the norm (as it in the *Gelasian Sacramentary,* below). Nonetheless, adults still came to the font. They were enrolled in the catechumenate at the beginning of Lent. Prominent in the rite was the renunciation of Satan, followed by the imposition of the celebrant's hand coupled with an exorcism that entailed hissing at the devil (exsufflation) and the administration of salt. As elsewhere and earlier, catechetical instruction was the Lenten fare, including daily exorcism.

Those catechumens demonstrably ready for baptism, together with infants, formed a special group, the elect. At some point early in Lent the creed was delivered to them (very likely at the beginning of the fourth week), after which they were considered both the elect and, according to John, the "living." Soon thereafter the scrutinies began (see above, Ambrose; also see below, *Gelasian Sacramentary* and ch. 2, Augustine), the purpose of which, Senarius learns, was to ferret out candidates whom the grip of Satan prevented from making a true profession of faith. The last scrutiny took place on what John calls the "Paschal Sabbath," Holy Saturday night. Immediately following it, the elect professed the creed *(redditio symboli),* after which the rite of "opening" *(aperitio)* the ears and nostrils, first described by Ambrose, took place. According to John, however, it was a sealing of the ears and nostrils, and it concluded with an anointing of the breast. Then came baptism by triple immersion, investiture with a white garment, anointing of the head, and covering it with white linen. The baptismal Eucharist then followed, including the long-traditional cup of milk and honey (see above, Hippolytus). The author links the postbaptismal anointing to the Israelite priestly and kingly anointings rather than to the sevenfold gift of the Holy Spirit, as it is in Ambrose and in the *Gelasian Sacramentary*.

John omits some baptismal rites, among them handing over the Lord's Prayer *(traditio orationis dominicae)*, anointing by the celebrant, and the episcopal consignation so clearly attested by Innocent and Leo (above) and the *Gelasian Sacramentary* and adverted to in the last section of the reading.

The text is John the Deacon, *Epistola ad Senarium,* ed. André Wilmart, *Analecta reginensia*, SeT 59 (Rome, 1933) 170-179. The reading comprises sections 2-7 in the letter, which deal with Sernarius' questions about baptism. For a valuable study, see Antoine Chavasse, "Les deux rituels romain et gaulois," in *Études de critique et d'histoire religieuses* (Lyon: 1948).

The Letter of John the Deacon to Senarius < *Roman Nobleman*

1. [This paragraph constitutes an extended introduction.]

2. You ask me [the following questions:] why a person is made a catechumen before baptism; what the word "catechizing" means; in what Old Testament rule it is established; whether the rule is new, deriving rather from the New Testament. Likewise, you also ask what a scrutiny is, why infants are scrutinized three times before Easter, and what benefit accrues to them by the concern and requirement of these scrutinies, and so forth.

3. I reply as follows. We are confident that you are well enough instructed to know that the entire human race, while still in its cradle, so to say, rightly fell into death by the waywardness of the first man. As a result, no redemption from [the Fall] was possible apart from what the grace of the Savior offered, who, though begotten of the Father before the world, did not refuse to become human for our salvation, [born] of a virgin mother alone. There is no doubt that, until born again in Christ, one is held bound by the power of the devil. Indeed, [one thus bound] should not approach the grace of the saving bath, unless, renouncing him [the devil] as part of the early rudiments of faith, one is extricated from his snares. In consequence, it is required that [candidates] enter first the schoolroom of the catechumens.

Catechesis is the Greek for "instruction." [Catechumens] are RADICAS> instructed through the church's ministry, by the blessing of the one who places his hand [on their heads], in order that [they] may realize who [they] are and who [they] are to become—in other words, that from being numbered among the damned [they] may become holy, from [being numbered] among the unjust, [they] may appear among the just, and finally, from [being numbered among the] servant[s they] may become son[s and daughters]. Thus, one whose first parentage brought perdition is restored by the boon of second parentage and becomes the possessor of a paternal inheritance.

SHIFT — BLOWING SATANIC FORCE OUT

[A catechumen], therefore, is exorcised by exsufflation that with the devil put to flight, entry may be prepared for Christ our Lord; that torn from power of darkness, he may be transferred to the kingdom of the glory of God's love [see Col 1:13]; and that until recently a vessel of Satan, he may now become a dwelling of the Savior. And so [Satan] is exorcised, because the ancient deserter [from God] merits such disgrace. He is exorcised—that is, he is commanded to get out and depart, acknowledging the advent of him whose upright image in Paradise he had cast down by perverse counsel.

[Next] the catechumen is signed with blessed salt, for just as all flesh is preserved healthy by salt, so the mind, drenched and driven by the waves of the world, is held on course by the salt of wisdom and of the preaching of God's word. Thus, may [the mind] arrive at settled permanence, with the turbulence of indigestion settled down by the soothing action of divine salt. [These effects] are achieved by the frequent imposition of hand[s] and by the blessing of the Creator invoked over [the catechumen's] head three times in honor of the Trinity.

4. And so, by his own efforts and those of others, the person who had recently received exsufflation from the snares of the devil and renounced his pomps now merits to receive the words of the creed handed down by the apostles. As a result, one who had just borne the name "catechumen" is now called "competent" or "elect." Conceived in the womb of mother church, such a person now begins to live, even though the time of sacred birth has not yet arrived. Then follows what church custom called "scrutinies." For we thoroughly test their hearts concerning faith to determine whether, since the renunciation of the devil, the sacred words [of the creed] have become fixed in their minds, whether they acknowledge the coming grace of the Redeemer, and whether they confess to believe in God, the Father almighty.

When it becomes clear from their replies that this is so—for it is written, "With the heart one believes for justification, but with the mouth saving confession is made" [Rom 10:10]—their

SEALING RITUAL

ears and also their nostrils are touched with the holy oil. The ears are touched [especially] because faith enters the mind, just as the apostle says: "Faith comes by hearing, and hearing by the word of God" [Rom 10:17]. Thus, the ears, protected by a kind of holy wall, will admit nothing noxious to entice them back.

5. Then, when their ears are touched, they are firmly warned that for as long as they inhale the breath of life through their nostrils they must faithfully abide in God's service and commandments. Thus, that holy man [Job] has said: "As God lives, who has taken away my judgment, the almighty, who has made my soul bitter, as long as my breath is in me, and the spirit of God is in my nostrils, my lips will not speak falsehood, nor will my tongue utter lies" [Job 27:2-4]. The anointing of the nostrils signifies also that [the nostrils], with the oil blessed in the name of the Savior, are to be led to his spiritual odor by a certain inexpressible sweetness [perceived by their] inner sense. Thus delighted, may [the elect] chant: "Your name is an ointment poured out; we shall run after the savor of your ointments" [Cant 1:3]. Thus, the nostrils, fortified by this mystery, are unable to allow the pleasure of the world to enter, nor anything that might seek to weaken the mind.

6. Next, their breast, the seat and dwelling place of the heart, is anointed with the consecrated oil, so that they may understand that [what] they promise with firm conscience and pure heart [is] to follow the commandments of Christ now that the devil has been driven out. They are required to proceed naked right down to their feet, so that, with the fleshly garments of mortality taken off, they may acknowledge that they journey on a road where nothing harmful can be found. Although the old books show no traces of these customs, the church has required [them to be done] over the years with watchful care. Then, when either the elect or the catechumens have progressed in the faith through these spiritual vehicles, so to speak, then it is also necessary to be consecrated in the baptism of the unique bath. For in this sacrament one is baptized by triple immersion, and rightly so. For whoever presents [himself] to be baptized in the name of the Trinity ought to signify the Trinity by a triple immersion and acknowledge his debt to the goodness of him who rose from the dead on the third day.

6TH C NUDITY

LIVING TRADITION OF CHURCH BEING MAINTAINED

Then, he is vested in a white garment, and his head is anointed with the unction of sacred chrism, so that the [newly] baptized may understand that in his person the kingdom and the priestly mystery have met. For priests and princes used to be anointed with the oil of chrism, that the former might offer God sacrifices and that the latter might govern the people. For a fuller expres- sion of the image of the priesthood the head of the reborn is covered with a linen cloth. For the priests of that [ancient] time always wore a certain mystical covering on the head; and indeed, all the reborn wear white clothes to enact the ascending church, just as our Lord and Savior himself was transfigured on the mount before certain disciples and prophets, as it was said: "His face shone as the sun; his clothing was made white as snow" [Matt 17:12]. This [rite] prefigured for the future, as has been indicated, the ascending church, about which it is written, "Who is this that ascends all in white?" [Cant 3:6; 8:5]. Thus, they wear white garments so that, although the ragged dress of ancient error has darkened the infancy of their first birth, the garment of the second birth may symbolize the garment of glory, so that attired in a wedding garment the [newly baptized] may approach the table of the heavenly bridegroom as a new person.

7. Lest I seem to have passed over something, I must clearly and quickly say that all these things are done even to infants, who by reason of their age understand nothing. Thus, you need to realize that by being sponsored by their parents or others, it is necessary that their salvation should come through the profession of others, especially since their damnation came by another's fault. . . .

8. [The remainder of par. 7 and this paragraph defend the requirement that the bishop consecrate the chrism.]

9. [This paragraph discusses heretical baptism. Citing Matt 28:19 ("Go, baptize all nations in the name of the Father and of the Son and of the Holy Spirit"), John tells Senarius that defects in Trinitarian faith (he mentions Arius by name) require baptism anew. Otherwise, heretics require the blessing of the bishop for reconciliation and incorporation in the Church.]

10. [In this paragraph, John distinguishes acolytes and exorcists.]

11. [This paragraph takes up the question of consecrating altars in Rome on Holy Saturday.]

12. You ask why milk and honey are [mixed] in the most sacred cup and offered with the Paschal Sabbath [the vigil Mass

on Holy Saturday]. The reason is the one written in the Old Testament and promised in figure to the new people: "I will lead you into the Promised Land, the land overflowing with milk and honey" [Lev 20:24]. The land of promise, then, is the land of resurrection to everlasting happiness; it is nothing else than the land of our body, which, in the resurrection of the dead, shall attain to the glory of incorruptibility and peace. This kind of rite is offered to the newly baptized, then, so that they may realize that only they, who share in the Body and Blood of the Lord, shall receive the land of promise: and as they start on the journey there, they are nourished with milk and honey like little children. Thus, they can chant, "How sweet are your words in my mouth, Lord, sweeter than honey and the honeycomb" [Ps 119:103; 19:11]. As new people, therefore, abandoning the bitterness of sin, they drink milk and honey, so that they, who in their first birth were nourished with the milk of corruption and first wept bitter tears, may, in their second birth, taste the sweetness of milk and honey in the entrails of the church. Thus nourished on such rites, may they be dedicated to the mysteries of everlasting incorruption.

13. [This paragraph discusses why the *Alleluia* is sung throughout the Easter season to Pentecost.]

14. [This final paragraph takes up the issue about one who dies without chrismation from the bishop. In view of the fact that it was a disputed question at the time, John gives his own opinion, which he argues as follows: Just as a person comes to life as a result of first birth, so one comes to justification as a result of second birth. Nothing needed for living natural life lacks in the first instance; similarly, nothing needed for living supernatural life lacks in the second. Thus, there is no obstacle to salvation.]

The Leonine Sacramentary

A sacramentary is a public and official liturgical document that contains the presider's parts for the celebration of the Mass and sacraments. Strictly speaking, then, the *Leonine Sacramentary* is not a sacramentary, nor, in fact, is it by Pope Leo (above). Rather, it is a sixth-century collection of Roman Mass propers from the late fourth century on. Compiled almost certainly at Verona (see above, Zeno) as a private work, the sacramentary, nonetheless, provided both the Roman Missal and the Book of Common Prayer with prayers remarkable for their "simplicity, practicality, great sobriety and self-control, clarity and dignity" (D. Hope, cited below).

The Mass prayers are grouped by month starting with January. Unfortunately, damage has obliterated most of January through April, effectively excising the Lenten and Easter baptismal Masses. The month of May, however, contains the baptismal Mass for Pentecost. The reading consists of those parts that relate particularly to baptism. Included also is the prayer over the baptismal font, which appears on the last leaf of the manuscript.

The text is *Sacramentarium Veronese,* ed. L. C. Mohlberg, *Rerum ecclesiasticarum documenta* 1 (Rome, 1956); the translation is that of E. C. Whitaker, DBL (1970) 153–154, altered for the reading. An important study is that of D. M. Hope, *The Leonine Sacramentary* (London: Oxford, 1971); for the above quote see p. 144.

The *Leonine Sacramentary*

At Pentecost, for Those That Come Up from the Font

(The Collect)

O ineffable and merciful God, grant that the children of adoption whom your Holy Spirit has called to himself may harbor nothing earthly in their joy, nothing alien in their faith; through . . .

(In the Canon)

We beseech you graciously to accept this obligation which we offer to you for these who have been regenerated by water and the Holy Spirit, granting them remission of all their sins; and command their names to be written in "the book of the living" [Ps 69:28]; through . . .

(A Blessing of Water, Honey, and Milk)

Bless also we beseech you, O Lord, these your creatures of water, honey, and milk, and give your servants drink of this fount of water of everlasting life, which is the spirit of truth, and nourish them with this milk and honey according as you promised our fathers, Abraham, Isaac, and Jacob, to lead them into the land of promise, a land flowing with honey and milk. Therefore, O Lord, unite your servants to the Holy Spirit, as this honey and milk is united, wherein is signified the union of heavenly and earthly substance in Christ Jesus our Lord, through whom all these . . .

(The Blessing of the Font)

We offer you [this] prayer, O Lord, the eternal begetter of [all] things, Almighty God, whose "Spirit was borne upon the waters" [Gen 1:3, Vulg.], whose eyes looked down from on high upon Jordan's stream when John was baptizing those who in penitence confessed their sins: and therefore we pray your holy glory that your hand may be laid upon this water that you may cleanse and purify the lesser man who shall be baptized therefrom: and that he, putting aside all that is deathly, may be reborn and brought to life again through the new man reborn in Christ Jesus, with whom you live and reign in the unity of the Holy Spirit, unto the ages of ages.

The Gelasian and the Gregorian Sacramentaries

The OLD Gelasian Sacramentary

The great value of "Church-order" books, which first make their appearance in the *Didache* (vol. 5, ch. 1) and the *Apostolic Tradition* of Hippolytus (above) is that they express in rite and symbol a Christian community's understanding of its inmost religious convictions. The sacramentaries continue the ancient tradition that people "express in worship what moves them most—worship is the index of belief" *(lex orandi, lex credendi).* The *Gelasian Sacramentary,* erroneously attributed to Pope Gelasius (492–496 C.E.), is the oldest extant sacramentary. Although it contains liturgical material that goes back even before Gelasius, the work was compiled at Rome considerably later (early seventh century) and remained in use there through the papacy of Gregory II (715–731). The earliest extant manuscript of the sacramentary, however, is a Frankish (Gallic) revision of the original. With the revisions removed, the original provides firsthand information about baptism at Rome in the interval between John the Deacon (ca. 500, above) and the liturgical reforms instituted during the reign of Charlemagne (742–814). Although the revisions indicate that there was an adult catechumenate in the kingdom of the Franks (ch. 71), these Roman chapters envision infant baptism. At some point between John the Deacon and Gregory

II the administration of infant baptism became the norm; the sacramentary is witness to the effect of the practice on the rites.

Chapters of Book 1 (30–44), which, abridged, comprise the reading, are without apparent revision and, thus, Roman. They focus on the presider's parts of the baptismal liturgy, beginning with enrollment and concluding with consignation, which, as noted in the General Introduction ("Anointing and the Holy Spirit"), will come to be called confirmation. The summons for candidates for baptism was formally made on the third Sunday of Lent. The rites started at 3:00 P.M. on Monday and are called "scrutinies."

The text for the *Gelasian Sacramentary* is *Sacramentarium Gelasianum; Liber sacramentorum Romanae Aeclesiae ordinis anni circuli,* ed. Dom Mohlberg. Rerum Ecclesiasticarum Documenta 4 (Rome: 1960) 42–74. For studies, see B. Moreton, *The Eighth-Century Gelasian Sacramentary: A Study in Tradition* (Oxford: Oxford University Press, 1976); also see C. Jones, G. Wainwright, E. Yarnold, *The Study of the Liturgy* (London: SPCK, 1978) 220–229.

The Gelasian Sacramentary: Book 1:30–44

Chapter 30: Prayers over the Elect for Making a Catechumen

Almighty and everlasting God, Father of our Lord Jesus Christ: graciously look on these your servants, whom you have considered worthy to summon to the beginning lessons of faith. Drive from them all blindness of heart, undo the bonds of Satan that have strapped them, open for them, Lord, the door of your compassion. Thus, bearing the sign of your wisdom [salt], may they shun the squalor of every lust, rejoice in the sweet odor of your commandments, and serve you zealously in the church. And may they progress [in virtue] from day to day, that once proficient through [your] healing treatment they may come to the grace of your baptism.

We ask, Lord, that you hear our prayers and safeguard by the cross of the Lord these your chosen, with which by its power we [ourselves] are signed and guarded, that, honoring your great glory from the outset, they may merit under the guidance of your commandments to come to the glory of rebirth. Through [our Lord].

God, who established the human race that you might restore it, look with favor on your adopted people, enroll the offspring of your new race in your new covenant, so that what these children of promise could not achieve by nature, they may joyfully receive by grace. Through our Lord.

Chapter 31–32: The Blessing and Giving of Salt

[Salt is exorcised in the name of the Trinity and spoken of as the "safeguard of the human race" and the "perfect medicine" for all who receive it. Then the infants receive a few grains each with the petition that they "receive the salt of wisdom as a token disposing them to eternal life." A final blessing is offered that the infants who "taste the salt as their first food may hunger only until satisfied with heavenly food."]

Chapter 33: Exorcism over the Elect

God of Abraham, God of Isaac, God of Jacob, God who appeared to Moses on Mount Sinai and led the children of Israel out of the land of Egypt, sending your angel to guard them day and night: we entreat you, Lord, please to send your holy angel that likewise he may watch over your servants and lead them to the grace of your baptism.

Therefore, accursed Devil, accept your sentence and give honor to the one, true God, and give honor to Jesus Christ his Son, and to the Holy Spirit: depart from these servants of God, for Jesus Christ our Lord has been pleased to lead them to his holy grace and blessing and to the font and grace of baptism. Through this sign of the holy cross, which we trace on their foreheads, accursed Devil, never dare to violate them.

Over the girls. God of heaven, God of earth, God of angels, God of archangels, God of prophets, God of martyrs, God of all who live well, God whom every tongue in heaven, on earth, and beneath the earth [Phil 2:10] confesses: I call upon you, Lord, please watch over and lead these your servants to the grace of baptism. [Then, "Therefore, accursed Devil . . ." is repeated.]

Likewise over the boys. Attend, accursed Satan, commanded by the name of the everlasting God and of our Savior the Son of God: since you and your envy are conquered, depart trembling. May there be nothing in common between you and the servants of God, who are already thinking about heavenly things, who are to renounce you and your kingdom, and [to be] blest with the immortality of the victorious one. Therefore, give honor to the Holy Spirit as he approaches: descending from the highest reaches of heaven, he will confound your deceits and will perfect these [boys] with hearts purified and sanctified from the divine font as the temple and dwelling for God. And thus freed from all the inner injuries of past sins, may they give thanks always to the everlasting God and bless his holy name forever: through Jesus Christ our Lord, who will come to judge the living and the dead and the world by fire.

And over the girls. God of Abraham, God of Isaac, God of Jacob, you admonished the tribes of Israel and freed Susannah from the false accusation of crime: I humbly entreat you, Lord, also to free these your servants, and deign to lead them to the grace of your baptism.

[Then, "Therefore, accursed Devil . . ." is repeated.]

Likewise over the boys. I exorcise you, unclean spirit, in the name of the Father and of the Son and of the Holy Spirit, that you go and depart from these servants of God. For the very one who walked on the sea with his feet and stretched out his right hand to Peter as he sank, commands you, cursed and damned one.

[Then, "Therefore, accursed Devil . . ." is repeated.]

And over the girls. I exorcise you, unclean spirit, through the Father and the Son and the Holy Spirit, that you go out and depart from these servants of God. For the very one who opened the eyes of the man born blind and raised Lazarus from the grave on the fourth day commands you, cursed and damned one.

[Then, "Therefore, accursed Devil . . ." is repeated.]

[Then there follows a prayer to be said by a priest.]

Lord, holy Father, all powerful and everlasting God of truth and light, I call on your eternal and most just piety on behalf of these your servants, that you deign to enlighten them with the light of your understanding. Cleanse and make them holy. Give them the knowledge so that they may advance to the grace of your baptism. Let them hold unshakable hope, right counsel, and holy teaching, so that they may be ready and able to receive your grace. Through . . .

[The second and third scrutinies took place respectively on the fifth and sixth Mondays of Lent; they included exorcisms, doubtless something like the above, but they are not recorded. Attached to the third scrutiny, however, were the rites of the delivery *(traditio)* of the Gospels, of the creed, and of the Lord's

Prayer, preceded by the rite of the opening of the ears (*aperitio,* see above, Ambrose). The Gospels were brought in by procession, placed at the four corners of the altar. A priest (the term in the text is always "presbyter") gave catechetical homilies, and a deacon read the beginning of each Gospel.]

Chapter 34: The Explanation of the Four Gospels to the Elect at the Opening of the Ears

Let the deacon proclaim: Stand in silence and listen attentively. ← RUBRICAL ADMONITION

And he reads the beginning of the Gospel According to Matthew up to: "For he will save his people from their sins" [Matt 1:22].

When he has finished reading, let a presbyter deliver these words: ALLEGORICAL EXPLANATION

Dearest brethren, lest we keep you too long, let us only explain for you the hidden meaning of the symbols [of the evangelists]; first, why Matthew has the symbol of a man. For in the beginning [of his Gospel] he speaks of the nativity of the Savior by giving his full genealogy. Thus he begins: "The book of the generation of Jesus Christ, son of David, son of Abraham." You see, not without merit is a human identity given this author, since he traces the birth [of the Savior] from his human lineage; not without merit, as we said, is the person Matthew signified in this mystery.

Then the deacon proclaims as above: Stand in silence and listen intently.

And he reads the beginning of the Gospel According to Mark up to: "I baptize you with water, but he has baptized [*sic*] you with the Holy Spirit" [Mark 1:8].

And the presbyter follows with these words:

Appearing in the form of a lion because of its solitude, the evangelist Mark says: "The voice of one crying in the desert: prepare the way of the Lord." He is not called a lion uselessly, for we find many examples of this lion who reigns unconquered: "Judah is a lion's whelp; from my seed, my son, you have grown up; crouching down, he slept as a lion and like a whelp of a lion; who will rouse him?" [Gen 49:9].

Then the deacon proclaims as above. And he reads the beginning of the Gospel According to Luke up to: "Ready a perfect people for the Lord" [Luke 1:17].

And the presbyter follows with these words:

The evangelist Luke has the appearance of a bull-calf, a type of our Savior sacrificed. For he begins the Gospel of Christ by speaking about Zachary and Elizabeth, from whom, at their advanced age, John the Baptist was born. Thus, Luke is compared to a bull-calf: for like tender things springing from the hard, he contained within himself two horns, that is, the two Testaments and the four hooves, that is, four Gospels.

Then the deacon proclaims as above. And he reads the beginning of the Gospel According to John up to: "Full of grace and truth" [John 1:14].

And the presbyter follows with these words:

John has the likeness of an eagle in that he soared; for he says, "In the beginning was the Word and the Word was with God and the Word was God. This was [the way things were] in the beginning with God." And David said about the person of Christ: "For your youth will be renewed like an eagle's" [Ps 103:5], that is, [the youth] of Jesus Christ our Lord, who, rising from the dead, ascended into the heavens. And so the church, now pregnant with your conception, rejoices that in these festal rites she is in labor to bring forth new lives subject to Christian law: thus, when the sacred day of the Pasch comes and you are reborn in the water of baptism, you, like all the saints, shall be worthy to receive the holy gift of birth [lit., infancy] from Christ our Lord, who lives and reigns throughout the ages.

Chapter 35: The Introduction of the Creed to the Elect

That is, before you recite the creed, you proceed with these words:

Our beloved, who seek to receive the rites of baptism and to be born as a new creature through the Holy Spirit, confident that you are to be justified, profess with your whole heart and mind the faith; with your minds turned in true conversation with God, who is the enlightener of our minds, approach, fresh from the rite of receiving the Gospels, this rite inspired by the Lord, instituted by the apostles, and a great mystery whose words are few indeed. For the Holy Spirit, who spoke these [words of the creed] to the teachers of the church, instituted this [profession of] faith with such eloquence and conciseness that what you are about to believe and always to profess can neither exceed [your] understanding nor burden [your] memory. With attentive minds you must learn the creed, and what we hand on to you just as we have received it you must write on the pages of your heart rather than on any easily destroyed material. And so the profession of faith which you have accepted begins with this introduction:

INFANT> *At this point an acolyte takes one of the boys, holds him on his left arm, and places his hand on his head. And the presbyter asks him:* In what language do they profess our Lord Jesus Christ? [*The acolyte*] *replies:* Greek. *The presbyter then says:* Proclaim their faith as they profess it. *And the acolyte responds by chanting the creed in Greek with these words, as he holds his hand on the boy's head:*

[The text gives the Nicene-Constantinopolitan Creed transliterated into the Roman alphabet together with an interlinear Latin translation:]

I believe in one God, the Father Almighty, maker of heaven and earth, and of all things visible and invisible. And in one Lord Jesus Christ, the only-begotten son of God; born of the Father before all ages, light of light, true God of true God, born, not made, of one substance with the Father; by whom all things were made; who for us humans and for our salvation came down from heaven; and was incarnate of the Holy Spirit and the virgin Mary, and was made human; he was also crucified for us under Pontius Pilate and suffered and died, rising on the third day, ascending into heaven, and sitting at the right hand of the Father; and he will come again in glory to judge the living and the dead; and whose kingdom shall have no end. And in the Holy Spirit, the Lord, and giver of life; who proceeds from the Father, who, together with the Father and the Son, is also adored and glorified, and who spoke through the prophets. [And] in one, holy, catholic and apostolic church. I confess one baptism for the remission of sins. I hope for the resurrection of the dead and for the world to come. Amen.

Beloved children, you have heard the creed in Greek; hear it also in Latin. *And you say:* In what language do they confess our Lord Jesus Christ? *He responds:* In Latin. Profess the faith as they profess it.

With his hand on the head of the boy, the acolyte chants the creed in these words: [A Latin text of the above creed follows.]

The presbyter continues with the following words:
[The explanation begins with a restatement of the creedal articles; when he comes to the articles on the resurrection and on baptism, he explains:]

Here finally is taught the summoning of the church, the remission of sins and the resurrection of the flesh. Thus, dearly beloved, we transform you from the "old man into the new" [Eph 4:22]: from fleshly to spiritual, from earthly to heavenly [see 1 Cor 15:42-58]. Believe in the resurrection with a steady and secure faith—a fact in the case of Christ, but still to be fulfilled in us—that what started in the head will follow in the rest of the body [see Col 1:18]. Moreover the very sacrament of baptism which you are about to receive expresses the form of this hope [for transformation]. For here in the sacrament is celebrated a kind of death and resurrection. "The old man is stripped off and the new put on" [Eph 4:22]. A sinner goes into the water and comes out justified. He is cast out who lures you to death, and he is put on who leads you back to life, he through whose grace you become "sons of God," not brought forth "by the will of the flesh" [John 1:13], but begotten by the power of the Holy Spirit. As a result you must allow this concise but abundant [creed] so to dwell in your hearts that through all time you may use it as your protection. For the power of such weapons cannot be overcome; it is at the service of every good soldier of Christ against all the snares of the enemy. The devil, who never desists from tempting humankind, must always find you protected by this creed. Thus, with the adversary whom you renounce defeated, and by the protection of him whom you profess, may you preserve the grace of the Lord pure and spotless to the end, so that, as you receive remission, may you also possess the glory of resurrection. Therefore, dearly beloved, you have now heard the creed of the catholic faith: go now and receive full instruction in what you have heard. Powerful is the mercy of God, mercy able both to lead you, as you seek after the faith of baptism, to the end of your search, and to bring us, who hand these mysteries over to you, together with you to the heavenly kingdom. Through the same Jesus Christ our Lord, who lives and reigns for ever and ever.

Chapter 36: The Introduction of the Lord's Prayer

[*The candidates*] *are admonished by the deacon as above* [Stand in silence and listen attentively.] [The Lord's Prayer was then chanted, doubtless by an acolyte.]

[*The infants*] *are then instructed by a deacon similar to the above:*

When the disciples sought to learn how they ought to pray, our Lord and Savior Jesus Christ, among the rest of his saving precepts, taught them the form of prayer which you have just heard. Let your love now hear how he teaches his disciples to pray to God the Father Almighty: "For when you pray, go into your room and, with the door closed, pray to your Father" [Matt 6:6]. When he says room, he does not mean some hidden place, but reminds us to open to him alone the secret places of our heart. That we should shut the door means that we should lock our breasts against evil thoughts with a mystical key and speak to God with sealed lips and pure mind. For our God hears the faith, not the voice. With the key of faith, therefore, may our breast be locked against the insidious adversary and open to God alone. [The breast] is his temple, as we know it to be, for he dwells in our hearts, so that he may be the advocate of our prayers. Therefore, the Word and Wisdom of God, Christ our Lord, taught us this prayer, so that we should pray thus.

Then you begin [your] instruction:
"Our Father who is in heaven." This is the language of liberty and complete trust. Therefore, you must live in such a way that you are able to be "sons of God and brothers of Christ" [Rom 8:17]. Would it not be effrontery for one to presume to call God Father, who turned away from his will? And so, dearly beloved, show yourselves worthy of divine adoption, since it is written: "To as many as believed in him he gave the power to become sons of God" [John 1:12].

"Hallowed be your name." This does not mean that God would be made holy by our prayers, for he is always holy, but that we want his name to be made holy in us, so that we who are sanctified in his baptism may persevere in that which we begin to be.

"Your kingdom come." You may wonder when God does not reign [in his kingdom], especially because his reign is immortal. But when we say, "Let your kingdom come," we are asking our kingdom to come, the kingdom promised us by God and sought with the blood and passion of Christ.

"May your will be done on earth as it is in heaven." This means that we on earth may do what you will in heaven, above reproach.

"Give us this day our daily bread." [In this petition] we are to understand spiritual food. For Christ is our bread, who said: "I am the living bread who came down from heaven" [John 6:41]. We say "daily," because we ought always to seek freedom from sin, so that we may be worthy of celestial nourishment.

"And forgive us our trespasses as we forgive those who trespass against us." This petition means that we cannot receive pardon for our sins unless and until we are first lenient with others who have sinned against us. Thus the Lord says in the gospel: "Unless you first forgive people their sins, neither will your Father forgive your sins" [Matt 6:15].

"And lead us not into temptation." This means, let us not undergo being led by him who tempts, the author of perversity. For the Scripture says: "God is not the tempter of the wicked" [Jas 13]. For it is the devil who is the tempter. To bring about his downfall, the Lord says: "Watch and pray that you do not enter into temptation" [Mark 14:38].

"But deliver us from evil." [The petition] reads thus, because the apostle has said: "You do not know what you ought to pray for" [Rom 8:26]. Our prayers must be offered to the one all-powerful God, so that, whenever human frailty is not up to being alert to and avoiding something, Jesus Christ our Lord may deign to grant us the [needed] strength, he who lives and reigns with God the Father in the unity of the Holy Spirit through all ages.

The deacon proclaims, as above: Stand in order and in silence and listen with attention.

You have heard, dearly beloved, the holy mysteries of the Lord's Prayer. As you go out now keep them ever new in your hearts, so that you may be perfect in Christ for praying and receiving the mercy of God. The Lord our God is powerful, and he is able to lead you who seek for faith to the waters of the bath of rebirth, and to bring you and us, who have delivered to you the mystery of the catholic faith, to the heavenly kingdom; he who lives and reigns with God the Father in the unity of the Holy Spirit through all ages.

Chapter 37: [The chapter concerns the Masses for Palm Sunday and the first three days of Holy Week.]

Chapters 38–39: [The chapters concern Holy Thursday Mass and prayers over those in public penance and the reconciliation of penitents, including the gravely ill.]

Chapter 40: [The chapter contains the prayers for the consecration of the oils, including the baptismal oils and those for anointing the sick. The prayers are part of the Holy Thursday "chrismal" Mass, celebrated both morning and evening. The following prayers of consecration are offered over the baptis-

mal oils at the end of the canon of the morning chrismal Mass
and after the Lord's Prayer has been chanted:]

@LASSIC ROMAN
EXORCISTIC CO

God, who bestows growth and progress in spiritual things,
who by the power of your Holy Spirit perfects the beginning
endeavors of simple minds, we beseech you, Lord, that you
grant cleansing of mind and body by the anointing of this element to those who are coming to the bath of blessed rebirth;
should any remnant of the evil spirit remain, may it depart at
the touch of this sanctified oil. May there remain no place for
evil spirits, no openings for retreating evil powers, no license
for the evil ones, who lie in wait, to hide. To your servants,
coming to the faith and about to be cleansed by the action of
the Holy Spirit, however, may this anointing we prepare avail
for salvation, which, through the birth of heavenly rebirth, they
are to attain in the sacrament of baptism: through our Lord
Jesus Christ, who will come to judge the world by fire.

Again, you say: The Lord be with you.
Response: And with you.

   Lift up your hearts.
Response: We have lifted them up to the Lord.

   Let us give thanks to the Lord our God.
Response: It is proper and right.

PROTOCOL → It is truly proper and right, fitting and helpful, that at all
times both here and everywhere we give thanks to you, Lord,
holy Father, almighty and eternal God. (For in the beginning, BODY
among other gifts of goodness and loving kindness, you commanded the earth to bring forth fruit-bearing trees. Thus, the
source of this rich essence, olive trees, was born that their fruit
might be used for this sacred chrism. David, foreseeing with
the prophetic spirit the sacraments of your grace, sang that our
faces should be made cheerful with oil [see Ps 104:15]. And
when of old the crimes of the world were to be expiated by the
flood, a dove, displaying in an olive branch the likeness of the
future gift, proclaimed the return of peace to the earth. Thus,
in these end times [these signs] have clear fulfillment when, as
the waters of baptism destroy all the sins committed, this ointment of oil makes our faces joyful and serene. Moreover, you
gave your commands to Moses, your servant, that he should
constitute his brother Aaron a priest, first washing him with
water, then by anointing him with this ointment. An even greater
honor came to this [chrism] when your Son, our Lord Jesus
Christ, sought to be washed by John the Baptist in the waves

of the Jordan, and the Holy Spirit was sent from above in the form of a dove on your only-begotten Son, in whom, as you showed from the voice which followed, you were well pleased [see Mark 1:11]. Thus, you established most clearly that this was what David sang of, namely, that he should be "anointed with the oil of gladness above his fellows" [Ps 45:7].

PETITION

Therefore, we beseech you, Lord, holy Father, almighty and everlasting God, through Jesus Christ, your Son and our Lord, that you deign to sanctify this rich element with your blessing and mix into it the power of the Holy Spirit, through the might of your Christ, from whose holy name chrism took its name. [This is] the chrism with which you anointed your priests, kings, prophets, and martyrs; for those who are to be born again of water and the Holy Spirit may it be the chrism of salvation, that you may bring them to participate in eternal life and share in the glory of heaven. Through the same your Son our Lord Jesus Christ.

DIFF. SPIRITUAL
WORD
STRATIFICATION
OF
PRAYER

At this point you mix the balsam with oil, and this exorcism follows:

I exorcise you, creature oil, in the name of God, the Father almighty, and in the name of Jesus Christ his Son, and of the Holy Spirit, by this invocation of the threefold might and by the power of the Godhead, may all the most evil powers of the adversary, all the enduring malice of the devil, all the clash of violence, every blind and disordered fantasy, be rooted out, depart, and be put to flight through this creature of oil that you have made for human use. May this ointment, purified by divine rites, bring about the adoption of flesh and spirit for all who are to be anointed with it, for the remission of all their sins; may it effect in them a pure heart made holy for every spiritual grace. Through the same Jesus Christ, our Lord, who will come in the Holy Spirit to judge the living and the dead and the world by fire: through our Lord.

FRAGMENT
OF A PREFACE

It is truly proper, almighty, everlasting God, who revealed to Noah's eyes the depths of your mysteries in showing him the branch carried in the mouth of the dove, that the dwellers of the ark might learn that the glory of the world's liberation would soon return to the world by the Holy Spirit and the chrism of the olive. Through our Lord Jesus Christ, who will come to judge the living and the dead and this world by fire.

When this has been explained, you come before the altar, drop a piece of the host in the chalice; you do not say The peace of the Lord, *nor give the kiss of peace; but* [the people] *receive*

Communion, and they reserve [the host] from this sacrifice for tomorrow's Communion. [The text follows with the proper parts of the evening Mass.]

Chapter 41: The order of the sixth day [Good Friday], the Passion of the Lord begins

[The chapter sets forth the Good Friday liturgy, which began at 3:00 P.M. and consists of prayers of petition, the reading of the passion, and Communion.]

Chapter 42: Holy Saturday

[In the morning the elect are exorcised, after which the celebrant touches their nostrils and ears with saliva in imitation of Jesus healing the deaf-mute (see Mark 7:35, *Ephphatha*). With exorcised oil he then anoints them on the breast and between the shoulder blades. Through their sponsors, they renounce Satan and his pomps and then recite the creed *(redditio symboli)*, which had been given and explained to them on the fourth Monday of Lent above.

In the evening, the Holy Saturday Vigil was celebrated; it began with long prayer, the theme of which is light, and included the blessing of grains of incense for the paschal candle (see below the *Exultet,* which replaces it in the *Gregorian Sacramentary*). The text then moves to the next chapter and more details about the vigil.]

Chapter 43: The Prayers for Each of the Holy Saturday Readings

[The elect have reassembled for prayer, biblical reading, and instruction. The focus is twelve lessons from the Old Testament, which present the axial events of salvation history. Although the text is not explicit about the precise texts, the selections revolve around the Creation account (Gen 1–2), Noah and the Flood (Gen 6–9), Abraham and Isaac (Gen 22), the Exodus from Egypt (Exod 14–15), Isaiah (54–55), Ezekiel (37), Isaiah again (4–5), the plagues in Exodus (7–12), Moses's death and canticle in Deuteronomy (31–32), and the apocalyptic passages in Daniel (presumably, ch. 7). At the end of the vigil, Ps 42 (41) is chanted: "As a hart longs for flowing streams, so longs my soul for you. . . ." A rubric outlining the baptism rite concludes the chapter:]

Then they proceed to the fonts for baptism, while a litany is sung. When baptism is finished, the infants are sealed by the bishop, as they receive the seven gifts of the Holy Spirit, and he places chrism on their foreheads. Then the priest returns to the sacristy with all the ranks of clergy. After a little while they begin the third litany; then they enter [the church] for the vigil Mass, when the [first] star appears in the sky. And they should so arrange things that the number of these litanies corresponds to the number in the Trinity.

Chapter 44: The Consecration of the Baptismal Font

[This chapter gives some of the details contained in the above rubric.]

The litany [is chanted] as you go down to the font.

Almighty, everlasting God, be present to the mysteries of your great and faithful devotion, be present at the rites and at the creation of a new people, whom the baptismal font brings forth; send forth the spirit of adoption and [grant] that what is to be done by our humble ministry may be fulfilled by the action of your power. Through . . . .

Next the consecration of the font.

God, who by your invisible power marvelously brings into being your sacraments: although we are not worthy to celebrate such great mysteries, do not forget the gift of your grace; instead, incline the ears of your goodness to our prayers. God, whose Spirit at the beginning of the world was "borne on the waters" [Gen 1:2], so that even the nature of water might conceive the power of sanctification; God who by the outrush of the flood, when you washed away the sins of a wicked world, signified a type of rebirth—by the mystery of the same element there might be [signified] both an end and a beginning. Look down, Lord, on the face of your church and multiply in her your generations, you who gladdened your city with the rush of the flood of your grace [see Ps 104:4], also open up the baptismal font for the renewal of all nations of the world that [they] may receive the grace of your Only-Begotten by the Holy Spirit at the command of your majesty. Let your Holy Spirit, by the hidden admixture of his light, give fruitfulness to this water prepared for the rebirth of humankind, that, with sanctification conceived in it, a heavenly offspring may come forth from the spotless womb reborn as a new creature, and that grace may be a mother to people of every age and sex, who are born into a common infancy. Lord, at your command let every unclean spirit go far from here; let all the wickedness of the devil's seduc-

4

tions stand off in the distance; let his mixture of opposing forces have no dwelling here; let him not fly about laying his snares; let him not slip silently in; let him not corrupt by infection. May this holy and innocent water be free from every incursion of the enemy and purified by the flight of evil. May the font be living, the water regenerating, the wave purifying, that all who are to be washed in this saving bath by the work of the Holy Spirit within them may be brought to the indulgence of perfect cleansing.

Here you sign the water.

MIDDLE > AGES

For this reason I bless you, creature water, through God the living, through God the holy, through God who in the beginning separated you from the dry land by his word and commanded you to water the whole earth in four rivers, who gave sweetness to your bitterness in the desert that people might drink you, and [who] brought you forth from the rock for a thirsty people. I bless you also through Jesus Christ his only Son our Lord, who changed you into wine at Cana of Galilee by his power in a marvelous sign, who walked upon you with his feet, and was baptized in you by John at the Jordan, who caused you to be gushed from his side with his blood, and commanded believers to be baptized in you, saying, "Go, teach all nations, baptizing them in the name of the Father and of the Son and of the Holy Spirit" [Matt 28:19].

Here you will change your tone. CONSECRATION OF FONT

CLASSIC ROMAN ADDRESS

Almighty God, be present among us with clemency as we observe your commandments, be kind and inspire us, bless these simple waters with your voice, that they may have the power to purify [the subjects'] minds beyond the natural purity that fits them for washing their bodies.

May the power of your Holy Spirit descend into every part of the water of this font and make fruitful the whole substance of the water for regeneration. Here may the stains of all sins be blotted out. Here may the nature that was founded on your image be restored to the honor of its origin and cleansed from all its ancient squalor, so that every person that enters this sacrament of regeneration may be reborn in a new infancy of true innocence. Through our Lord, Jesus Christ, your Son, who will come in the Holy Spirit to judge the living and the dead and the world by fire.

Then, when the font is consecrated, you baptize each one in order, [asking] these questions:

SAME AS HIPPOLYTES

	Do you believe in God the Father almighty?
Response:	I believe.

	And do you believe in Jesus Christ his only Son our Lord, who was born and suffered?
Response:	I believe.

	And do you believe in the Holy Spirit, the holy church, the remission of sins, the resurrection of the flesh?
Response:	I believe.

Then singly you dip [each infant] three times in the water.

When an infant has emerged from the font [the third time] the presbyter signs him [her] on the head with chrism, with these words:

Almighty God, Father of our Lord Jesus Christ, who has regenerated you from water and the Holy Spirit [see John 3:5] and has given you remission of all your sins, he it is who anoints you with the chrism of salvation for eternal life in Christ Jesus our Lord.

[The sponsor] responds: Amen.

Next the sevenfold gift is given to them by the bishop. To seal them he imposes his hand on them with these words:

Almighty God, Father of our Lord Jesus Christ, who has regenerated your servants from water and the Holy Spirit [see John 3:5] and has given them the remission of all sins: Lord, send upon them your Holy Spirit, the Paraclete, and give them the spirit of wisdom and understanding, the spirit of counsel and might, the spirit of knowledge and faithful devotion, and fill them with the spirit of fear of God [see Isa 11:2], in the name of our Lord Jesus Christ, with whom you live and reign always God with the Holy Spirit throughout every age of ages. Amen.

Then he signs them on the forehead with chrism, saying:

	The sign of Christ for eternal life.
Response:	Amen.

	Peace be with you:
Response:	And with you.

[At this point the *Gloria in excelsis Deo* of the paschal vigil Mass is intoned. The prayers proper to the Easter season are given for the Mass. The following chapters (46–78) give the propers for the Easter season, which included the feast of the Ascension of Christ. The season ended with Pentecost, which started with a vigil similar but not identical in structure with the Easter Vigil. It was also a time of solemn baptism, but the sacramentary does not contain the ritual (chs. 77–80).]

The Gregorian Sacramentary

The *Gregorian Sacramentary,* also of erroneous attribution (to Pope Gregory the Great, 590–604), combines papal liturgical usage some fifty years before Pope Hadrian (772–779) and the Frankish (Gallic) liturgical traditions of Charlemagne (742–814). In its present form (compiled about 800), the sacramentary consists of what Pope Hadrian called the "sacramentary of Gregory in pure form" (as it turns out, a beautiful manuscript but incomplete) and a supplement, which may also go back to Pope Gregory, yet has much Frankish liturgical tradition. The reading from the sacramentary is the celebrated hymn of praise *(Praeconium paschale)* which served as a liturgical preface for the blessing of the paschal candle at the Easter Vigil (and continues to do so, save for the last two paragraphs, which differ from the more recent versions). The custom of the paschal candle and its blessing can be traced back as far as late fourth-century North Africa and Italy. Some have thought Augustine its author, very likely because he composed a short eulogy on the candle *(On the City of God* 15:22); other candidates have been proposed as well, among them Jerome (347–420), Ambrose (above), and Leo (above). In fact, however, the reading that follows comprises the earliest version of the hymn, often called the *Exultet* from its opening word. It celebrates the turning points in the biblical history of salvation, teaching the meaning of baptism in the process.

The text is that of H. A. Wilson, *The Gregorian Sacramentary Under Charles the Great* (London: The Henry Bradshaw Society [69], 1915) 151–153. The *Exultet* is contained in the largely Frankish supplement. There is no trace of it in the *Gelasian Sacramentary.*

The *Exultet*

Let the angelic hosts of heaven now rejoice; let the divine mysteries rejoice; and let the trumpet of salvation sound the victory of so great a King. Let the earth also rejoice, made radi-

ant by such splendor, and, enlightened with the brilliance of
the eternal King, let us realize that the darkness has fled. Let
mother church also rejoice, adorned with the splendor of so
great a light; and may this sanctuary resound with the swelling
voices of the people. And so, dearest brethren, now made lu-
minous with the clarity of this light, to invoke with me the mercy
of almighty God, that he, who deigned to number me among
the Levites without any merit of mine, may endue me with the
grace of his light to render fulsome the praise of this candle.
Through the Lord . . .

> Let us lift up our hearts.
> We have lifted them to the Lord.
> Let us give thanks to the Lord our God.
> It is proper and fitting so to do.

It is indeed proper and fitting to proclaim with full affection
of mind and heart and by the service of [my] voice that God
invisible and everlasting, the Father of his only begotten Son,
Jesus Christ our Lord, who repaid to his Father Adam's debt,
and cancelled the bond of our ancient crime by the devoted shed-
ding of [his] blood. For this is the paschal festival, in which
is slain the true Lamb by whose blood the door posts of the
faithful are made sacred. This is the night in which you first
led our fathers, the children of Israel, out of Egypt and led them
dry-shod through the Red Sea. This is the night that scattered
the darkness of sin with the pillar of fire. This is the night
throughout the world that restores those who believe in Christ
at this season to grace, severing from them the gloom of sin
and bonding them to holiness. This is the night when Christ,
having broken the shackles of death, ascended victorious from
hell. For it would have profited us nothing had we not profited
by being redeemed.

How wonderful the reaching down to us of your devoted fi-
delity! How incomparable the preference of your charity: you
gave up your own Son that you might ransom your servant!
How truly necessary was Adam's sin that it be destroyed by
the death of Christ! O happy fault that merited so great a
Redeemer! How blessed this night which alone was worthy to
know the season and the hour at which Christ rose again from
hell! This is the night about which it was written: "And the
night shall be illumined by the day, and the night is my light
for the things I delight in." Thus, it is that the sacredness of
this night banishes crime, washes away sin, and restores inno-

cence to those that have fallen and gladness to those that are sad. It drives out crime, brings peace, curbs arrogance.

In the grace of this night, then, holy Father, receive as the evening sacrifice this incense [very likely, the deacon blessed and inserted five grains of incense in the paschal candle cross-wise, as he did in later rites], which holy church renders to you in the solemn offering of this candle of wax, fashioned by bees, at the hand of her ministers. Through the praises sung, now we know about this column, whose red glow flames up to the honor of God. [At this point the deacon very likely lit the candle, as in later rites.] Though divided into parts, still it suffers no loss from the light which it shares. For it is fed from the melted wax which the mother bee made for the substance of this precious lamp. [Possibly three reeds were also lit, from which the lamps and the candles of the congregation were lit, as in later rites.]

Concerning the bees, they excel all other animals known to humans. Although in body slight, still in this small space [the bee] possesses strong spirit in its heart. However strong in mind we dull humans are, an example near at hand may help. When gray winter [of hibernation] has spread gray whiteness over nature, and icy old age keeps at bay springtime moderation, the bees have already risen and are out plying their trade, scattered here and there through the fields. With small wings spread and legs hanging loose, they pick small blossoms with their mouths and return to their nests to make their food. Then with clever skill some [of the swarm] construct cells with strong glue, others attend to the [making] of honey, others turn the flowers into wax, others nourish the newborn, and others encase the honey with collected leaves. Truly blest and wonderful is the bee, whose sex males do not violate nor fetuses shatter, and whose chastity children do not destroy. Just so did Mary conceive as a virgin, bore her child as a virgin, and has remained a virgin. Truly blessed is the night which despoiled the Egyptians and enriched the Hebrews! the night in which the things of heaven are joined to those of earth.

We pray, therefore, that this wax consecrated to the honor of your name, Lord, may last out this night without fail in spite of the destruction wrought by the [candle's] fire, that, received in the odor of sweetness, it may be mixed with the lights on high, and that the morning star may find its flames. That morning star, I say, who knows no setting; he it is, returned from the dead, who serene sheds light on the human race. We beseech you, therefore, Lord, that you deign to guard us your family—all your clergy and most devoted people, together with our father the Pope—and grant us a quiet season for these paschal joys. Through our Lord.

Chapter 2

North Africa

The center of North African Christianity was Carthage, now a town (Qartajanneh) of five thousand (and an archaeological site) a few miles northeast of modern Tunis. Celebrated in Virgil's *Aeneid* as the city of Dido, Carthage was founded in 841 B.C.E. and long dominated the western Mediterranean. It fell to Rome and was destroyed in 146 B.C.E. Rebuilt in 29 B.C.E., Carthage became the capital of Roman Africa and vied with Alexandria as second city in the empire. The Vandals seized the city in 439 C.E., then the Byzantines in 533, and finally the Arabs in 698, after which it largely disappears from Christian view.

The first clear record of Christians in North Africa is a document based on the court record of the trial involving twelve Christians of Scillium (location not known). They were executed at Carthage July 17, 180, for being Christians. The next record, twenty-three years later, is a similar but more celebrated document, *The Martyrdom of Saints Perpetua and Felicity.* An apocalypse apparently based on the martyrs' words, the account records the trial, imprisonment, and death of Vibia Perpetua, a twenty-two-year-old woman of high birth, her slave Felicity, a male slave, two young men, and a catechumen. In between these two recorded events, intermittent trouble between the city's Christians and the authorities prompted Tertullian (below), North Africa's most brilliant Christian spokesman prior to Augustine (below), to launch an ecclesiastical career that issued in apologetic works of consummate artistry.

All three—court records, apocalypse, and Tertullian—attest that Christianity had penetrated deeply into the fabric of North African life by the end of the second century. With some justice Tertullian could chide the Proconsul Scapula about the havoc his anti-Christian policy would wreak on Carthaginian society if continued: Carthage would reel, many families would be scarred including some of senatorial rank, and even members of his own entourage would fall (*To Scapula* 5:2; also *Apology* 37:4). And Carthage was not alone, for Christianity had spread into the major cities and the countryside as far as Mauritania (Morocco).

Unfortunately, none of the three witnesses speak about the early years, which peer through the obscurity only through the hints given by the Synoptic Gospels (see Mark 15:21 and parallels) and the Acts of the Apostles (see 2:10) that there may have been Christians in Libya quite early. Nonetheless, the pattern that existed elsewhere is doubtless true of Carthage and its environs. Immigrant Jewish Christians, largely artisans and traders, came to the city, associating themselves with the city's synagogues. The strong Jewish heritage in North African Christianity suggests that Christians moved out of the synagogues only slowly, and a clear apocalyptic strain indicates that in the process, they clashed sharply with the city's Greco-Roman culture as the work of the devil, producing Christians like the Scillitan martyrs, Perpetua and her companions, and many others.

This militant rejection of Greco-Roman culture remained a permanent characteristic of North African Christianity. It is hardly an accident that baptism bore the name and evoked the image of the military oath (*sacramentum,* see General Introduction, "Baptism: Sacrament as Sign"), that homiletic appeal was continually made to the baptismal renunciation of Satan, and that close attention was given to the baptismal scrutiny (see ch. 1; also see below, Augustine) as the decisive, almost "saving" moment in the process of conversion.

A second characteristic of the Church in North Africa was its conciliar structure. Early in the third century (ca. 225) seventy bishops met in council at Carthage to consider a question that would surface again and again: whether one baptized in heresy needed rebaptism (see below, Cyprian). A second council was held in the next decade, and some two decades later Bishop Cyprian (below) held five councils at Carthage, three of which (252, 253,

256) reexamined the question of heretical baptism. Indeed, with Cyprian the conciliar pattern was set and in him found its first theoretician. He held that taken collectively the bishops were at once the sign and the source of both the Church's unity and the authenticity of Church teaching and practice. Taken individually, they shared in this totality; as a result, to contravene the bishop was to contravene the Church (*On the Unity of the Catholic Church* 1–6). When the bishops met in council, then, they embodied the Church and its authority; when they worked in their own Churches, they embodied something of the whole, especially as the teachers of catechumens and faithful and as the celebrants of the sacraments.

Still another characteristic of the North African Church was the emphasis placed on the Holy Spirit in the Church. This emphasis first surfaced in the *Martyrdom of Saints Perpetua and Felicity* and then acquired a champion in Tertullian, who ended his life as a Montanist and champion of the "church of the Spirit" embodied in the poor and the martyrs. The emphasis finally threatened the very existence of the Church in North Africa during the long Donatist controversy (see below, Optatus and Augustine).

Two related issues were involved: whether the Church is a communion of saints or of sinners, and whether the character of the celebrant of the sacraments affects their validity. Like other Christians, the North Africans thought of the Church as that community where humankind had access to the saving action of Christ the Savior. But they tended to draw its boundaries narrowly, holding that outside the visible community centered around the bishop and the bishops, that is, the Catholic Church, there was no salvation. In effect this denied Christian status to any but Catholics. An important result was the North African conciliar teaching, promulgated under Cyprian, that those baptized in heresy and returning to the Church required rebaptism.

But this narrow definition of boundaries had further repercussions. When the first empire-wide attempt to destroy Christianity struck North Africa in 250, many Christians apostatized. Called *lapsi* (the fallen), they posed a divisive question when the persecution ceased: Ought the repentant among them be reconciled to the Church? Inspired by Novatian (ch. 1), some answered a sharp no, arguing that the Church was composed of the steadfast, who alone possessed the Spirit. Cyprian, however, argued for reconciliation through the penitential discipline, grounding his position in the conviction that the Church is the place of salvation and must be accessible to sinners.

The divisions between the Novatianists and the Catholics, however, persisted underground until the second imperial attempt to crush Christianity struck under Diocletian (303). After the persecution subsided in 311, the issue about the boundaries of the Church flared again, this time with long-term results for North African Christianity. The question, however, was more sharply focused: Were those sacraments valid that were celebrated by a bishop or priest who had betrayed the Church during the persecution? Like their Novatianist predecessors, some North African Christians, who came to be led by a bishop named Donatus, were convinced that the true Church is the Church of the martyrs (and of the poor): Only they possessed the Spirit of holiness. The Donatists, as they came to be called by the Catholics, argued that since clergy who betrayed the Church were by that fact outside the Church, they could not give what they did not have, namely, holiness and its source, the Spirit. They concluded, therefore, that the sacramental minister who lacked the holiness of the Spirit could not confer a valid sacrament. The Donatist position enlisted capable exponents and organizers who secured the intellectual and spiritual upper hand for the Donatists during the fourth century. The Catholics did not find their voice until the appearance of Optatus of Milevis and Augustine of Hippo.

Nonetheless, the controversies about the nature of the Church secured the foundation of baptismal teaching important for later centuries: (1) Given the intent to do what the Church does, the moral condition of the celebrant does not affect the validity of baptism (or any sacrament); (2) baptism properly celebrated imprints a character ("seal," indelible mark) on the baptized in virtue of which the gifts of baptism, if not received or if lost, revive; and (3) heretical and schismatic baptisms are valid.

With respect to baptismal liturgy, close bonds are evident between early Christian North Africa and Italy. Tertullian and Cyprian testify to the importance of Roman practice to the North African Christians; Augustine looks to Milan (see Ambrose, ch. 1), which in turn looks to Rome. But for the development of Western baptismal teaching, the student of baptism must look primarily to North African baptism, the architects of which constitute the readings: Tertullian, Cyprian, Optatus, and Augustine.

For a valuable treatment of the development of early Christianity in North Africa, see Timothy D. Barnes, *Tertullian: A Historical and Literary Study*, 2nd. ed. (Oxford: Clarendon, 1985). See also W. H. C. Frend, *The Donatist Church: A Movement of Protest in Roman North Africa* (New York: Oxford University Press, 1971).

Tertullian

The earliest treatise on baptism in East or West is Tertullian's homily *On Baptism*. The author was born of pagan parents about 160 in Carthage (a suburb of modern Tunis, capital of Tunisia), North Africa. His father was a professional army officer (a centurion) in the Roman legions, which gave the son access to education and upward mobility. A man of high education, a gifted writer in both Latin and Greek, and a rhetorician (the equivalent of a modern lawyer), Tertullian became a Christian about 190. From that point on he dedicated his wit, intelligence, and considerable talent to those issues of the day that affected Christians. The earliest Christian on record to write in Latin, he left a legacy of theological terms (some of which he mined from his Old Latin version of the Bible) that remain at the service of Western Christianity even today, among them terms so influential as almost to be English: *persona* (person), *substantia* (substance), *trinitas* (trinity), and *sacramentum* (sacrament).

About 206, he began to show interest in the Montanist movement, the members of which lived in the ready expectation of the imminent outpouring of the Holy Spirit on the Church. In 213 he separated from the Catholic Church in Carthage to join the Montanists. Toward the end of his life he parted from the Montanists, apparently over a dispute about the bodily constitution of the soul. Traces of his group, the "Tertullianists," were present in North Africa until the end of the fourth century, when their basilica in Carthage was given over to the Catholics.

Tertullian is the most important and original Latin Christian author and thinker prior to Augustine (below). In all his works—apologetical, disciplinary, and theological—he proves ever the controversialist. This is true even of the work at hand, *On Baptism*. It was occasioned by a woman missionary of a small Cainite Gnostic sect who argued (apparently with much success) that baptism was neither necessary nor effective because enmeshed in matter—particularly trivial matter at that, water. She reinforced her argument by pointing out that the pagan mystery rites were far more impressive. Tertullian responds with a defense of baptism that emphasizes the centrality of water and the Holy Spirit in God's plan for human salvation (chs. 1–9). Then he turns to questions about baptism disputed among the city's Christians (10–16): the effect of John's baptism; why Jesus did not baptize; how the apostles and the patriarchs of Israel were saved apart from baptism; whether faith is enough; the validity of heretical baptism; and second baptism. He concludes his treatise with pastoral considerations: the proper minister of the sacrament; delaying baptism; and the most appropriate seasons for solemn baptism (17–20).

Delivered to a mixed congregation of catechumens (the primary audience) and faithful at the turn of the third century, *On Baptism* presupposes and permits glimpses of the baptismal rites of North Africa's principal Church, rites which had by then become traditional. Tertullian's corpus of works reveals a picture of baptism not unlike that of Rome, though not as clearly articulated and demanding (see ch. 1, *Apostolic Tradition*).

That prebaptismal instruction was required is clear; the extent of it is not, though several years is a reasonable supposition. In the treatise we learn that the period of preparation was punctuated with frequent prayer, fasting, kneeling, nightlong vigils, and the confession of past sinfulness (20). At a point close to baptism, those chosen for baptism (he calls them *ingressuri,* "those about to enter," 20) renounced Satan in the presence of the bishop, a rite repeated at baptism itself, where renunciation also embraced the world and took place outside the church. Whether baptism itself took place in the Mediterranean, in the vast Baths of Antoninus, or in a church building is not clear (4). The water, however, was consecrated and the candidates were accompanied by their sponsors. Triple immersion was the custom and the baptismal formula, Trinitarian, based on the Carthaginian creed (6), which very likely formed the syllabus of instruction. On coming out of the baptismal font, the newly baptized (Tertullian calls them "novices") were anointed with consecrated oil (whether from head to foot or just on the head is not clear) and probably sealed with the cross, after which the presider (normally, the bishop) imposed his hand in invitation and welcome to the Holy Spirit (7–8). Indeed, Tertullian ascribes the descent of the Holy Spirit to this anointing (see ch. 1, Ambrose). The candidates then joined the congregation for the Eucharist, at which, as in Rome, they received a cup of mixed milk and honey. A week of celebrations centering on the "novices" followed, almost certainly around the Eucharist, with continued instruction on the requirements and expectations of their new baptismal state.

Tertullian regards the baptismal liturgy as at once simple and powerful, the very attributes of God himself (2). Even the demons (i.e., the mystery religions, 5) imitate the rites. The liturgy's power is disclosed especially in the biblical types or figures (Tertullian's usual term is *figura*), which reveal the waters as the "worthy chariot" (or "throne") of God (3). The types are, primarily, the creation of the world from water (3–4); Israel's Exodus from Egypt and the forty years in the desert (9); John's baptism (6); the baptism of Christ and the "water" events of Christ's life, especially the wound in his side from which bursts forth water (9, 19). Such is the "religious significance" (10) of baptism, which at once wipes away guilt and the penalty of sin and restores the image and likeness of God given Adam in Paradise (6).

Of particular note is Tertullian's sacramental conviction, namely, that water is capable of regenerating the candidate because of God's spirit, which it bears. The very fact that water can penetrate to the hiddenmost inner recesses of the physical world discloses that it penetrates to the very spirit of the baptismal candidate. Thus, the candidate's spirit is physically washed, while the body is spiritually cleansed in the very same waters (4).

The text is that of Ernest Evans, ed., *Tertullian's Homily on Baptism* (London: SPCK, 1964) and of R. F. Refoulé, M. Drouzy, eds., SC 35 (1952), both of which contain valuable introductions and notes as well as facing translations, respectively in English and French. Tertullian's text is difficult due both to its transmission and to the fact that Tertullian assumes things familiar to his audience. The translation that follows has in mind the general reader. As a result it incorporates the Evans and Refoulé notes and commentary for clarity in reading.

On Baptism

1. The Occasion of the Work

The present work treats our sacrament of water that washes away the sins contracted at the time of our original blindness and releases us into eternal life. It will not be without value if [our discussion] instructs both those being systematically formed [in the faith] and those who have simply believed without having examined the grounds for what the baptismal rites have conferred on them; they bear a faith open to temptation. Indeed, a certain woman—a most venomous viper from the Cainite heresy—recently arrived among us, carrying off many with her teaching. That she made the destruction of baptism her first aim fully accords with what we know from nature—vipers and asps and even serpents usually frequent dry and waterless places. But we little fish, like our great Fish, Jesus Christ, are born in water, nor can we be saved in any other way than by remaining permanently in the water. And so this monster of a woman, who would not lawfully be allowed to teach even sound doctrine, found the most effective means of killing these little fish: by taking them out of the water.

2. Simplicity and Faith

In fact, this heresy has such powerful perversity, whether for shattering faith or for completely impeding it, that it uses as its weapons the very fundamentals on which faith rests. For there is nothing which hardens people's minds more than the simplicity of the divine works which one sees in action and the wonder their effects summon. Here indeed is such simplicity: without display, without innovative contrivances [Tertullian has in mind the theatrical productions in Carthage's two theaters], and, not least, without cost [the mystery religions charged a fee for initiation], a person is immersed and baptized to the accompaniment of a few words, emerging little or no cleaner. Yet the resultant effect, eternity, is said to be beyond belief. Deplorable unbelief that denies to God his own distinctive properties, simplicity and power. Is it, after all, so astonishing that death is dissolved by washing? Since it is a work of wonder, ought it not for that very reason to be believed? It should be believed all the more readily, for is it not a characteristic of divine works that they are beyond astonishment? Even so, we too are astonished, precisely because we believe. As for the others, their incredulity marvels, because they do not believe: it marvels at simplicity as ineffective, at grandeur as impossible. Grant that

it is as you [might] think, God's proclamation spoken long ago
is applicable to both simplicity and grandeur: "Yet to shame
the wise, God has chosen foolish things" [1 Cor 1:27]; and
again, "What is difficult for humans is easy for God" [Luke
18:27]. . .[In a few sentences Tertullian expands his point].

3. Waters and Creation

Mindful of this proclamation laid down as if it were a standing rule, are we nevertheless to consider it impossible or foolish that one is formed anew [*reformari*] by water? Nevertheless,
since this liquid matter has merited a function of such high dignity, I think that its significance requires explanation. Indeed,
from the very beginning it has possessed great significance. For
before the world was set in order, water was one of the elements resting in the hands of God. "In the beginning," we read,
"God made heaven and earth: earth, however, was invisible
and chaotic, and there was darkness over the deep, and the spirit
of God was borne on the waters" [Gen 1:1-2]. Humans, you
must first hold in reverence the age of the waters, for they are
an ancient substance, and next, [recognize] the honor done them
as the throne of the divine Spirit, more pleasing to him than
the other elements. Consider the pervasive unformed darkness
as yet without the adornment of the stars, and [that] joyless
abyss, the earth unshaped: the flowing water alone—ever perfect, fertile and simple, and of itself pure— submitted itself to
be the worthy chariot of God [Carthage was famous for its cir-
cus and charioteers]. Must one also summon the order of the
world, an order which consists, so to speak, of God's arrange-
ment of its parts? In order to hang the vault of heaven, he divided the waters in the middle; in order to establish the solid
earth, he gathered together the waters and made it emerge. Then,
with the world thus ordered, when it was time that inhabitants
be provided, a command was given to the primordial waters
to bring forth living creatures [see Gen 1:20]. Granted that the
liquid was first to bring forth what should have life, is it any
wonder in baptism that the waters know how to bring forth life?
As for the task of creating humanity, did not the waters assist
[see Gen 2:7]? Matter was taken up from the earth. Nonetheless, it was only workable by being moistened and wet, specifically, the waters, gathered together into their own place four
days before, had changed into mud by their moist residue.

[Continuing, Tertullian comments that, should he go on to
speak about water and the rest of the matter in the world, he

would be composing a panegyric on water rather than an instruction on baptism. He then concentrates on his first example:]

4. Water, the Holy Spirit, and Sacrament

Finally, it suffices to recall quickly those original events which help us to know the religious significance of baptism: the Spirit of God, who by his conduct was already at work prefiguring baptism, he who, since the beginning was borne on the waters [see Gen 1:2] would dwell on the waters as baptizer. Indeed, something holy was borne on something holy, or rather, that which bore borrowed from that which it bore. . . . Thus, the nature of the waters, made holy from the holy, itself conceived the power to make holy. Let no one, then, ask, "Are we baptized in the very same waters as those in the beginning?" Not the very same, yet still the same from the standpoint of a single species, though there are many individual instances: for the characteristics of the species overflow into its individual instances. So it makes no difference whether one is baptized in the sea or a pond, in a river or a fountain, in a cistern or a tub: nor is there a difference between those whom John baptized in the Jordan and those whom Peter baptized in the Tiber—unless it be that [from the standpoint of disposition] the eunuch, whom Philip baptized in the water found by chance [see Acts 8:36] received more or less salvation. Therefore, once God is invoked [in the consecration], all water participates in the mystery of sanctification from this ancient prerogative that marked it from the beginning. For as soon as the invocation is offered, the Spirit descends from heaven and comes to rest on the waters, rendering them holy by his presence; thus, they absorb the power of making holy. Perhaps a simile about an ordinary act would [clarify the work of] baptism: we are defiled by sins as if by dirt, so we are washed clean by water.

[At this point Tertullian shifts his attention to the Cainite teacher and Gnostics in general.] However, just as sins are not visible in the flesh—no one carries on his face the traces of idolatry or adultery or fraud—so it is the spirit, the true author of these sins, that soils. The spirit is master and the flesh is servant. Yet both communicate to each other the grounds for guilt: the spirit by its orders, the flesh by its service. Therefore, when the water received healing power through the intervention of the angel [see John 5:4], the spirit was washed by the body and the flesh purified in the same waters by the spirit.

5. Baptism: Pagan and Christian

[In this chapter Tertullian argues that the ritual washings in Greco-Roman religions are the devil's imitation of divine rites; nonetheless, they do testify that water can be the vehicle for spiritual power. As evidence, he cites the custom of murderers seeking to expunge their crimes in purifying waters, of participants in some of the new Roman games submerging themselves for purification before the contest, of the sacred washings of the initiation rites in the mystery cults of Isis and Mithra prevalent in the major Roman cities like Carthage, and of the festive processions in which devotees carried their god in the form of a statue to a stream for the annual ceremonial bath. In his development he asserts that evil spirits, imitating the Holy Spirit in Genesis 1:2, settle upon the "shady springs, all sorts of out-of-the-way streams, pools in the (public) baths, aqueducts, and domestic cisterns." The "settling" image reminds him of the gospel account of the angel at the "Sheep Pool" at the Bethesda (Bethsaida) gate who would stir the waters, healing the first to enter (see John 5:1-15). Tertullian concludes the paragraph with a discussion of the incident as a type of baptism and may have in mind that the bishop is the ritual counterpart of the angel:]

Why have I brought up these things? So that no one should think it any harder for the holy angel of God to be present stirring up the waters for the salvation of a human being, when an unholy angel of the evil spirit engages in the business with the same elements [but] for human perdition. If the intervention of the angel on the waters seems a novelty, there is a precedent. At the pool in Bethsaida an angel used to enter the waters to stir them up; those seeking a cure waited expectantly for him; for anyone who got down into the waters before the others lost the reason for complaint [i.e., was healed]. This physical healing disclosed in figure the spiritual healing, in conformity with the law that physical realities always come first as figures of spiritual realities. Thus it is that the grace of God continually progresses in everything: the water and the angel [of the gospel account] demonstrate increased power. They used to repair temporal defects, now they restore eternal life; long ago they freed people one at a time, now they save people daily, destroy death by the remission of sins—just think: as the fault is remitted the punishment is also taken away. So it is that humankind is restored to God, to the likeness of him [Adam] who had once been in the image of God [see Gen 1:26]—the "image" was rooted in the first human God had formed, the "likeness" designates that which is eternal—for there is returned to him the spirit of God that he had received from God's breath, but only after he had lost it through sin [see Gen 2:7].

6. The Trinity and Baptism

This is not to say that the Holy Spirit is in the water, but that purified in the water through the work of the angel, we are made ready for the Holy Spirit. Here also the figure had come first. For just as John was the precursor of the Lord, preparing his way, so also the angel, who presides at baptism, gets the way ready for the Holy Spirit, who is to come next. This he does by taking away sins, an absolution granted by faith sealed in the Father and the Son and the Holy Spirit. For, if every word shall be corroborated by three witnesses [see Deut 19:15], how much more so the gift of God? Through the blessing [i.e., form] of baptism we have as the witness of the faith the very ones who offer salvation. The number of the divine names itself is the confident ground of our hope. Yet because the three have taken in pledge the profession of faith and the offer of salvation, necessarily the mention of the church is added: for where the three are—the Father and the Son and the Holy Spirit—there is the church, the body of three [see Matt 18:20; in Roman law three was the minimum for a corporation, or *collegium*].

7. Chrismation

After we have emerged from the baptismal font we are anointed with consecrated oil, following that ancient [Israelite] practice according to which one was anointed with oil from the horn: thus was Aaron anointed by Moses [see Exod 29:7; 30:30; Lev 8:12]. The reason the [high priest] is called a "christ" [Lev 4:3-5, LXX] is from "chrism," the Greek word for anointing, which also gave the Lord his title [one reading adds: "the name 'Christians' comes from it as well"]. Thus it says in Acts: "For indeed they are gathered together in this city [the Jewish leaders in Jerusalem] against your Son whom you have anointed" [4:27]. For us also the oil flows on the flesh, but we profit in the spirit, just as in the rite of baptismal immersion itself there is an act that touches the flesh with a spiritual effect, namely that we are liberated from sins.

8. Typology and the Imposition of Hands

Next follows the imposition of hand[s] together with a blessing that summons and welcomes the Holy Spirit. For if human ingenuity can combine air with water [the reference is to the ancient water organ] such that with these two elements joined the musician's hand is able to make the mixture live with a new [sonorous] beauty, shall not God be permitted, by the use of holy hands [the minister's], to play a sublime melody with an instrument of his own making? Yet this [imposition and blessing] also recalls that ancient rite in which Jacob blessed his grandsons, the sons of Joseph, Ephraim, and Manasseh [see Gen 48:14], by placing his hands interchanged on their heads, thus forming a cross and announcing at that early date the blessing that would come to us in Christ.

At this point the very Holy Spirit, coming from the Father, gladly descends on the bodies purified and blessed; he comes to rest upon the waters of baptism as though returning to his primordial throne [see Gen 1:2], the very one who, in the form of a dove, descended on the Lord. In this descent the nature of the Holy Spirit is revealed, simplicity and innocence, for even physically the dove is without gall. This is why [the Lord] says, "Be simple, like doves" [Matt 10:16]. [The saying] is related to the type that preceded it: after the waters of the flood had washed away the ancient iniquity—after the baptism of the world, so to speak—the dove, sent from the ark and returning with an olive branch [see Gen 8:10-11], heralded to earth peace from the wrath of heaven, this [sign, the dove] too is offered as a sign of peace to the Gentiles. Even so, by the same ordinance, whose effect is spiritual, the dove, that is, the Holy Spirit, flies untrammeled to earth, that is, to our flesh as it emerges from the bath, now washed clean of its ancient sins.

You might [reasonably] object, "But the world fell back into sin, making the parallel between baptism and the flood invalid!" Exactly so, this is why the world is appointed to fire, just as humans are, who fall back into sin after baptism. Let this be taken as a warning sign to us.

9. The Typology of Baptism

Consider how many the advocates [of baptism] in nature, how many the special provisions of grace, how many the solemn rituals, [i.e.,] the scaffolding of types that have shaped the sacred use of water! The first is [the Exodus], when the people, freed from Egypt, crossing the water, escaped from the Egyptian king's power; the water destroyed the king himself with all his troops [see Exod 14:25-31]. What type could be more pertinent to the sacrament of baptism? The Gentiles are freed from the world and leave behind in the water their ancient master, the

devil, drowned. Another type is the water that Moses cured of
its bitter bite and restored to its normal sweetness by [plunging
into it] the tree [see Exod 15:22–25]. That tree was Christ, transforming [healing] from within himself nature's springs, previously poisoned and made bitter, into the health-giving water
of baptism. This is the same water that flowed for the people
from the rock which followed them [see Exod 17:6]. For if this
rock is Christ [thus, Paul: see 1 Cor 10:4], without any doubt
we realize that baptism receives its consecration from the water
[flowing from] Christ.

For confirming the significance of baptism, see how great
the grace of baptism before God and his Christ. Christ is never
without water! He himself was baptized with water [see Matt
3:16-17 and parallels]. Invited to a wedding [in Cana: see John
2:1-11], he inaugurates with water the first use of his power.
When he preaches [the kingdom], he invites the thirsty [to drink]
everlasting water [see John 4:14-15]. When he teaches about
charity, he reveals that a cup of water offered to a little one
is [counted] among the works of love. He recuperates his
strength near a spring [called Jacob's well: see John 4:6]; he
freely walks on the water [see Matt 14:22-27]; he ministers to
his disciples with water [washes their feet: see John 13:5]. He
continues these testimonies to baptism right up to his passion:
indeed, when he is sentenced to the cross, water still intervenes:
the hands of Pilate feel it [see Matt 27:24]; when he is wounded,
water flows from his side, as the soldier's lance announces [see
John 19:34].

10–14. Controversial Issues About Baptism

[Tertullian has divided his treatise into two parts: the first
(chs. 1–9) is a response to the Gnostic challenge and sets forth
the sacred significance of baptism and its liturgy. At this point,
he considers what he calls a series of questions about baptism,
some of which he calls "small questions" of controversy in the
Church at Carthage (10–14). He then goes on to consider matters of practice and policy (15–19).

The first controversial issue (ch. 10) concerns the effect of
John's baptism. Some thought it a "divine service that brought
forgiveness of sins." Tertullian concedes that Christ gave John
authority over repentance and that he prepared the way for the
Messiah, who would come baptizing "in the Spirit and fire";
but the catechist insists that John's baptism conferred neither
remission nor the gift of the Spirit. Another question (ch. 11)

concerned the baptism performed by the apostles during Jesus' life: Did it obtain for the baptized remission and the Spirit? Tertullian responds that these gifts of baptism had to await the ascension of Jesus. To those who wondered about the baptism of the apostles themselves (ch. 12), the catechist advises that their "original promotion (to apostleship) and, thereafter, of inseparable companionship might be understood to confer a bypassing of baptism." These issues about the sacrament and the precise moment of salvation leads him to reflections about the salvation of the pre-Christian just, like Abraham and the prophets; his answer has a twist (ch. 13). Before "our Lord's passion and resurrection," he argues, "salvation was by faith unattired; you know that faith has been enlarged for those who believe in his nativity and passion and resurrection, the sacrament has been expanded, and the seal of baptism added, in some cases a clothing for faith previously unattired." A final issue (ch. 14) was whether Paul, in insisting that Christ had not sent him to baptize (see 1 Cor 1:17), had abrogated baptism. Tertullian answers in the negative, explaining that Paul's denial was tactical to counter the schisms in Corinth, which had their roots in allegiance to those who baptized the members of the factions—the so-called baptismal camps.

Tertullian then turns his attention to what he regards as more pressing matters. The first is the unity of baptism (ch. 15). In view of the fact, he says, that "we have only one baptism, . . . one God . . . and one church that is in heaven" (Eph 4:4-5), what about heretics and baptism? In reply he gives voice to a policy that had long and loud effect in North Africa, as will be evident in the selections that follow Tertullian.]

15. Heretical Baptism

I know of no additional matters that are causing controversy about baptism. . . . We have only one baptism, according to the gospel of the Lord and the letters of Paul, and only one church in heaven [see Eph, above]. Concerning what ought to be customary practice about heretics, would that there were one more competent than I to treat the matter in depth. Since the Scriptures were addressed to us alone, heretics have no part in our rites; the very fact that they have no part in our communion testifies that they are outsiders. [Tertullian argues as a Roman lawyer from the law of *praescriptio:* The Scriptures belong to the Carthaginian Church; therefore, heretics have no right to use them.] I ought not acknowledge in their behalf the precept that applies only to us, because they do not have the same God as we nor have they the one, that is, the same Christ [he has in mind Gnostics and Marcionites]. As a result, they do not have the one, because not the same, baptism. Since they do not have it correctly [he seems to mean both the proper rite and the correct understanding of the sacrament], they do not have it at all, and cannot list it among their possessions. Also, they cannot have [the sacrament] given to them, because they cannot confer it. However, we have already treated this matter at length in Greek [the reference is to a lost treatise].

So then, we enter the baptismal font only once, and only once are our sins washed away, for we ought not to repeat them. By contrast Israel [the reference is to Jewish sects, including some Jewish Christian sects] washes daily, because the people defile themselves daily. That this might not happen among us, only one washing was prescribed. Happy the water that washes once for all, that is not a sport for sinners, and that is not tainted by repeated doses of dirt, defiling once more those whom it [seeks] to cleanse!

16. Baptism of Blood

As a matter of fact, we do have a second baptism; it too is once-for-all, that of blood, about which our Lord says, "I have a baptism to be baptized with" [Luke 12:50], after he had already been baptized. As John had written [see John 19:34], he had come by water and blood, so that he would be washed by water and glorified by blood. Likewise, by water he called us and by blood elected us. These two baptisms gushed forth from the wound in his pierced side [see John 19:34], because those who believed in his blood were washed by water, and those who had washed in the water would need also [to be washed] in blood. This second baptism replaces the baptism of water, when the latter has not been received, and it restores what has been lost [by postbaptismal sin].

17. The Ministers of Baptism

[Tertullian here discusses the North African tradition about who can lawfully baptize. The bishop is the primary minister of baptism, though with his approval, presbyters and deacons may lawfully baptize. The right (and at times duty) to baptize, however, belongs to lay Christians also, although they should exercise it "in emergencies, when conditions of place or time or person require it." He adverts again to the Cainite woman missionary who both taught and baptized in Carthage, which reminds him also of the apocryphal work (still extant), *The Acts of Paul,* which describes Thecla, authorized by Paul, teaching and baptizing. In the process he labels the work a forgery of a well-intentioned "Asian presbyter," and seems to exclude women from administering baptism validly, arguing that Paul (in 1 Cor 14:35) required women to keep silence in church and "ask their husbands at home."]

18. The Candidates for Baptism

[Apparently, there was some pressure to expedite the giving of baptism. Some cited the example of Philip and the Egyptian eunuch (see Acts 8:26-40), Paul's own speedy baptism (see Acts 9:15), and Jesus' encouragement (often applied to baptism): "Do not forbid (the little ones) to come to me" (Matt 19:14). Although Cyprian (below) speaks of the eighth day after birth (the Jewish custom for circumcision) as the usual time, Tertullian favors deferring baptism, a widespread custom in the fourth and following centuries. He advises:]

With respect to children, it is preferable to defer baptism in accord with each candidate's character and even age. . . .So let them come when they are growing up, when they are of an age to be instructed, when they have acquired the knowledge of what [estate] they are coming to. Let them become Christians when they have the capacity to know Christ. Why should innocent infancy hurry to the remission of sins? [Tertullian holds that infants do not inherit original sin. Although separated from God at birth, they bear no guilt for the separation—see below, Augustine—and are able to sin only when they have the use of reason. Nonetheless, demons lie in wait for them in their innocence and inexperience: see his *On the Soul* 39-40.] One acts with more caution in worldly affairs; should one who withholds earthly goods [from children] go on to confer divine gifts on them? Let [children] learn how to ask for salvation, so that it will be clear that salvation is given only to those that ask [see Matt 5:42].

For a reason no less serious, baptism ought to be put off for the unmarried, for temptation lies in wait for them, and also for girls until they reach maturity, and for widows because they have too little to do [see 1 Tim 5:13]. Delay baptism until they are either married or well established in continence. For if [people] understand the obligations of baptism, they will fear more receiving than delaying it: fully realized faith is assured of salvation.

19. The Seasons for Solemn Baptism

The Passover is the most solemn day for baptism, since it commemorates the passion of the Lord into which we are baptized. It is not interpreted irrationally as a type of [baptism], since, when the Lord was about to celebrate his last Passover, he sent his disciples to make preparations, saying: "You shall meet a man carrying water" [Mark 14:13]. By the sign of water he indicated the place for celebrating the Passover.

Next after [Passover], Pentecost is the most propitious season for baptism, for it is the time when the risen Lord showed himself frequently to the disciples, when the grace of the Holy Spirit was communicated, and [when] the hope of the Lord's [second] coming was made evident. Indeed, at that time, [namely,] when he was received back into heaven, the angels said to the apostles that he would come [from heaven] just as he had entered heaven—specifically at Pentecost. Thus, Jeremiah, in this passage, "I will reunite them from the ends of the earth on the feast day" [Jer 31:8, LXX], also means Pentecost, which is a proper feast day. Even so, every day is a Lord's day: any hour, any season, is suitable for baptism. Such matters [as season] impinge on the rite; they make no difference to the grace.

20. The Immediate Preparations for Baptism

Those who are about the enter baptism [the "elect" or the "competent"] ought to invoke God with frequent prayers, fasts, genuflections, and vigils. These ought to be coupled with the confession of their former sins, reminiscent of the baptism of John: "They were baptized," we read, "confessing their sins" [Matt 3:6]. We are fortunate that we are not called upon for the public confession of our sins and wickedness.

[Tertullian then addresses himself to postbaptismal temptations that assailed the apostles, Christ, and Israel in the wilderness, concluding his instruction as follows:]

Therefore, Blessed Ones, you for whom the grace of God is waiting, when you come up from that most sacred washing of the new birth [Titus 3:5] and for the first time spread out your hands with your brethren in your mother's house, ask your Father, ask the Lord, as a special gift, for an abundance of spiritual gifts [*charismatum,* see 1 Cor 12:1-31]. "Ask," he says, "and you will receive" [Matt 7:7-8]. Now that you have searched and found, knocked and it has been opened for you, I ask only that, as you ask, you will remember Tertullian, a sinner.

Cyprian

Tertullian was the first African theologian in a distinguished line that would end with Augustine; Cyprian, who spoke of Tertullian as "the great master," was the second. Born about 205, he grew up in a wealthy and cultivated pagan family, surrounded by all the best Carthage had to offer. High status all but assured that he would receive the best education and achieve prominence as a rhetorician and public servant. In midlife, however, he became disenchanted with public life, turned to Christianity, was baptized, ordained a priest, and in 249, elected bishop of Carthage. Unfortunately, within a year Emperor Decius (249–251) instituted the first concerted imperial effort to stamp out Christianity. Convinced that his presence was unnecessarily provocative, Cyprian went into hiding (*Letter* 20), emerging only after Decius was killed in battle (251). When Emperor Valerian renewed the persecution in 257 he was arrested and banished; a year later he was beheaded outside his native city, the first African bishop to be executed for being a Christian.

Whereas Tertullian was a man of thought and controversy, Cyprian was a man of action and affairs. Although he left behind him a variety of practical treatises (*Concerning the Lapsed* and *On the Unity of the Church* are his best known), his wide correspondence (sixty-five letters are extant) provides a unique window through which to view the problems and controversies that faced the Western Church at mid-third century. They deal with matters of discipline (*Letters* 1–4), with problems that arose as a result of imperial hostility, especially the reconciliation of apostates and struggles with heretics and schismatics (*Letters* 5–68, 76–81), and with baptism (*Letters* 69–75).

Cyprian's correspondence about baptism was occasioned by what he and other Africans saw as a burning issue: whether heretics should be baptized upon reentering the Church. The issue was not abstract. Followers of Novatian (ch. 1), insisting that Catholics who sought entry among them must be baptized anew, had established themselves in Carthage. Likewise, some Novatians sought to join (or rejoin) the Catholics; Cyprian and his African colleagues also required their baptism ("rebaptism" is technically impossible: One is either baptized or not). The Novatianist insistence on rebaptism was grounded in the conviction that they embodied the true Church. Similarly, the Catholics. Cyprian, for instance, argued (*Letter* 66:8) that just as the Church was one with and embodied Christ, so the properly established bishop was one with and embodied the Church. Indeed the bishops united to each other, according to Cyprian, were the cement that bonds the Church together. As a result, Cyprian held that he who was not with the bishop was not in the Church.

The matter was further complicated by the fact that the Roman Church (and the majority of the other Churches) held that baptism, as long as it was properly celebrated (i.e., in the faith and name of the Trinity), was indeed valid. Thus, the Romans argued, a person baptized in heresy should enter the Church through the reconciling rite of the imposition of hands rather than by rebaptism. From Cyprian's correspondence we learn that the Roman bishop Stephen (254–257) argued strongly against Cyprian and the Africans on the grounds that apostolic tradition sanctioned reconciliation rather than rebaptism (*Letter* 74). Although there seems to be a hint in *Letter* 75 that Stephen threatened the Africans with excommunication, the matter was not settled ecclesiastically until the Council of Arles (314), whose members affirmed the validity of heretical baptism, if celebrated in the name and faith of the Trinity. Wide acceptance for the validity of heretical baptism, however, awaited the championship of Optatus and Augustine (below).

Two other baptismal issues receive some notice in Cyprian's letters. Tertullian had recommended that baptism be postponed until children were old enough to know Christ (*On Baptism* 18). Cyprian and his fellow bishops, on the contrary, argued that baptism be conferred as early as possible, not even waiting the customary eight days (*Letter* 74). His reason was that infants, although without personal sin, nonetheless bear the sin of Adam (see ch. 3, Origen). But he agreed with Tertullian on the second issue, namely, that there is another baptism, richer in grace, more sublime in power, and more precious in effect than water baptism: martyrdom, or the baptism of blood. (There is a good deal of evidence, even apart from Cyprian's fate, that Africans received this baptism frequently.)

With respect to the liturgy of baptism in Carthage, one learns little from Cyprian save that (1) baptismal candidates renounced the world as well as the pomps of the devil, (2) the baptismal water was consecrated, (3) the baptismal formula was Trinitarian, and (4) "those who are baptized in the church are offered to the bishops of the church and, through our prayer and the imposition of hands, may receive the Holy Spirit and be signed with the seal of the Lord" (*Letter* 73:9). The rites were substantially those found in Tertullian's Carthage.

The readings consist of *Letter* 69 and *Letter* 70. The former is Cyprian's letter written in 255 to Magnus, an African whom he advises on two problems, Novatianist baptism and clinical baptism (the baptism of those in danger of death). The latter is in fact the letter of the Council of African bishops on heretical baptism, held at Carthage under Cyprian's presidency in 255.

The text is that of W. von Hartel, ed., CSEL 3, 2 (1871); the translation (abridged), that of Rose Bernard Donna, FC 51 (1964). A recent study on Cyprian is M. Sage, *Cyprian* (Cambridge, England: The University Press, 1975); and of rebaptism, Maurice Bevenot, "Cyprian's Platform in the Rebaptism Controversy," *Heythrop Journal* 19 (1978) 123-142. But see also G. W. Clarke, ACW 7 (1986) 32-45 (and endnotes on 172-191), 54-69 (and endnotes on 218-233).

Letter 69

[In chapter 1, Cyprian rejects in advance the validity of Novatianist baptism because he regards all heretics and schismatics as "abiding outside the church and acting against the peace and love of Christ." He marshalls texts to show how the Bible regards dissidents and then turns his attention to the "one" baptism and the unity of the unity of the Church.]

2. That the church is one, the Holy Spirit declares in the Canticle of Canticles, saying in the person of Christ: "One is my dove, my perfect one; she is the only one of her mother, the chosen of her parent" [Cant 6:8]. Concerning this again, he says furthermore: "An enclosed garden is my sister, my bride . . . a fountain sealed . . . a well of living water" [Cant 4:12, 15]. But if the garden enclosed is the spouse of Christ, which is the church, a thing enclosed cannot lie open to outsiders and profane men. And if the fountain is sealed, there is no access to the fountain to anyone placed outside either to drink or to be sealed therewith. The well of living water, also, if it is one, is the same which is within; he who is situated outside cannot

be vivified and sanctified by that water of which it is granted only to those who are within to have all use and drink.

And Peter, showing that there is one church and that those alone who are in the church can be baptized, asserted and said: "In the ark of Noah, a few, that is, eight souls of men were saved through water. Its counterpart, baptism, will now save you also" [1 Pet 3:20-21], proving and testifying that one ark of Noah was the type of the one church. If, in that baptism of the purged and purified world, he who was not in the ark of Noah could then be saved by water, he who is not in the church to which alone baptism has been granted can now be vivified through baptism!

But Paul, making this same matter clearer and more open, in addition, writes to the Ephesians and says: "Christ loved the church, and delivered himself up for her, that he might sanctify her, cleansing her in the bath of water" [Eph 5:25-26]. But if there is one church which is loved by Christ and that alone is purged by his washing, how can he who is not in the church either be loved by Christ or washed or purged by his washing?

3. Because of this, since the church alone has the life-giving water and the power of baptizing and of cleansing men, he who says with Novatian that anyone can be baptized and sanctified must first show and teach that Novatian is in the church or presides over the church. For the church is one and what is one cannot be both within and without. For if it is with Novatian, it was not with Cornelius. If it was, in truth, with Cornelius [the bishop of Rome], who succeeded Bishop Fabian by a legitimate ordination and whom the Lord also glorified beyond the honor of the bishopric with martyrdom, Novatian is not in the church; nor can he be counted as a bishop, who, succeeding to no one and despising evangelical and apostolic tradition, has sprung from himself. For he who was not ordained in the church can neither have nor keep the church in any way.

4. But the faith of the divine Scripture manifests that the church is not outside and that it cannot be rent or divided against itself, but that it holds the unity of an inseparable and indivisible house since it is written concerning the rite of the Passover and of the lamb, which lamb signifies Christ: "It shall be eaten in one house; you shall not take any of its flesh outside the house" [Exod 12:46]. We also see this expressed concerning Rahab, who herself also signified a type of the church, to whom it was entrusted and said: "Gather your father and your mother and your brothers and all the house of your father to yourself

into your house. And whosoever shall go out of the door of your house, he will be responsible for himself" [Josh 2:18-19].

In this mystery it is declared that in one house alone, that is, in the church, there ought to be assembled together those who will live and escape from the destruction of the world. But whoever will go out from the elect gathered together, that is, if anyone whoever, having found grace in the church, has withdrawn and departed from the church, he will be responsible, that is, the fact that he may perish will be imputed to him. The Apostle Paul explains this, teaching and instructing that a heretic must be avoided as perverse and a sinner and condemned by himself [see Titus 3:10-11]. For this is the man who will be responsible for himself, not cast out by the bishop, but having fled from the church of his own will, with heretical presumption condemned by himself.

5. And, therefore, the Lord, suggesting to us the unity coming from divine authority, asserts and says: "I and the Father are one" [John 10:30]. Recalling his church to that unity, he again says: "And there shall be one fold and one shepherd" [John 10:16]. But if there is one flock, how can he who is not in the number of the flock be numbered in the flock? Or, when the true shepherd remains and presides in the church of God after a valid ordination, how can he be considered as a shepherd who, succeeding no one but beginning from himself, has become foreign and strange, an enemy of the peace of the Lord and of divine unity, not living in the house of God, that is, in the church of God, in which none live except the peaceful and those of one mind, since the Holy Spirit speaks in the psalms and says: "God makes men of one mind to dwell in a house"? [Ps 67:7]. Finally, the very sacrifices of the Lord declare that Christian unanimity is bound to itself with a firm and inseparable charity. For when the Lord calls bread made from the union of many grains his body, he indicates our people whom he bore united; and when he calls wine pressed from the clusters of grapes and many small berries and gathered in one his blood, he, likewise, signifies our flock joined by the mixture of a united multitude. If Novatian is joined to this bread of the Lord, if he himself is also united to the chalice of Christ, he may also be able to seem to have the grace of the one ecclesiastical baptism if it is established that he holds the unity of the church.

6. [Cyprian cites two biblical examples of how God dealt with those "who make a schism and, after having abandoned their

bishop, appoint for themselves another false bishop from without" (4 Kgs 17:20-21; Matt 10:5).]

7. But if anyone objects—to say that Novatian holds the same law as the Catholic church holds, baptizes with the same symbol with which we baptize, knows the same God the Father, the same Christ the Son, the same Holy Spirit, and, because of this, can usurp the power of baptizing because he seems not to differ from us in the questioning of baptism—let whoever thinks that this must be objected know first that there is not one law of symbol for us and the schismatics nor the same questioning. For when they say: "Do you believe in the remission of sins and life everlasting through the Holy church?" they lie by their questioning because they do not have a church. Then, also, by their voice they themselves confess that the remission of sins cannot be given except by the holy church, which, not having, they show that sins cannot be remitted there.

8-9. [Cyprian then returns to biblical examples, this time to the three priests who rebelled against Aaron, the high priest, and to their punishment (see Num 16).]

10. [Inveighing against "the men who, as enemies of the bishops," usurp the right to baptize, Cyprian mounts an argument that would long live in North Africa among the Donatists (see below, Augustine). Indeed, they would continually cite him as the master.] Since these, indeed, stubborn and indocile as they are in other matters, yet confess this, that all either heretics or schismatics do not have the Holy Spirit and, therefore, can baptize but they cannot give the Holy Spirit, in that very matter they are held by us that we may show that those who do not have the Holy Spirit cannot baptize at all.

11. For since in baptism his sins are forgiven for each one, the Lord proves and declares in his gospel that sins can be forgiven through them alone who have the Holy Spirit. For, after the resurrection, sending his disciples, he spoke to them and said: " 'As the Father has sent me, I also send you.' When he had said this, he breathed upon them, and said to them, 'Receive the Holy Spirit; whose sins you shall forgive, they are forgiven him; and whose you shall retain, they are retained' " [John 20:21-23]. In this place, he shows that he alone who has the Holy Spirit can baptize and give the remission of sins.

Finally, John, who was to baptize Christ our Lord himself, previously had received the Holy Spirit when he was still in his mother's womb, so that it might be certain and manifest that only those who have the Holy Spirit can baptize. Therefore, let those who defend heretics or schismatics answer us whether they have the Holy Spirit or whether they have not. If they have, why are hands placed upon the ones baptized there when they come to us to receive the Spirit since he would have already been received there if he could have been given?

But if all heretics and schismatics from without do not give the Holy Spirit and, therefore, hands are imposed by us that here he may be received because there he is not and cannot be given, it is clear that the remission of sins cannot be given through those men who, it is certain, do not have the Holy Spirit. And, therefore, that, according to the divine plan and the evangelical truth, they may be able to obtain the remission of sins and to be sanctified and to become the temples of God, all who come from adversaries and antichrists to the church of Christ must, indeed, be baptized in the baptism of the church.

12. You have asked also, dearly beloved Son, what I thought about those who gain the grace of God in infirmity and illness, as to whether they are to be considered as legitimate Christians because they have not been bathed in the water of salvation, but sprinkled with it. In this matter, our reserve and moderation prejudge no one so that each one should perceive what he thinks best and should act according to his conscience. We, as far as our poor ability conceives of the problem, think that the divine benefits can in nothing be mutilated or weakened and that nothing else can occur there when, with full and complete faith of both the giver and of the receiver, there is received what is drawn from the divine gifts. . . . [Cyprian then cites warrants in the Hebrew Bible for aspersion: Ezech 36:25-26; Num 8:5-7; Num 19:8-13.]

13: [Apparently some in Carthage called those baptized in the emergency situation of grave illness "clinicals" and did not consider them to be "legitimate Christians." He denies any suggestion that they are not fully Christian and rejects out of hand the requirement that they should be baptized again "should they overcome the incovenience of their sickness and become well." As a matter of fact, Novatian himself was baptized in grave illness, and there was some sentiment that because the rites of clinical baptism were slender, the gifts of baptism thus given were equally slender in their measure, especially the Holy Spirit.]

14. Nay, rather, the Holy Spirit is not given from a measure, but is poured out completely upon the believer. For if the day

is born to all equally, and if the sun shines upon all with equal and similar light, how much more does Christ, the Sun and the True Day, bestow equally in his church the light of eternal life with equal measure! We see that the pledge of this equality is celebrated in Exodus, when the manna from heaven fell and, with a prefiguring of the future, showed the nourishment of heavenly bread and the food of the coming Christ. For there, without distinction either of sex or of age, a measure was collected for each equally.

Whence it appears that the mercy of Christ and the heavenly grace following after are divided among all equally; without regard for sex, without discrimination of age, without respect of persons, the gift of spiritual grace is poured forth upon all of the people of God. Assuredly, that same spiritual grace which is received equally in baptism by the believers afterward either diminishes or increases in our manner of living and in our action as, in the gospel, the seed of the Lord is sowed equally, but, according to the variety of the soil, some is taken away; some brings forth an abundant supply, either thirtyfold or sixtyfold or one hundredfold with abundant fruit. But still, when each one is called to the penny reward, why is it that what has been evenly distributed by God is lessened by human interpretation?

15. But if anyone is disturbed in this that certain of those who are baptized while ill are still tempted by unclean spirits, let him know that the wickedness of the devil remains strong all the way up to the saving water, but, in true baptism, it loses all the virus of its malice. This example we see in the king Pharaoh, who, having resisted for a while and having delayed in his perfidy for so long a time, could resist and prevail until he came to the water; when he had come thither, he was both conquered and destroyed. The blessed Apostle Paul declares that the sea was a pledge of baptism, saying: "For I would not have you ignorant, brethren, that our fathers were all under the cloud, and all passed through the sea, and all were baptized in Moses and in the cloud and in the sea." And he added, saying: "Now all these things came to pass as examples to us" [1 Cor 10:1-6].

This is being carried out even today that through exorcists, by means of the human voice and the divine power, the devil is lashed out and burned out and tortured and, although he says often that he is going out and leaving the man of God, yet he deceives in what he has said and does what was first done through Pharaoh with the same lying of obstinacy and of fraud.

Yet when it comes to the water of salvation and to the sanctification of baptism, we ought to know and to trust that the devil is oppressed there and that the man dedicated to God is freed by the divine mercy. For if scorpions and serpents which prevail in dry land, when hurled into water can prevail or retain their poison, evil spirits, also, which are called scorpions and serpents, and yet are trodden under foot by the power given through us by the Lord, can remain in the body of man, in whom, baptized and after that sanctified, the Holy Spirit begins to dwell.

16. We have found out this finally also through the things themselves: that with urgent necessity in illness those who are baptized and have gained grace are freed from the unclean spirit by which formerly they were urged on and live praiseworthy and approved in the church and accomplish much through each day in the increase of heavenly grace through an increase of faith; and that, on the contrary, often some of those who are baptized in good health, if afterward they begin to sin, are distressed by the return of the unclean spirit; that it is manifest that the devil is excluded in baptism by the faith of the believer; and that he returns afterward if faith should fail.

Unless it seems just to some people that those who are polluted among adversaries and antichrists by profane water outside the church should be considered baptized! But those who are baptized in the church seem to have gained less of mercy and of divine grace, and so great honor should be considered for the heretics that, when they come, they should not be questioned as to whether they were bathed or sprinkled, whether they were patient or peripatetic; but among us there is detraction from the whole truth of faith and its majesty and sanctity are taken away from ecclesiastical baptism.

17. I have written an answer to your letter, dearly beloved Son, as far as my moderate ability availed and I have shown as well as possible, prescribing for no one, that every prelate, who will render an account of his actions to the Lord, should decide what he thinks best, according to what the blessed Apostle Paul writes in his Epistle to the Romans and says: "Every one of us will render an account for himself. Therefore let us not judge one another" [Rom 14:12-13]. I trust that you, dearly beloved Son, are always well.

Letter 70
[The greeting is "Cyprian," followed by the names of the fifty bishops who took part in the Council of Carthage, 225 C.E.]

1. When we were together in council, dearly beloved Brethren, we read your letter which you wrote concerning those who seem baptized among heretics and schismatics, as to whether they ought to be baptized when they come to the catholic church, which is one. Concerning this matter, although you yourselves there hold the truth and firmness of the catholic rule, yet, because you thought that we ought to be consulted in accordance with our mutual love, we express our judgment, which is not new, but we join with you with a like agreement in one already decreed by our predecessors long ago and observed by us, judging plainly and holding for certain that no one can be baptized outside, without the church, since there is one baptism appointed in the holy church. And it is written in the words of the Lord: "They have forsaken me, the source of living water; and they have dug themselves broken cisterns, that cannot hold water" [Jer 2:13]. And again the divine Scripture warns and says: "Abstain from strange water and do not drink from a strange fountain" [Prov 9:18, LXX].

But the water ought to be first cleansed and sanctified by the bishop that it may be able to wash away in its baptism the sins of the man who is baptized since the Lord says through Ezechiel: "And I will sprinkle clean water upon you, and you shall be cleansed from all your impurities and from all your idols. And I will cleanse you. And I will give you a new heart and place a new spirit within you" [Ezech 36:25-26]. But how can he who is himself unclean and with whom the Holy Spirit is not cleanse and sanctify water since the Lord says in Numbers: "Whatever the unclean person touches will be unclean" [19:22]. Or how can one who baptizes grant to another the remission of sins who, himself outside the church, cannot put aside his own sins?

2. But the very question which is used in baptism is a witness of the truth. For when we say: "Do you believe in eternal life and the remission of sins through the holy church?" we know that the remission of sins is not given except in the church. But among the heretics where the church is not, sins are not forgiven. They who agree with the heretics, therefore, either change the questioning or vindicate the truth unless they claim the church for those who, they contend, have baptism.

It is necessary also for him who is baptized to be anointed that, having received chrism, that is anointing, he can be anointed of God and have in himself the grace of Christ. But, in turn, it is by the Eucharist that the oil by which the baptized are anointed is sanctified on the altar. But he who has neither altar nor church cannot sanctify the creature of oil. Thus neither can spiritual anointing be had among the heretics since it is evident that oil cannot be sanctified among them, nor the Eucharist be held among them at all. But we ought to know and remember that it is written: "Let not the oil of the sinner anoint my head" [Ps 140:5]. Before in the psalms, the Holy Spirit warned of this lest any going astray and wandering from the path of truth should be anointed among the heretics and adversaries of Christ.

But what prayer can the sacrilegious and sinful priest make on behalf of the baptized since it is written: "God does not hear the sinner; but if anyone is a worshiper of God, and does his will, him he hears" [John 9:31]? But who can give what he himself does not have or how can he accomplish spiritual deeds who himself has lost the Holy Spirit? And, therefore, he who comes ignorant to the church must be baptized and renewed that he may be sanctified within through the holy ones since it is written: "Be holy, for I am also holy, says the Lord" [Lev 19:2]. Thus he who has been seduced into error and baptized without may put this aside also in the true and ecclesiastical baptism because a man coming to God, while he seeks the bishop, runs into a sacrilegious one by the fraud of error.

3. As for the rest, it is to approve of the baptisms of heretics and schismatics to agree to it that they have baptized. For part cannot be void and part be valid there. If one could baptize, he could also give the Holy Spirit. But if he cannot give the Holy Spirit because, established outside, he is not with the Holy Spirit, he cannot baptize the one who comes since baptism is also one, and the Holy Spirit is one, and the church founded by Christ our Lord upon Peter in the origin and established plan of unity is also one.

Thus it happens that, since all things are useless and false among those men, none of those things which they have done ought to be approved by us. For how can that be ratified and firm with the Lord which those do who the Lord says in his gospel are his enemies and adversaries, stating: "He who is not with me is against me; and he who does not gather with me scatters" [Luke 11:23]. And the blessed Apostle John, also keeping the commands and precepts of the Lord, put in his epistle: "You have heard that Antichrist is coming, so now many antichrists have been made; whence we know that it is the last hour. They have gone forth from us, but they were not of us. For

if they had been of us, they would have continued with us"
[1 John 2:18-19].

Whence we also ought to assemble and to consider whether they who are the adversaries of the Lord and have been called antichrists can give the grace of Christ. Wherefore, we who are with the Lord and hold the unity of the Lord and administer his priesthood in the church according to his condescension ought to repudiate and to reject and to consider as impious whatever his adversaries and antichrists do. And we ought to give through all of the sacraments of divine grace the truth of unity and faith to those who, coming from error and depravity, recognize the true faith of the one church. We trust that you, dearly beloved Brethren, are always well.

Optatus of Milevis

With Cyprian's death a long literary night (over one hundred years) fell on North African Christianity. Relieved only by the works of Arnobius of Sicca (253–327) and Lactantius (d. after 317), it deepened with the final Roman attack against Christianity under Diocletian and his successors (303–311) and grew ever darker in the extended religious controversy that was its aftermath.

The controversy was over heroes and traitors during the persecution. The former were those who stood fast against the authorities; the latter were those who did not, especially clergy who handed over to the authorities the Scriptures and sacred vessels of the Church. When Constantine's edict of religious toleration (311/313) ended the persecution, a grave issue flamed up: Granted that the sacraments convey grace, did the sacraments celebrated by clergy who had betrayed the Church *(traditores)* convey grace? Underneath the issue lay the old issue that Cyprian had had to face: Was the Church composed of those who stood with the properly established bishop (Cyprian) and his episcopal colleagues or with the spirit-filled prophets and martyrs (Novatian)?

A group of African Christians, for whom the true Church was the Church of the poor and the martyrs, denied that traitorous clergy could convey grace in their ministrations. They argued, as Cyprian had, that one cannot give what one does not have; the traitors had severed themselves wholly from the Church and had banished the Holy Spirit from their midst. These African Christians had great appeal among the ordinary people, who were poor, suffered at the hands of the Roman provincial government, and stood militantly against Rome. The movement spread rapidly across North Africa, especially under the skillful leadership of a bishop, Donatus (d. ca. 335), becoming known as the Donatist Church. About 336 Donatus wrote a letter (now lost) about baptism, in which he maintained that the members of the Catholic Church, that is, the Church of the betrayers, precisely because they stood outside the true Church were deprived of grace and the Spirit. As a result, they could not be considered Christians, their baptism (as well as the other sacraments, including ordination) was of no value, and a Catholic who sought to become a member of the (Donatist) Church needed to be rebaptized.

Donatus was succeeded by an even more skillful leader, Parmenian (362–392), who secured Donatist intellectual dominance in Africa down to Augustine's time. Among other things, he gave the Donatists a theology of the Church in a work called *Against the Church of the Traitors;* in the process, he addressed himself also to baptism (which he calls *fons*) and anointing *(sigillum).*

The fact that none of the Donatist works have survived, coupled with the absence of equally skillful Catholic leaders, accounts for the long literary night. One leader, however, eventually broke out into the light of day—Optatus, bishop of Milevis in the province of Numidia. Almost nothing is known of him save that he wrote a systematic reply to Parmenian's work, *Against Parmenian the Donatist.* The manuscript evidence indicates that the first edition, consisting of the first six books, appeared between 370 and 374; the second, comprising scattered revisions and the seventh book, about 390.

Optatus devotes the fifth book to a discussion respectively of Donatist and Catholic baptism. Following Donatus, Parmenian argues that although there are two baptisms, Catholic and Donatist, only one is valid, namely, Donatist, because the holiness of the minister enters into the very constitution or "body" of the sacrament. Optatus responds with a view that deeply influenced Augustine's thinking on the subject of sacramental validity, which, in turn, conditioned all subsequent Catholic thinking on the dynamics of sacrament.

True or valid baptism, Optatus argues, has three components or "elements," which make up the body of the sacrament: the action of the Trinity, the faith of the recipient, and the action of the minister. Only the first two are indispensable. In any effective baptism, the Trinity is the primary agent who accomplishes the blessings of the sacrament. As a result, the Trinitarian faith of the subject is important, specifically, the conviction that the Trinity comprises three persons participating in the one divine nature. Therefore any defect of Trinitarian faith invalidates the sacrament (see above, Cyprian).

As for the minister, the sacrament is effective for holiness through the Trinity and faith, not through the holiness of the minister. He is only contingently necessary, an instrument in the hands of the Trinity, not a cause in his own right. Thus, if one is properly disposed and the sacrament properly administered, it will be effective for holiness quite independent of ministerial holiness. Augustine (below) will modify Optatus on the subject of proper dispositions and baptism's effect.

With respect to the liturgy of baptism in Milevis, it is doubtful that it differed in any substantial way from the liturgy in Augustine's Hippo (below), the principal city in Numidia. Nor would it have differed much, if at all, from the Donatist liturgy. Optatus considers Catholic and Donatist to have the same ecclesiastical practices, the same Scriptures, the same faith, the same sacraments, and the same creed. Indeed, Optatus sharply distinguishes between heretics, whose belief about the persons of the Trinity is erroneous, and schismatics, who, like the Donatists, have split from the Church because of faith as related to practice. With Optatus the distinction between heresy and schism becomes technical.

The text of the fifth book is *S. Optati Milevitani Libri VII,* ed. Carl Ziwsa, CSEL 26, 118–141. The translation and abridgment is based on O. R. Vassall-Phillips, trans., *The Work of Saint Optatus Against the Donatists* (London: Longmans, 1917) 203–245. See also W. H. C. Frend, *The Donatist Church: A Movement of Protest in Roman North Africa* (New York: Oxford, 1971) especially 191–207. A helpful study is Robert B. Eno, "The Work of Optatus as a Turning Point in the African Ecclesiology," *Thomist* 37 (1973) 668–685.

The Fifth Book

. . . We must speak at this point about baptism. In the matter at present to be considered the whole question consists in this, that you have dared to do violence to baptism—that you have repeated what Christ has commanded to be done but once. . . .

[Parmenian had argued that there are two baptisms, one the "true water" (Donatist) and the other "lying water" (Catholic). Optatus argues that just as among the "types" of baptism there is only one circumcision and one flood, so there is one baptism, concluding:]

That water alone is true which has been sanctified not from any place, nor by any [human] person, but by the Trinity. . . . It remains to show that you have praised baptism in such a way as to bring forward many things which tell both for you and for us [Augustine, below, shares the same attitude], but something that tells against you. Whatever we share with you is in favor of both. For this reason does it favor you, because from us you went out. Thus, for example, you and we have one ecclesiastical discipline, we read from the same Scriptures, we possess the same faith, the same sacraments of faith, the same mysteries. With reason, therefore, you have praised baptism, for who among the faithful is unaware that the one baptism is life for virtues, death for evil deeds, birth to immortality, the attainment of the heavenly kingdom, the harbor of innocence, and [as you have said] the shipwreck of sins? These are the blessings conferred upon every believer, not by the minister of this sacrament, but by the faith of him who believes and by the Trinity.

Then you will ask what you have, when praising baptism, said against your selves. Listen! But first you must acknowledge something which not one of you will be able to deny. You said that the Trinity counts for nothing, unless you be present.

If you think little of us, at least reverence the Lord, who is first in the Trinity, who with his Son and the Holy Spirit effects and completes all things even when no person is present.

[At this point Optatus cites the Genesis account to show that the Trinity created life out of water with no human being at all present. He continues:]

You have said that there was only one deluge and that circumcision could not be repeated, while we have taught that the heavenly gift is bestowed upon every believer by the Trinity, not by man—why have you thought it right to repeat baptism not after us, but after the Trinity?

Concerning this sacrament, no small contention has been engendered, and the question is discussed whether it be lawful to do this a second time after the Trinity [has baptized], in the name of the same Trinity. You say: "It is lawful," while we say, "It is not lawful." Between your "It is lawful," and our "It is not lawful," the souls of the multitude hesitate and sway backwards and forwards. Let no one believe you or us. We are all like litigants in a suit. Judges must be sought for . . .

[Optatus argues that they cannot be Christians, because of conflict of interest, nor pagans, because of ignorance, nor Jews, because of enmity. He then proceeds to make the case for the Catholic position from the gospels, concluding:]

And thus did he make his declaration concerning the washing which he had commanded to be done through the Trinity: . . . "Go, baptize all nations in the name of the Father and of the Son and of the Holy Spirit" [Matt 28:19]. This was the washing of which he said: "He that has washed once has no need of being washed a second time" [John 13:20]. In saying "once" he forbade it to be done again and spoke of the thing, not of the person [i.e., the minister]. For if there had been a difference [to be considered between persons], he would have said, "He that has been rightly washed once." By not adding the word "rightly," he points out that whatever has been done in the [name of the Trinity] is done rightly. This is the reason why we receive those who come from you to us without rebaptizing. When Christ says: "He has no need of being washed a second time," this is a general, not a particular declaration, for if these things had been said to Peter [only], Christ would have said: "Because you have been once washed, you have no need of being washed a second time."

[Optatus then insists that there is one God, one Christ, one faith (creed), one baptism, all violated by Donatist rebaptism. Then he comes to the heart of his exposition:]

It is clear that in the celebration of this sacrament of baptism there are three elements, which you will not be able either to decrease or diminish, or to put on one side. The first is in the Trinity, the second in the believer, the third in him who gives the sacrament. For I perceive that two are necessary, and that one is quasi-necessary. The Trinity holds the chief place, without whom the work itself cannot be done. The faith of the believer follows next. Then comes the office of the "minister," which cannot be of equal authority. The first two remain always unchangeable and unmoved. For the Trinity is always itself; and the faith is the same in everyone. Both [the Trinity and faith] always preserve their own efficacy. Therefore the office of the minister cannot be equal to the other two elements [in the sacrament of baptism], because it alone is liable to change.

You will have it that between you and us there is a distinction, though the office is the same, and, judging yourselves to be more holy than we, you do not hesitate to place your pride higher than the Trinity, although the person of the "minister" can be changed, but the Trinity cannot be changed. And, whereas it is baptism which should be longed for by those who receive it, you put yourselves forward as the person to be eagerly sought after [i.e., because they are deemed holy].

Since you are—among others—"ministers" of the sacrament, show what is the nature of the place that you occupy in this mystery, and whether you can belong to its "body"!

The name of baptism is but one. It possesses its own "body," a body which has its well-defined members, to which nothing can be added, in which nothing can be taken away. All these members [i.e., the Trinity and faith and, by implication, the matter and form] are both at all times and once for all with this "body," and cannot be changed, whereas the "ministers" are changed every day, both as to place and to time, and in their own persons. For it is not one man only who baptizes always or everywhere. This work is now done by different men from those who did it of old. In the time to come it will be done by yet others. . . . Since therefore you see that all who baptize are laborers not lords [Luke 10:2], and that the sacraments are holy through themselves, not through men [i.e., the ministers], why do you claim so much for yourselves? Why is it that you try to shut God out from his own gifts? Allow him to bestow those things which are his own. For that gift, which belongs to God, cannot be given by man. . . .

[Here Optatus brings to bear prophetic texts to show that it is God who does the washing: Ps 50:9, 40; Isa 4:4; Isa 1:18. He then turns to the New Testament:]

Go back to the gospel, and see what Christ has promised for the salvation of the human race. When the Samaritan woman refused water to the Son of God, then he said that which gives his answer to your contentions: "He who shall drink the water which I give shall not thirst for ever" [John 4:13]. He said "the water which *I* give." He did not say: "which *they* shall give, *who deem themselves holy,*" as you think yourselves to be; but he did say that *he* would give. He himself, therefore, it is who gives, and that which is given is his own. What, therefore, is it that which you strive, with absolute unreasonableness, to vindicate for yourselves?

[At this point, Optatus offers one final biblical proof of the contingency of the minister in baptism: John the Baptist. He argues that John validly baptized for the forgiveness of sins until the risen Jesus mandated the form of baptism before the ascension: "Go, teach all nations, baptizing them in the name of the Father and of the Son and of the Holy Spirit. . ." (Matt 28:19). John's baptism was no longer valid; rather the disciples, as the ministers of the new law, replaced him. "Nor," he continues, citing Acts 19:3; 1 Cor 1:13; Luke 9:49-50, "do they baptize in their own names, but in the name of the Trinity."]

For to them the command had been given that their work should be sanctification by the Trinity, and that they should not baptize in their own name, but in the name of the Father and of the Son and of the Holy Spirit. Therefore it is the name which sanctifies, not the work.

[Optatus concludes the section on the minister with a discussion of 1 Cor 3:5-23, where Paul, reflecting on his role and that of Apollo in the work of baptism, argues that both are laborers of the Lord, who grants the growth:]

Accordingly, in all those who serve there is not ownership but service. Now, therefore, my brother Parmenian, you see that of the three elements [in baptism] which I have mentioned above, the one which is threefold [the Trinity] comes first, is immovable, is supreme and unchangeable, but that the person of any individual minister remains only for a time. . . .

[Optatus then turns to the third element which constitutes the "body" of baptism, the faith of the candidate. For him faith is an unchangeable member of the "body," and his biblical examples all emphasize faith's role. He has in view, of course, adult baptism, which, as has been noted, remained the norm until the mid-to-late fifth century (ch. 1, John the Deacon). He ends the book by acknowledging that he has, perhaps, made "a mistake in bringing forward so many proofs." Nevertheless, he adds one more in the form of sarcasm about the power of Donatist holiness: If it is not strong enough to raise the dead to life, how can it help the living (presumably, to the new life of baptism)?]

Augustine of Hippo

Born in Thagaste, Numidia (modern Souk-Ahras, Algeria), in 354, Aurelius Augustinus was destined to become the towering figure in Western Christian antiquity. Although of Berber stock, his parents were Roman in outlook, Latin in speech, and minor gentry in social status.

After local schooling, Augustine did the equivalent of high school in Madaura, a few miles to the south, and then went on to Carthage for his advanced studies in rhetoric (371–375). Subsequently, he pursued an academic career as a rhetorician first in Africa, then in Rome, and finally in Milan, where he held the municipal chair of rhetoric (384–385).

Augustine's mother, Monica, was a Catholic Christian, and his father, Patricius, became one shortly before he died (370). As for Augustine, he was an infant when inscribed as a catechumen and reared in his mother's African Christianity, which he abandoned when he went to Carthage. Eventually, he settled down there with a mistress, fathered a son, Adeodatus, discovered philosophy, and became a Manichee, a religious sect of Persian origin and Gnostic timbre that appeared in Africa as a reform movement within Christianity. He remained a "hearer" in the sect for nine years (375–384).

When he went to Italy (382), however, Augustine encountered Neoplatonic philosophy, ascetic Christianity, and a combination of both in the cultured Ambrose (ch. 1), bishop of Milan. As a result, he became an adult catechumen (387), resigned his chair of rhetoric, and received baptism at the Milanese Easter Vigil in 387 with his son, Adeodatus, and a longtime friend, Alypius.

Augustine and his companions decided to return to Africa, there to establish themselves in monastic seclusion, but his mother died suddenly, delaying their return. When the company finally reached Africa, they established a monastery at Thagaste. Unfortunately, death struck suddenly once again, carrying off Adeodatus. In 391 at Hippo (modern Bone, Algeria), Augustine was ordained a priest and in 395, Catholic bishop of the city, which he served for thirty-five years. He died in August 430 at the age of seventy-six during the Vandal siege of the city, which fell the following May. With the coming of the Vandals, North African Christianity gradually sank from view.

By his own count Augustine left behind ninety-three treatises in 270 volumes. The list, however, does not include thirteen works written between 426 and 430, nor his seventy-six extant letters, nor close to one thousand sermons. From his works, four selections have been made for the readings. The first, doctrinal, is taken from his handbook *(Enchiridion)* on Christian teaching, which so deeply influenced medieval Christianity. The second, taken from his Easter homilies on baptism, depicts the liturgical process of conversion. The third, his autobiographical *Confessions*, recounts the conversion of the Neoplatonic philosopher Marius Victorinus at Rome (362), including his public profession of faith *(redditio symboli),* as well as Augustine's own entry into the catechumenate and his feelings about baptism. Several short chapters from his treatise *On Baptism, Against the Donatists* make up the fourth reading. A modern classic on Augustine's life and thought is Peter Brown, *Augustine of Hippo: A Biography* (Berkeley: University of California Press, 1965). For a concise and valuable treatment of his thought, see Henry Chadwick, *Augustine* (New York: Oxford, 1986). The Christian basilica at Hippo has been excavated, for which see H. I. Marrou, "La basilique chrétienne d'Hippone d'après le résultat des dernières fouilles," *Revue des Études Augustiniennes* 6 (1960) 109–154. See also T. M. Finn, "It Happened One Saturday Night: Ritual and Conversion in Augustine's North Africa," *Journal of the American Academy of Religion* 58 (1990) 589–616.

Enchiridion on Faith, Hope, and Love

Two major controversies engaged Augustine the bishop, Donatism and Pelagianism. The former had direct effect on his baptismal teaching, as will be evident from the final reading. The latter had a more pervasive effect, because it concerned the "old" or "fallen" humankind, which was the subject of baptismal rebirth. The Pelagians, influenced by ascetic Christianity, held that although Adam's fall infected his descendants with suffering and death, it did not touch the human spirit. Humans retain the power of free will, the capacity to love, and the ability to achieve salvation.

Augustine's understanding of the human condition, which came quickly to dominate Western thinking about human nature and salvation, was quite different. As a result of Adam's original sin, humankind is born corrupt in body and spirit, incapable of anything but self-serving thought and action, and powerless before the need for salvation.

The first reading, drawn from Augustine's *Enchiridion for Laurentius, on Faith, Hope, and Love,* addresses original sin and the role of baptism. Composed about 421 for a highly placed layman who wanted a "handbook" of Christian teaching, it represents Augustine's fully matured thought and his only attempt to synthesize his theology. Based on the Apostles' Creed and the Lord's Prayer, both of which he regularly explained to catechumens, the work had a profound influence on medieval Christianity.

The text is that of Ernest Evans, CCL 46 (1959) 72–79; the translation, that of Albert C. Outler, *Augustine: Confessions and Enchiridion,* LCC 7 (1955) 354–368. See also his valuable introductory study.

Enchiridion 8

[In this first selection, paragraphs 24–27, Augustine addresses himself to the plight of humans after the Fall:]

24. This was the primal lapse of the rational creature, that is, his first privation of the good. In train of this there crept in, even without his willing it, ignorance of the right things to do and also an appetite for noxious things. And these brought along with them, as their companions, error and misery. When these two evils are felt to be imminent, the soul's motion in flight from them is called fear. Moreover, as the soul's appetites are satisfied by things harmful or at least inane—and as it fails to recognize the error of its ways—it falls victim to unwholesome pleasures or may even be exhilarated by vain joys. From these tainted springs of action—moved by the lash of appetite rather than a feeling of plenty—there flows out every kind of misery which is now the lot of rational natures.

25. Yet such a nature, even in its evil state, could not lose its appetite for blessedness. There are the evils that both men and angels have in common, for whose wickedness God hath condemned them in simple justice. But man has a unique penalty as well: he is also punished by the death of the body. God had indeed threatened man with death as penalty if he should sin. He endowed him with freedom of the will in order that he

might rule him by rational command and deter him by the threat
of death. He even placed him in the happiness of paradise in
a sheltered nook of life where, by being a good steward of righteousness, he would rise to better things.

26. From this state, after he had sinned, man was banished,
and through his sin he subjected his descendants to the punishment of sin and damnation, for he had radically corrupted them,
in himself, by his sinning. As a consequence of this, all those
descended from him and his wife (who had prompted him to
sin and who was condemned along with him at the same time)—
all those born through carnal lust, on whom the same penalty
is visited as for disobedience—all these entered into the inheritance of original sin. Through this involvement they were
led, through divers errors and sufferings (along with the rebel
angels, their corruptors and possessors and companions), to that
final stage of punishment without end. "Thus by one man, sin
entered into the world and death through sin; and thus death
came upon all men, since all men have sinned" [Rom 5:12].
By "the world" in this passage the apostle is, of course, refer-
ring to the whole human race.

27. This, then, was the situation: the whole mass of the human
race stood condemned, lying ruined and wallowing in evil, being plunged from evil into evil and, having joined causes with
the angels who had sinned, it was paying the fully deserved penalty for impious desertion. Certainly the anger of God rests,
in full justice, on the deeds that the wicked do freely in blind
and unbridled lust; and it is manifest in whatever penalties they
are called on to suffer, both openly and secretly. Yet the Creator's goodness does not cease to sustain life and vitality even
in the evil angels, for were *this* sustenance withdrawn, they
would simply cease to exist. As for mankind, although born
of a corrupted and condemned stock, he still retains the power
to form and animate his seed, to direct his members in their
temporal order, to enliven his senses in their spatial relations,
and to provide bodily nourishment. For God judged it better
to bring good out of evil than not to permit any evil to exist.
And if he had willed that there should be no reformation in
the case of men, as there is none for the wicked angels, would
it not have been just if the nature that deserted God and, through
the evil use of his powers, trampled and transgressed the precepts
of his Creator, which could have been easily kept—the same
creature who stubbornly turned away from his light and violated the image of the Creator in himself, who had in the evil

use of his free will broken away from the wholesome discipline of God's law—would it not have been just if such a being had been abandoned by God wholly and forever and laid under the everlasting punishment which he deserved? Clearly God would have done this if he were only just and not also merciful and if he had not willed to show far more striking evidence of his mercy by pardoning some who were unworthy of it.

[In the next few paragraphs (28–32) Augustine insists again and again that God's mercy (grace) "predisposes a man before he wills, to prompt his willing. It follows the act of willing, lest one's will be frustrated" (32). He then argues that God's mercy required that he send his Son, Jesus Christ, who, with the Holy Spirit, embodies grace (33–40). He concludes with a discussion of baptism and original sin and baptismal death and resurrection.]

41. Since he was begotten and conceived in no pleasure of carnal appetite—and therefore bore no trace of original sin— he was, by the grace of God (operating in a marvelous and an ineffable manner), joined and united in a personal unity with the only-begotten Word of the Father, a Son not by grace but by nature. And although he himself committed no sin, yet because of "the likeness of sinful flesh" [Rom 8:3] in which he came, he was himself called sin and was made a sacrifice for the washing away of sins.

Indeed, under the old law, sacrifices for sins were often called sins. Yet he of whom those sacrifices were mere shadows was himself actually made sin. Thus, when the apostle said, "For Christ's sake, we beseech you to be reconciled to God," he straightway added, "Him, who knew no sin, he made to be sin for us that we might be made to be the righteousness of God in him" [2 Cor 5:20-21]. He does not say, as we read in some defective copies, "He who knew no sin did sin for us," as if Christ himself committed sin for our sake. Rather, he says, "He [Christ] who knew no sin, he [God] made to be sin for us." The God to whom we are to be reconciled has thus made him the sacrifice for sin by which we may be reconciled.

He himself is therefore sin as we ourselves are righteousness—not our own but God's, not in ourselves but in him. Just as he was sin—not his own but ours, rooted not in himself but in us—so he showed forth through the likeness of sinful flesh, in which he was crucified, that since sin was not in him he could then, so to say, die to sin by dying in the flesh, which was "the likeness of sin." And since he had never lived in the old manner of sinning, he might, in his resurrection, signify the new life which is ours, which is springing to life anew from the old death in which we had been dead to sin.

42. This is the meaning of the great sacrament of baptism, which is celebrated among us. All who attain to this grace die thereby to sin—as he himself is said to have died to sin because he died in the flesh, that is, "in the likeness of sin"—and they are thereby alive by being reborn in the baptismal font, just as he rose again from the sepulcher. This is the case no matter what the age of the body.

43. For whether it be a newborn infant or a decrepit old man—since no one should be barred from baptism—just so, there is no one who does not die to sin in baptism. Infants die to original sin only; adults, to all those sins which they have added, through their evil living, to the burden they brought with them at birth.

44. But even these are frequently said to die to sin, when without doubt they die not to one but to many sins, and to all the sins which they have themselves already committed by thought, word, and deed. Actually, by the use of the singular number the plural number is often signified, as the poet said, "And they fill the belly of the armed warrior" [Virgil, *Aeneid,* 2:1.20], although they did this with many warriors. And in our own Scriptures we read: "Pray therefore to the Lord that he may take from us the serpent" [Num 21:7, LXX]. It does not say "serpents," as it might, for they were suffering from many serpents. There are, moreover, innumerable other such examples.

Yet, when the original sin is signified by the use of the plural number, as we say when infants are baptized "for the remission of sins," instead of saying "for the remission of sin," then we have the converse expression in which the singular is expressed by the plural number. Thus in the gospel, it is said of Herod's death, "For they are dead who sought the child's life" [Matt 2:20]; it does not say, "He is dead." And in Exodus: "They made," [Moses] says, "to themselves gods of gold," when they had made one calf. And of this calf, they said: "These are thy gods, O Israel, which brought you out of the land of Egypt" [Exod 32:4], here also putting the plural for the singular.

45. Still, even in that one sin—which "entered into the world by one man and so spread to all men" [Rom 5:12], and on account of which infants are baptized—one can recognize a plurality of sins, if that single sin is divided, so to say, into its separate

elements. For there is pride in it, since man preferred to be under his own rule rather than the rule of God; and sacrilege too, for man did not acknowledge God; and murder, since he cast himself down to death; and spiritual fornication, for the integrity of the human mind was corrupted by the seduction of the serpent; and theft, since the forbidden fruit was snatched; and avarice, since he hungered for more than should have sufficed for him—and whatever other sins that could be discovered in the diligent analysis of that one sin. . . .

[In 46 and 47, Augustine expands his argument, the point of which is that "the new birth *(regeneratio)* would not have been instituted except for the fact that the first birth *(generatio)* was tainted."]

48. That one sin, however, committed in a setting of such great happiness, was itself so great that by it, in one man, the whole human race was originally and, so to say, radically condemned. It cannot be pardoned and washed away except through "the one mediator between God and men, the man Christ Jesus" [1 Tim 2:5], who alone could be born in such a way as not to need to be reborn.

49. They were not reborn, those who were baptized by John's baptism, by which Christ himself was baptized. Rather, they were *prepared* by the ministry of this forerunner, who said, "Prepare a way for the Lord" [Matt 3:13], for him in whom alone they could be reborn.

For his baptism is not with water alone, as John's was, but with the Holy Spirit as well. Thus, whoever believes in Christ is reborn by that same Spirit, of whom Christ also was born, needing not to be reborn. This is the reason for the voice of the Father spoken over him at his baptism, "Today have I begotten thee" [Ps 2:7], which pointed not to that particular day on which he was baptized, but to that "day" of changeless eternity, in order to show us that this man belonged to the personal unity of the Only Begotten. For a day that neither begins with the close of yesterday nor ends with the beginning of tomorrow is indeed an eternal "today."

Therefore, he chose to be baptized in water by John, not thereby to wash away any sin of his own, but to manifest his great humility. Indeed, baptism found nothing in him to wash away, just as death found nothing to punish. Hence, it was in authentic justice, and not by violent power, that the devil was overcome and conquered: for, as he had most unjustly slain him who was in no way deserving of death, he also did most justly lose those whom he had justly held in bondage as punishment for their sins. Wherefore, he took upon himself both baptism and death, not out of a piteous necessity but through his own free act of showing mercy—as part of a definite plan whereby one might take away the sin of the world, just as one man had brought sin into the world, that is, the whole human race.

50. There is a difference, however. The first man brought sin into the world, whereas this one took away not only that one sin but also all the others which he found added to it. Hence, the apostle says, "And the gift [of grace] is not like the effect of the one that sinned: for the judgment on that one trespass was condemnation; but the gift of grace is for many offenses, and brings justification" [Rom 5:16]. Now it is clear that the one sin originally inherited, even if it were the only one involved, makes men liable to condemnation. Yet grace justifies a man for many offenses, both the sin which he originally inherited in common with all the others and also the multitude of sins which he has committed on his own. . . .

[Augustine then pursues a discussion of Christ's mediatorial work (51–55), after which he considers the last articles of the creed (on the Holy Spirit in the Church) and other issues he thinks his manual should contain.]

Sermon *227*

Augustine gave numerous sermons, both to prepare catechumens for baptism and to instruct them after baptism. This second reading is a baptismal homily that Augustine delivered to the newly baptized on Easter morning. The primary subject is the Eucharist (cf. Ambrose, ch. 1; also Cyril of Jerusalem and Theodore of Mopsuestia, vol. 5, ch. 1). Nonetheless, in the image of bread making he calls attention to the catechumenate at Hippo. It was a complex process, which began when an inquirer (as Augustine once was) became seriously interested in Christianity. He or she sought initial private or semipublic instruction. (Augustine's *First Catechetical Instruction* was composed for the purpose.) Upon completion, the inquirer, if willing and accepted, became an adult catechumen through the rite of inscription, involving exorcism, the imposition of hands, the sign of the cross, and the ingestion of salt (it was the rite for infants as well). At this point one became a catechumen, attended the instructional part of the Eucharist, and was otherwise gradually integrated into the community. He or she would remain such for the better part of two years, which were devoted largely to catechetical instruction and moral reformation.

Those catechumens whose conversion was evident and who felt ready for baptism were urged to hand in their names at the beginning of Lent during a rite that included the chanting of Psalm 42 (41): "As a hart longs for flowing streams, so longs my soul for you, O God. . . ." From that point on they were called *competentes* (those who together seek baptism), obliged to abstain from wine, meat, the baths, entertainment, and the use of marriage. In addition, they were instructed daily and exorcized frequently.

The first rite of immediate baptismal preparation took place on Saturday two weeks before Easter. It consisted in the oral delivery of the creed to the candidates *(traditio symboli)* coupled with creedal instruction. During the week that followed, sponsors (and family) helped the candidates commit the creed to memory.

On the following Saturday evening (eight days before Easter), they assembled for the first of two vigils. The vigil began with the rite of lamp lighting *(lucenarium)* and was devoted to prayer, psalmody, biblical readings, and homiletic instruction. At cockcrow the pivotal rites of the whole process of conversion began with a solemn exorcism called the "scrutiny." In the eerie light of first dawn the candidates stood barefoot on coarse animal skins *(cilicium),* naked and with head bowed. Invoking the power of Christ and the Trinity, voicing vituperative biblical condemnations of Satan, and imposing hands, the exorcist hissed in the faces of competents, peremptorily commanding the Evil One to depart. There followed a physical examination to determine whether any of the competents showed evidence of a disease, which signaled the continued inhabitation of Satan. Granted that they passed scrutiny, the competents, each in her or his own voice, then renounced Satan, his pomps, and his service. The rites concluded in morning's light with each competent reciting the creed *(redditio symboli)* before the assembled congregation, much as he or she would do a week later in the Easter Vigil (see below, *Confessions*). Custom dictated that a homily (or homilies) accompany the rites, and at least one such homily of Augustine survive (*Sermon* 215, 216; see also Quodvultdeus, *On the Creed* 1, 2, 3).

The rites were pivotal because they represented the culmination of the competents' formal turning away from the past (in Augustine's term, *aversio*): The "old man" had begun to die. At the same time that they turned away, they turned toward Christ (Augustine: *conversio*) by their recitation of the creed: The "new man" began to be.

In close association with the rite (very likely, at the Palm Sunday Eucharist) was the oral delivery of the Lord's Prayer *(traditio orationis dominicae)*, which the candidates appear to have recited at baptism as "new-born" sons and daughters of the Father. Prominent in the rite was the chanting of Psalms 34 (33): "I will bless the Lord. . . . I sought the Lord, and he answered me, and delivered me from all my fears. . . ." and 27 (26): "The Lord is my light and my salvation; whom shall I fear? . . ." The homily was built around the petitions presented successively.

On Wednesday of Holy Week, the liturgy faced the passion squarely, with the lessons at the Eucharist devoted to the Lamentations of Jeremiah (Jer 9) and to Matthew's account of the unknown woman who anointed Jesus for his burial (Matt 26:1-13). The psalm of the day was Psalm 41 (42), by now quite familiar to the competents.

On Thursday, bathing was permitted and the fast relaxed for a meal in conjunction with the Eucharist. The custom commemorated the Last Supper and included the foot washing recounted in John 13:1-11 (see ch. 1, Ambrose; also see vol. 5, ch. 2, Aphrahat).

Friday was devoted to the commemoration of Christ's crucifixion, with rites that included the reading of the Passion According to Matthew, coupled with a homily. The order of the day also called for fasting in solidarity with the competents as they approached the end of their long and exacting journey.

Thus was set the stage for Saturday and what Augustine calls the "mother of all holy vigils" (*Sermon* 219). Devoted to biblical lessons, responsive prayers (largely psalms), and biblical homilies (several of Augustine's survive), the Vigil lasted from the lighting of the paschal candle, signaling the arrival of evening, to cockcrow, heralding the dawn, when the rites of baptism proper began. A central event of the Vigil was the second recitation of the creed, this time an extremely solemn public moment, the drama of which Augustine has preserved in his account of the conversion of the celebrated Neoplatonic philosopher Marius Victorinus about 360 in Rome (see below, *Confessions*).

The baptismal rites were celebrated in the baptistery and the consignatorium of Hippo's major basilica and included (1) the consecration of the baptismal water; (2) the procession of the competents to the baptismal font, chanting Psalm 42 (41); (3) the removal of their penitential tunics of animal skin; (4) their standing waist deep in the water, answering interrogations about their faith and good will; and (5) their triple immersion in the names of the Father and of the Son and of the Holy Spirit.

When they emerged (very likely praying the Lord's Prayer, see vol. 5, ch. 1, Chrysostom), the bishop imposed his hand on them, anointed their heads with chrism, and traced on their foreheads the sign of the cross (consignation), a rite which some think gave shape to Augustine's doctrine of sacramental character. In any case, he associates this "sealing" or consignation in a special way with the gift of the Holy Spirit. One is born of the Spirit and sins are forgiven, to be sure, but he distinguishes between being born of the Spirit and being nourished continually by the Spirit; indeed, he calls this anointing "the sacrament of the Holy Spirit."

The newly baptized then dressed in white, received a baptismal candle, the embrace of the congregation, and then celebrated their first Eucharist, which included a cup of milk and honey mixed (see ch. 1, *Apostolic Tradition*).

The newly baptized returned to church for the Easter morning Eucharist, when they would have heard the following instruction. Each morning for the rest of the week postbaptismal instruction was given on the four gospel accounts of the resurrection, because, according to Augustine, baptism is the sacrament of the resurrection. On the following Sunday, the octave day, they put away their white garments (thus, "White" Sunday). Their task then was to preserve unstained the radiance of their baptismal renovation.

The text is that of Suzanne Poque, ed., SC 116 (1966) 234–242; the translation is that of Mary Sarah Muldowney, FC 17 (1959) 195–198, which contains a number of Augustine's baptismal catecheses. The definitive study is Benedictus Busch, "De initiatione christiana secundum sanctum Augustinum," *Ephemerides Liturgicae Analecta* 52 (1938) 159–178, 385–483. Philip Weller has translated thirty catecheses in his *Selected Easter Sermons of St. Augustine* (St. Louis: B. Herder, 1959). For the most recent study of baptism in Hippo and Augustine, see Poque, 26–39.

Sermon on Easter Morning (227)

I am not unmindful of the promise by which I pledged myself to deliver a sermon to instruct you, who have just been baptized, on the sacrament of the Lord's table, which you now look upon and of which you partook last night. You ought to know what you have received, what you are going to receive, and what you ought to receive daily. That bread which you see on the altar, consecrated by the word of God, is the Body of Christ. That chalice, or rather, what the chalice holds, consecrated by the word of God, is the Blood of Christ. Through those accidents [i.e., elements] the Lord wished to entrust to us his Body and the Blood which he poured out for the remission of sins. If you have received worthily, you are what you have received, for the apostle says: "The bread is one; we, though many, are one body." Thus he explained the sacrament of the Lord's table: "The bread is one; we, though many, are one body." So, by bread you are instructed as to how you ought to cherish unity [i.e., the catechumenate]. Was that bread made of one grain of wheat? Were there not, rather, many grains? However, before they became bread, these grains were separate; they were joined together in water after a certain amount of crushing. For, unless the grain is ground and moistened with water, it cannot arrive at that form which is called bread. So, too, you were previously ground, as it were, by the humiliation of your fasting and by the sacrament of exorcism [Lenten exorcism, the scrutiny, and the renunciation of Satan]. Then came the baptism of water; you were moistened, as it were, so as to arrive at the form of bread. But, without fire, bread does not yet exist. What, then, does the fire signify? The chrism. For the sacrament of the Holy Spirit is the oil of our fire. Notice this when the Acts of the Apostles are read. (Soon the reading of the book is going to begin; today the reader is beginning that book which is called the Acts of the Apostles.) He who wishes to advance has the source of advancement. When you come to church, put aside empty talk; concentrate your attention on the Scriptures. We are your books. Attend, then, and see that the Holy Spirit will come on Pentecost. And thus he will come: he will show himself in tongues of fire. For he enkindles charity by which we ardently desire God and spurn the world, by which our chaff is consumed and our heart purified as gold. Therefore, the fire, that is, the Holy Spirit, comes after the water; then you become bread, that is, the body of Christ. Hence, in a certain manner, unity is signified.

You now have the rites in their order. At first, after the prayer, you are admonished to lift up your heart. This befits the members [1 Cor 10:17] of Christ. For, if you have become members of Christ, where is your head? Members have a head. If the head had not preceded, the members would not follow. Where has your head gone? What did you recite in the creed? "On the third day he rose again from the dead; he ascended into heaven; he sits at the right hand of the Father." Therefore, our head is in heaven. Hence, when the "Lift up your heart," is said, you answer: "We have [them lifted up] to the Lord." Then, because this lifting up of your hearts to God is a gift of God and lest you should attribute to your own strength, your own merits, and your own labors the fact that you have your hearts thus lifted up to the Lord, after the answer, "We have our hearts lifted up to the Lord," the bishop or priest who is officiating also says: "Let us give thanks to the Lord our God, because we have our hearts raised up to him. Let us give thanks to him, because if he did not give [the grace], we would have our hearts fixed on the earth." And you bear witness to this, saying: "It is right and just for us to give thanks to him who caused us to raise our hearts up to our head."

Then, after the consecration of the holy sacrifice of God, because he wished us also to be his sacrifice, a fact which was made clear when the holy sacrifice was first instituted, and because that sacrifice is a sign of what we are, behold, when the sacrifice is finished, we say the Lord's Prayer which you have received and recited. After this, the "Peace be with you" is said, and the Christians embrace one another with the holy kiss. This is a sign of peace; as the lips indicate, let peace be made in your conscience, that is, when your lips draw near to those of your brother, do not let your heart withdraw from his. Hence, these are great and powerful sacraments. Do you wish to know how they are commended? The apostle says: "Whoever eats the body of Christ or drinks the cup of the Lord unworthily, will be guilty of the body and blood of the Lord" [1 Cor 11:27]. What does it mean to receive unworthily? To receive in mockery, to receive in contempt. Let the sacrament not appear of trifling value to you because you look upon it. What you see passes; but the invisible, that which is not seen, does not pass; it remains. Be-

hold, it is received; it is eaten; it is consumed. Is the body of
Christ consumed? Is the church of Christ consumed? Are the
members of Christ consumed? God forbid! Here they are
cleansed; there they will be crowned. Therefore, what is signified will last eternally, even though it seems to pass. Receive,
then, so that you may ponder, so that you may possess unity
in your heart, so that you may always lift up your heart. Let
your hope be, not on earth, but in heaven; let your faith be
firm and acceptable to God. Because you now believe what you
do not see, you are going to see there where you will rejoice
eternally.

The Confessions

Unique among Augustine's works is the *Confessions,* from
which the third reading is drawn. Composed between 397 and 401,
it is something of a library: autobiography, manifesto of the inner world, profession of faith, prayer of praise, confession of sin,
testimony to grace, Neoplatonic treatise. It is also a journal of
Augustine's journey to the baptismal font, providing a unique
insight into the struggle of a late fourth-century intellectual to
become a Christian.

In the following selections from the work, Augustine records
the public profession of the creed *(redditio symboli)* at Rome by
the celebrated Neoplatonic philosopher-convert, Marius Victorinus (ca. 360), already mentioned in the introduction to the second reading. In addition, he gives an account of the feelings that
surrounded his own baptism.

The selections are from Books 8, chapters 3–5; and 9, chapters
6–7; the text is that of Lucas Verheijen, ed., CCL 27 (1981); the
translation, that of Albert C. Outler, *Augustine: Confessions and
Enchiridion*, LCC 7 (Philadelphia: Westminster Press, 1955)
159–161, 186–187.

Book 8:3–5 (The Conversion of Marius Victorinus)

3. I went, therefore, to Simplicianus, the spiritual father of
Ambrose (then a bishop), whom Ambrose truly loved as a father. I recounted to him all the mazes of my wanderings, but
when I mentioned to him that I had read certain books of the
Platonists which Victorinus—formerly professor of rhetoric at
Rome, who died a Christian, as I had been told—had translated into Latin, Simplicianus congratulated me that I had not

fallen upon the writings of other philosophers, which were full
of fallacies and deceit, "after the beggarly elements of this
world" [Col 2:8], whereas in the Platonists, at every turn, the
pathway led to belief in God and his Word.

Then, to encourage me to copy the humility of Christ, which
is hidden from the wise and revealed to babes, he told me about
Victorinus himself, whom he had known intimately at Rome.
And I cannot refrain from repeating what he told me about him.
For it contains a glorious proof of your grace, which ought to
be confessed to you: how that old man, most learned, most
skilled in all the liberal arts; who had read, criticized, and explained so many of the writings of the philosophers; the teacher
of so many noble senators; one who, as a mark of his distinguished service in office had both merited and obtained a statue
in the Roman Forum—which men of this world esteem a great
honor—this man who, up to an advanced age, had been a worshiper of idols, a communicant in the sacrilegious rites to which
almost all the nobility of Rome were wedded; and who had inspired the people with the love of Osiris and

> "The dog Anubis, and a medley crew
> Of monster gods who 'gainst Neptune stand in arms
> 'Gainst Venus and Minerva, steel-clad Mars" [Virgil,
>   *Aeneid* 8, 698],

whom Rome once conquered, and now worshiped; all of which
old Victorinus had with thundering eloquence defended for so
many years—despite all this, he did not blush to become a child
of your Christ, a babe at your font, bowing his neck to the yoke
of humility and submitting his forehead to the ignominy of the
cross.

4. O Lord, Lord, "who did bow the heavens and did descend,
who did touch the mountains and they smoked" [Ps 144:5],
by what means did you find your way into that breast? He used
to read the Holy Scriptures, as Simplicianus said, and thought
out and studied all the Christian writings most studiously. He
said to Simplicianus—not openly but secretly as a friend—"You
must know that I am a Christian." To which Simplicianus replied, "I shall not believe it, nor shall I count you among the
Christians, until I see you in the church of Christ." Victorinus
then asked, with mild mockery, "Is it then the walls that make
Christians?" Thus he often would affirm that he was already
a Christian, and as often Simplicianus made the same answer;
and just as often his jest about the walls was repeated. He was

fearful of offending his friends, proud demon worshipers, from the height of whose Babylonian dignity, as from the tops of the cedars of Lebanon which the Lord had not yet broken down, he feared that a storm of enmity would descend upon him.

But he steadily gained strength from reading and inquiry, and came to fear lest he should be denied by Christ before the holy angels if he now was afraid to confess him before men. Thus he came to appear to himself guilty of a great fault, in being ashamed of the sacraments of the humility of your Word, when he was not ashamed of the sacrilegious rites of those proud demons, whose pride he had imitated and whose rites he had shared. From this he became bold-faced against vanity and shamefaced toward the truth. Thus, suddenly and unexpectedly, he said to Simplicianus—as he himself told me—"Let us go to the church; I wish to become a Christian." Simplicianus went with him, scarcely able to contain himself for joy. He was admitted to the first sacraments of instruction, and not long afterward gave in his name that he might receive the baptism of regeneration. At this Rome marveled and the church rejoiced. The proud saw and were enraged; they gnashed their teeth and melted away! But the Lord God was your servant's hope and he paid no attention to their vanity and lying madness.

5. Finally, when the hour arrived for him to make a public profession of his faith—which at Rome those who are about to enter into your grace make from a platform in the full sight of the faithful people, in a set form of words learned by heart—the presbyters offered Victorinus the chance to make his profession more privately, for this was the custom for some who were likely to be afraid through bashfulness. But Victorinus chose rather to profess his salvation in the presence of the holy congregation. For there was no salvation in the rhetoric which he taught: yet he had professed that openly. Why, then, should he shrink from naming your Word before the sheep of your flock, when he had not shrunk from uttering his own words before the mad multitude?

So, then, when he ascended the platform to make his profession, everyone, as they recognized him, whispered his name one to the other, in tones of jubilation. Who was there among them that did not know him? And a low murmur ran through the mouths of all the rejoicing multitude: "Victorinus! Victorinus!" There was a sudden burst of exaltation at the sight of him, and suddenly they were hushed that they might hear him. He pronounced the true faith with an excellent boldness, and all desired to take him to their very heart—indeed, by their love and joy they did take him to their heart. And they received him with loving and joyful hands.

Book 9:13–14 (Augustine on His Baptism)

13. Now that the vintage vacation was ended, I gave notice to the citizens of Milan that they might provide their scholars with another word-merchant. I gave as my reasons my determination to serve you and also my insufficiency for the task, because of the difficulty in breathing and the pain in my chest.

And by letters I notified your bishop, the holy man Ambrose, of my former errors and my present resolution. And I asked his advice as to which of your books it was best for me to read so that I might be the more ready and fit for the reception of so great a grace. He recommended Isaiah the prophet; and I believe it was because Isaiah foreshows more clearly than others the gospel, and the calling of the Gentiles. But because I could not understand the first part and because I imagined the rest to be like it, I laid it aside with the intention of taking it up again later, when better practiced in our Lord's words.

14. When the time arrived for me to give in my name, we left the country and returned to Milan. Alypius also resolved to be born again in you at the same time. He was already clothed with the humility that befits your sacraments, and was so brave a tamer of his body that he would walk the frozen Italian soil with his naked feet, which called for unusual fortitude. We took with us the boy Adeodatus, my son after the flesh, the offspring of my sin. You had made of him a noble lad. He was barely fifteen years old, but his intelligence excelled that of many grave and learned men. I confess to you your gifts, O Lord my God, Creator of all, who has power to reform our deformities—for there was nothing of me in that boy but the sin. For it was you who inspired us to foster him in your discipline, and none other—your gifts I confess to you. There is a book of mine, entitled *De Magistro*. It is a dialogue between Adeodatus and me, and you know that all things there put into the mouth of my interlocutor are his, though he was then only in his sixteenth year. Many other gifts even more wonderful I found in him. His talent was a source of awe to me. And who but you could be the worker of such marvels? And you did quickly remove his life from the earth, and even now I recall him to mind with a sense of security, because I fear nothing for his childhood or youth, nor for his whole career. We took him for our com-

panion, as if he were the same age in grace with ourselves, to be trained with ourselves in your discipline. And so we were baptized and the anxiety about our past life left us.

Nor did I ever have enough in those days of the wondrous sweetness of meditating on the depth of your counsels concerning the salvation of the human race. How freely did I weep in your hymns and canticles; how deeply was I moved by the voices of your sweet-speaking church! The voices flowed into my ears; and the truth was poured forth into my heart, where the tide of my devotion overflowed, and my tears ran down, and I was happy in all these things.

On Baptism

The final reading is from Augustine's *On Baptism, Against the Donatists*. Composed about 400, it is a refutation of the Donatists (see above, Optatus), who remained a powerful force in North African Christianity until their final disappearance well after the death of Augustine. He has in view especially their practice of rebaptizing those whom they regarded as heretics (Catholics) and their conviction that the effectiveness of baptism depends on the minister's holiness.

Much of the work (bks. 2–7) seeks to recapture from the Donatists both Cyprian and African conciliar teaching on rebaptism (see above, Cyprian). In the first book, however, he develops the position already espoused by Optatus, namely, that baptism (and ordination) has an enduring validity and effect quite independent of the moral character of the minister or of the recipient. The reason, he argues (developing Optatus), is that the primary minister is the Church, more accurately, Christ, whose body and bride the Church is. As a result, he continues, baptism immediately affects even the deceitful candidate in one of two ways: (1) Either the sacrament gives him something (the seal or character of Christ) in virtue of which the "benefit" of the sacrament revives when he is contrite and reconciled (1:12, 18); or (2) the power of the sacrament forgives sin at the moment of reception, even though the sin may return immediately afterward to engulf the ill disposed. Elsewhere in the work (6:1, 1) Augustine argues the first position (seal/character) as his own. His distinction between the validity of the sacrament and its fruitfulness were fundamental to Western medieval sacramental thinking.

The text is PL 43, 116–150; the translation is adapted from that of J. R. King, NPNF 4, series 1 (1987) 417–421. For studies see W. H. C. Frend, *The Donatist Church: A Movement of Protest in Roman North Africa* (New York: Oxford, 1971) and P. Brown, *Augustine of Hippo*, 212–243.

On Baptism, Against the Donatists: Book 1:1–19

Chapter 1:1–2. [Augustine had previously written (see above) that baptism can be conferred outside the Catholic communion just as within it. He continues the argument here: Apostates retain their baptism when they leave, and should they return, they are reconciled rather than baptized anew. So also the ordained: They retain their ordination quite apart from their separation. In the following passage Augustine uses the terms "rightly" *(recte)*, "profitably" *(utile)*, and "unprofitably" *(inutiliter)*, which gave rise to the medieval distinction between "fruitful" and "valid." He means that baptism rightly or profitably received (fruitful) accomplishes its full effects, whereas baptism unprofitably (i.e., valid but not fruitful) received seals the person as Christ's; in virtue of the seal or character, baptism becomes profitable when the "deceit" changes to "charity."]

So those, too, who in the sacrilege of schism depart from the communion of the church, certainly retain baptism, which they received before their departure, seeing that, in case of their return, it is not again conferred on them; whence it is proved, that what they had received while within the unity of the church, they could not have lost in their separation. But if it can be retained outside, why may it not also be given there? If you say, "It is not rightly given outside"; we answer, "As it is not rightly retained, and yet is in some sense retained, so it is not indeed rightly given, but yet it is given." But as, by reconciliation to unity, that begins to be profitably possessed which was possessed to no profit in exclusion from unity, so, by the same reconciliation, that begins to be profitable which without it was given to no profit. Yet one cannot be permitted to say that what was given was not given, nor that any one should reproach a man with not having given this, while confessing that he had given what he had himself received. For the sacrament of baptism is what the person possesses who is baptized; and the sacrament of conferring baptism is what he possesses who is ordained. And as the baptized person, if he depart from the unity of the church, does not thereby lose the sacrament of baptism, so also he who is ordained, if he depart from the unity of the church, does not lose the sacrament of conferring baptism. For neither sacrament may be wronged. If a sacrament necessarily becomes void in the case of the wicked, both must become void; if it remain valid with the wicked, this must be so with both. If, therefore, the baptism be acknowledged which he could not lose who severed himself from the unity of the church, that baptism must also be acknowledged which was administered by one who by his secession had not lost the sacrament of conferring baptism. For as those who return to the church, if they had been baptized before their secession, are not rebaptized, so those who return, having been ordained before their secession, are certainly not ordained again; but either they again exercise their former ministry, if the interests of the church require it, or if they do not exercise it, at any rate they retain the sacrament of their ordination; and hence it is, that when hands are laid on them, to mark their reconciliation, they are not ranked with the laity.

Chapter 2:3. [Some pastoral advice on the subject of Donatist baptism:] And so the Donatists in some matters are with us; in some matters have gone out from us. Accordingly, those things wherein they agree with us we do not forbid them to do; but in those things in which they differ from us, we earnestly encourage them to come and receive them from us, or return and recover them, as the case may be; and with whatever means we can, we lovingly busy ourselves, that they, freed from faults and corrected, may choose this course. We do not therefore say to them, "Abstain from giving baptism," but "Abstain from giving it in schism." Nor do we say to those whom we see them on the point of baptizing, "Do not receive the baptism," but " Do not receive it in schism." For if any one were compelled by urgent necessity, being unable to find a Catholic from whom to receive baptism, and so, while preserving Catholic peace in his heart, should receive from one without the pale of Catholic unity the sacrament which he was intending to receive within its pale, this man, should he forthwith depart this life, we deem to be none other than a Catholic. But if he should be delivered from the death of the body, on his restoring himself in bodily presence to that Catholic congregation from which in heart he had never departed, so far from blaming his conduct, we should praise it with the greatest truth and confidence; because he trusted that God was present to his heart, while he was striving to preserve unity, and was unwilling to depart this life without the sacrament of holy baptism, which he knew to be of God, and not of men, wherever he might find it. But if any one who has it in his power to receive baptism within the Catholic church prefers, from some perversity of mind, to be baptized in schism, even if he afterwards decides to come to the Catholic church, because he is assured that there that sacrament will profit him, which can indeed be received but cannot profit elsewhere, beyond all question he is perverse, and guilty of sin, and that the more flagrant in proportion as it was committed wilfully. For that he entertains no doubt that the sacrament is rightly received in the church, is proved by his conviction that it is there that he must look for profit even from what he has received elsewhere.

Chapter 3:4. [Issues of controversy between Donatist and Catholic:] There are two propositions, moreover, which we affirm, that baptism exists in the Catholic church, and that in it alone can it be rightly received, both of which the Donatists deny. Likewise there are two other propositions which we affirm, that baptism exists among the Donatists, but that with them it is not rightly received, of which two they strenuously confirm the former, that baptism exists with them; but they are unwilling to allow the latter, that in their church it cannot be rightly received. Of these four propositions, three are peculiar to us; in one we both agree. For that baptism exists in the Catholic church, that it is rightly received there, and that it is not rightly received among the Donatists, are assertions made only by ourselves; but that baptism exists also among the Donatists, is asserted by them and allowed by us.

[Augustine explores in the rest of this section and in 3:6 the possible choices one might make about the best road to baptism—Donatist or Catholic. His interlocutor is a doubting "strawman" whom he engages in rhetorical dialectic not entirely easy to follow.]

Chapter 6:7-8. [Donatist factions: An element in the "doubter's" quandary must be the factions among the Donatists. Two major groups were those headed by Primianus, bishop of Carthage, and the followers of the dissident, Maximianus. Augustine continues:] But this brings us to consider next, whether those men do not seem to have something to say for themselves, who refuse communion with the party of Primianus, contending that in their body there remains greater sincerity of Donatism, just in proportion to the paucity of their numbers.

And even if these were only the party of Maximianus, we should not be justified in despising their salvation. How much more, then, are we bound to consider it, when we find that this same party of Donatus is split up into many most minute fractions, all which small sections of the body blame the one much larger portion which has Primianus for its head, because they receive the baptism of the followers of Maximianus; while each endeavors to maintain that it is the sole receptacle of true baptism, which exists nowhere else, neither in the whole of the world where the Catholic church extends itself, nor in that larger main body of the Donatists, nor even in the other minute sections, but only in itself.

Chapters 7:9–9:12. [At this point in the discussion Augustine turns to the New Testament "to prove," as he says, "how rightly and truly in the sight of God it has been determined, that in the case of every schismatic and heretic, the wound which caused his separation should be cured by the medicine of the Church; but that what remained sound in him should rather be recognized with approbation than wounded by condemnation."]

Chapter 10:13–14. [The Church and the roots of baptism's validity and fruitfulness:] For the Donatist church is severed from the bond of peace and charity, but it is joined in one baptism. And so there is one church which alone is called Catholic; and whenever it has anything of its own in these communions of different bodies which are separate from itself, it is most certainly in virtue of this which is its own in each of them that it, not they, has the power of generation. For neither is it their separation that generates, but what they have retained of the essence of the church; and if they were to go on to abandon this, they would lose the power of generation. The generation, then, in each case proceeds from the church, whose sacraments are retained, from which any such birth can alone in any case proceed, although not all who receive its birth belong to its unity, which shall save those who persevere even to the end. Nor is it those only that do not belong to it who are openly guilty of the manifest sacrilege of schism, but also those who, being outwardly joined to its unity, are yet separated by a life of sin. For the church had herself given birth to Simon Magus through the sacrament of baptism; and yet it was declared to him that he had no part in the inheritance of Christ [Acts 8:13–21]. Did he lack anything in respect of baptism, of the gospel, of the sacraments? But in that he lacked charity, he was born in vain;

and perhaps it had been well for him that he had never been born at all. . . .

Chapter 11:15–17. [The "profitability" of Donatist baptism.
The question at issue in this chapter is whether Donatist baptism forgives sins. Augustine puts the question to his interlocutors: "Whether there is any remission of sins where there is not charity; for sins are the darkness of the soul." He replies with biblical citations about schism and hatred of one's brother. He then concludes:]

17. They think that they solve this question when they say: "There is then no remission of sins in schism, and therefore no creation of the new man by regeneration, and accordingly neither is there the baptism of Christ." But since we confess that the baptism of Christ exists in schism, we propose this question to them for solution: Was Simon Magus endued with the true baptism of Christ? They will answer, Yes; being compelled to do so by the authority of Holy Scripture. I ask them whether they confess that he received remission of his sins. They will certainly acknowledge it. So I ask why Peter said to him that he had no part in the lot of the saints. Because, they say, he sinned afterwards, wishing to buy with money the gift of God, which he believed the apostles were able to sell.

Chapter 12:18–19. [Baptism in deceit, is it effective? In this chapter Augustine comes to the nub of his argument, namely, that when baptism is rightly performed although unprofitably received, it nonetheless has a permanent effect in virtue of which the "benefit" of the sacrament (remission and rebirth) revives. Augustine's position here enunciated undergirds medieval sacramental teaching about the validity and fruitfulness of the sacrament (i.e., *ex opere operato*). Augustine continues with the discussion launched in chapter 17:]

18. What if he approached baptism itself in deceit? were his sins remitted, or were they not? Let them choose which they will. Whichever they choose will answer our purpose. If they say they were remitted, how then shall "the Holy Spirit of discipline flee deceit" [Wis 1:5], if in him who was full of deceit he worked remission of sins? If they say they were not remitted, I ask whether, if he should afterwards confess his sin with contrition of heart and true sorrow, it would be judged that he ought to be baptized again. And if it is mere madness to assert this, then let them confess that a man can be baptized with the true baptism of Christ, and that yet his heart, persisting in malice

or sacrilege, may not allow remission of sins to be given; and so let them understand that men may be baptized in communions severed from the church, in which Christ's baptism is given and received in the said celebration of the sacrament, but that it will only then be of avail for the remission of sins, when the recipient, being reconciled to the unity of the church, is purged from the sacrilege of deceit, by which his sins were retained, and their remission prevented. For, as in the case of him who had approached the sacrament in deceit there is no second baptism, but he is purged by faithful discipline and truthful confession, which he could not be without baptism, so that what was given before becomes then powerful to work his salvation, when the former deceit is done away by the truthful confession; so also in the case of the man who, while an enemy to the peace and love of Christ, received in any heresy or schism the baptism of Christ, which the schismatics in question had not lost from among them, though by his sacrilege his sins were not remitted, yet, when he corrects his error, and comes over to the communion and unity of the church, he ought not to be again baptized: because by his very reconciliation to the peace of the church he receives this benefit, that the sacrament now begins in unity to be of avail for the remission of his sins, which could not so avail him as received in schism.

19. But if they should say that in the man who has approached the sacrament in deceit, his sins are indeed removed by the holy power of so great a sacrament at the moment when he received it, but return immediately in consequence of his deceit: so that the Holy Spirit has both been present with him at his baptism for the removal of his sins, and has also fled before his perseverance in deceit so that they should return: so that both declarations prove true—both, "As many of you as have been baptized into Christ have put on Christ"; and also, "The holy spirit of discipline will flee deceit"—that is to say, that both the holiness of baptism clothes him with Christ, and the sinfulness of deceit strips him of Christ; like the case of a man who passes from darkness through light into darkness again, his eyes being always directed towards darkness, though the light cannot but penetrate them as he passes; if they should say this, let them understand that this is also the case with those who are baptized outside the church, but yet with the baptism of the church, which is holy in itself, wherever it may be; and which therefore belongs not to those who separate themselves, but to the body from which they are separated; while yet it avails even

among them so far, that they pass through its light back to their own darkness, their sins, which in that moment had been dispelled by the holiness of baptism, returning immediately upon them, as though it were the darkness returning which the light had dispelled while they were passing through it.

[Augustine then cites the example of the "unjust" steward who, forgiven by his master, nonetheless refuses to forgive the debts of his debtors (see Matt 18:23-25). He concludes:] Yet the fact that he had not yet forgiven his fellow-servant, did not prevent his lord from forgiving him all his debts on the occasion of receiving his accounts. But what advantage was it to him, since they all immediately returned with redoubled force upon his head, in consequence of his persistent lack of charity? So the grace of baptism is not prevented from giving remission of all sins, even if he to whom they are forgiven continues to cherish hatred towards his brother in his heart. For the guilt of yesterday is remitted, and all that was before it, nay, even the guilt of the very hour and moment previous to baptism, and during baptism itself. But then he immediately begins again to be responsible, not only for the days, hours, moments which ensue, but also for the past—the guilt of all the sins which were remitted returning on him, as happens only too frequently in the church.

Chapters 13:21-19:29. [In the chapters that conclude *On Baptism,* Augustine again makes the point that "it is the church that gives birth to all, either within her own womb; or beyond it, of the seed of her bridegroom" (15:23). He continues to explore biblical texts from both the Hebrew Bible and the New Testament and concludes with a defense of Cyprian and his teaching on the basis of his humility and charity: "I take it that the reason why the Lord did not reveal the error in this (the requirement of rebaptism in Cyprian's letters and the conciliar decree above) to a man of such eminence was that his pious humility and charity in guarding the peace and health of the church might be made manifest, and might be noticed, so as to serve as an example of healing power, so to speak, not only to Christians of that age, but also to those who should come after" (18:27).]

Chapter 3

Egypt

In 30 B.C.E. Egypt became a Roman imperial province, and Alexandria, its central city and the cultural gem of the Mediterranean world, became the empire's intellectual capital. The citizenry of the city was Greek; the majority of the inhabitants, however, were native Egyptians; and the largest and oldest ethnic minority were deeply Hellenized Jews. Christianity arrived there early (ca. 50) with the first Jewish Christian immigrants from Palestine, especially Judaea. They settled among the diverse groups of Jews that made up the flourishing and influential Jewish community. In the city's synagogues they encountered the Gentiles, spread to the surrounding countryside, and then up the Nile into Ethiopia.

Although nurtured in the city's synagogues, Egyptian Christianity became increasingly Gentile in time and appears to have gone its own way in the first decades of the second century, when serious political troubles all but decimated Alexandria's Jewish community. Nonetheless, Jews and Christians remained in continual contact, and Judaism left its offspring a rich legacy of belief and practice, including the Bible in Greek (the Septuagint); a distinctive typological approach to biblical interpretation often called "allegorical" or "mystical" (see below, Origen); and a philosophical tradition mediated by Philo, the celebrated Alexandrian Jewish thinker whose works Egyptian Christians preserved. Indeed, the early Alexandrian Christians differed little from their non-Christian Jewish brethren, save in their conviction that Jesus was the Messiah.

The Alexandrian School

There were other aspects of the legacy as well, especially Jewish diversity in the city. As a result of its Jewish heritage the Alexandrian Church, when it appeared on its own in the mid-second century, was composed of small and to some extent separate communities, or schools. The principal division was between Gnostic Christian schools like the Valentinians (see below, *Excerpts of Theodotus*) and those who appealed to the "traditions of the Fathers," like Pantaenus and Clement (below). Toward the end of the second century, however, the bishop, Demetrius (189–231), emerged as strong and centralizing leader of the traditionists. He is credited with the rise of the Egyptian Church as Catholic rather than Gnostic.

Alexandrian Christianity achieved intellectual eminence several decades later in Origen, who, in spite of his controversial stature in both life and death, still stands as the towering theological figure in Eastern Christianity. Alexandria maintained eminence, however, because of intellectual and spiritual leaders like Dionysius the Great (d. ca. 265), Athanasius (ca. 296–373), Didymus the Blind (d. 398, below), and Cyril (d. 444, below). Not to be overlooked, however, is its celebrated catechetical school, the origins of which lie in the "schools" tradition of the early second century. Not a few of the city's Christian intellectual leaders, like Origen and Didymus the Blind, were also heads of the school, which rivaled the school at Antioch for intellectual leadership in the developing Church (see vol. 5, ch. 1).

Alexandrian biblical interpretation runs toward allegory rather than history and the strict construction of the text, which characterizes the Antiochenes. The Alexandrian baptismal homilies, for instance, luxuriate in baptismal typology and seek to find the meaning inspired by the Spirit buried in biblical word and liturgical rite alike. In addition, their understanding of Christian life strongly emphasizes the journey motif, ascetical practices, and transformation to the point of deification, an emphasis quite consistent with their preoccupation with the divinity of Christ and their Platonic philosophical tradition.

Where the Antiochenes tended to distinguish too sharply between the Son of God and the man Jesus (see vol. 5, ch. 1, Theodore; also see vol. 5, ch. 2, Narsai), the Alexandrians tended to blur the distinction. They ran the risk of devaluing Jesus' humanity to the point that it could seem to be but borrowed flesh—the clothing of corporeity. Once the Council of Nicaea (325) and its defenders established that the Son of God was identical in nature to his Father, the issue shifted to whether and to what extent he was identical in nature to humans. Raised in the mid-fourth century, the issue sparked sharp controversy between the two schools of thought, with far-reaching consequences for Christianity.

To assure the integrity of Christ's humanity in the work of salvation, for instance, the Antiochene Nestorius, Patriarch of Constantinople (428–431), taught that Jesus Christ was composed, on the one hand, of the man Jesus, who was of the "seed of David" and, on the other, of the divine Word, who dwelled in Jesus, uniting the two natures. Nestorius' Christology, understood to assert two separate persons in Christ, was condemned at the Council of Ephesus (431; Nestorius was deposed and eventually exiled) and again at the Council of Chalcedon (451).

Fearing that an overemphasis on Christ's humanity jeopardized the work of salvation, Alexandrians and those influenced by them adopted the formula "after the union [incarnation], one nature of the Incarnate Word." One influential advocate, Eutyches (d. 454), appears to have taken the formula to mean that Christ's human nature had no concrete, individual existence, that it was absorbed by his divine nature, and that his body was not truly human. Whatever he intended, his teaching was condemned at the Council of Chalcedon, and he was exiled.

Midway between them stood Cyril, Patriarch of Alexandria, the determined, resourceful, and at times ruthless antagonist of Nestorius, who secured the latter's demise at Ephesus. Although Eutyches was his friend and disciple, Cyril interpreted the "one nature" formula in a way that anticipated the teaching of Chalcedon. After Cyril and the controversies about Christ's humanity and divinity (see below, Coptic Rite), Egyptian Christianity, strongly opposed to Chalcedon, gradually lost prominence until, like North African Christianity, it virtually disappeared from the larger Christian canvas with the Islamic conquests in the seventh century.

The Readings

The texts here selected are representative of what is characteristic of Egyptian baptismal tradition. Three selections are devoted to the liturgy of baptism as it developed in Egypt: the *Sacramentary of Serapion,* the *Canons of Hippolytus,* and the Coptic Rite. As for the liturgy itself, given the influence of the *Apostolic Tradition* of Hippolytus, one is not surprised to find strong similarity with Rome (see ch. 1). In any case, its development is treated with each selection. Five selections are devoted to baptismal instruction. In two (Theodotus and Clement) baptism is revealed as the true "mystery," which transforms one from death to life. For the third (Origen), it is the indispensable first stage of a journey into the "mysteries of God," which reenacts Israel's passage through the Red Sea and the River Jordan into the Promised Land. In the fourth, Didymus the Blind concentrates on the fact that the sacrament restores the image and likeness of God, lost in original sin. And in the fifth, Cyril of Alexandria considers why Christ was baptized and what it meant about him and for those who are baptized. His Christology is integral to the instruction.

Suggested Reading

Burghardt, W. J. "On Early Christian Exegesis." TS 11 (1950) 78–116.

Pearson, Birger A. and James E. Goehring, eds. *The Roots of Egyptian Christianity.* Philadelphia: Fortress, 1986.

Sellers, R. V. *Two Ancient Christologies: A Study in the Christological Thought of the Schools of Alexandria and Antioch* (London: SPCK, 1940).

Excerpts of Theodotus

A dominant strain of early Christianity in Egypt was Gnostic. Gnostic Christians tended to gather around teachers and to form schools, the most flourishing of which were the schools of Basilides, Marcion, and Valentinus. The Valentinians (see vol. 5, ch. 2, *Gospel According to Philip*), East and West, were perhaps the most numerous.

Clement of Alexandria (below), in his attempt to understand the teaching of the more prominent Gnostic schools, collected passages from their leading teachers. Someone, probably a disciple of Clement, appended excerpts, together with some of Clement's reflections and a collection of prophetic testimonies, to his *Car-*

pets (Stromata) as its eighth book. Thus, eighty-six fragments are gathered under the title "Excerpts from the Works of Theodotus and from the Oriental School of Valentinus" *(Excerpta Theodoto)*. Those that make up the reading (the last ten) concern baptism.

Almost nothing is known about Theodotus save that he was an important Gnostic Christian teacher. He seems to have been a contemporary of Clement and originally an Alexandrian, achieving prominence between 160 and 170. As a Gnostic Christian he tended to depreciate matter and the physical, to emphasize spirit and the spiritual, to seek insight from the Scriptures through strongly allegorical interpretation, and to reflect the world-view and terminology of contemporary Platonic philosophy. These traits, coupled with the fact that the offerings are fragmentary and visionary, render access to his meaning difficult. Nonetheless, they are the earliest extant record of a Gnostic Christian view of baptism.

In general, Theodotus' view of the human plight is that people's destiny is controlled by the stars and the evil powers they embody. As Savior, Christ is the "new star" who brings release. In truth, it is baptism that accomplishes release, for it brings about the death of the old or entrapped self and rebirth of a new self and life. Baptism transforms one's spirit and consists primarily of knowledge *(gnosis)* about "who we were or where we were placed, whither we hasten, from what we are redeemed, what birth is, and what rebirth" (frag. 78). Thus transformed, the baptized radiate a new power that prevails over every evil.

Theodotus' teaching, however, was at once cognitive and experiential. It presupposed and was based on a baptismal liturgy, the main elements of which seem to have been the common possession of second-century Alexandrian Christians. There was a catechumenate of indeterminate length that consisted of fasting, prayer, exorcism, and oral instruction (frag. 84). Baptism was by immersion and involved anointing in the name of "Father, Son, and Holy Spirit" (frag. 80, 86). Solemn exorcism and perhaps the renunciation of Satan seem to have preceded the rite (frag. 77, 81), and the Eucharist followed it (frag. 82). The rite bears the name "seal," which may refer to the anointing.

Where Theodotus differed from Clement and others was in the interpretation of baptism. One notices the prominence assigned to the soul, or spirit, and to the Holy Spirit, and learns that "name(s)" denote the essential being of Christ and of the Trinity and that "Ogdoad" is the state of final unity with God (the eighth heaven). Nevertheless, much of the New Testament underlies the excerpts.

The text is that of F. Sagnard, ed., SC 23bis (1970) 198–212; the translation, that of Robert P. Casey, ed., *The Excerpta ex Theodoto of Clement of Alexandria*, Studies and Documents 1 (London: Christophers, 1934) 87–91. Both works have excellent introductory studies. For Valentinian Gnosticism, see Bentley Layton, ed., *The Gnostic Scriptures* (Garden City: Doubleday, 1987).

Excerpts of Theodotus

76. As, therefore, the birth of the Savior released us from "becoming" and from fate, so also his baptism rescued us from fire, and his passion rescued us from passion in order that we might in all things follow him. For he who was baptized for God advanced toward God and has received "power to walk upon scorpions and snakes" [Luke 10:19], the evil powers. And he commands the disciples "When you go about, preach, and them that believe baptize in the name of the Father and of the Son and of the Holy Spirit" [Matt 28:19], in whom we are born again, becoming higher than all the other powers.

77. Therefore baptism is called death and an end of the old life when we take leave of the evil principalities, but it is also called life according to Christ, of which he is sole lord. But the power of the transformation of him who is baptized does not concern the body but the soul, for he who comes up [out of the water] is unchanged. From the moment when he comes up from baptism he is called a servant of God even by the unclean spirits and they now "tremble" at him whom shortly before they obsessed [see Jas 2:19].

78. Until baptism, they say, fate is real, but after it the astrologists are no longer right. But it is not only the washing that is liberating, but the knowledge of who we were, and what we have become, where we were or where we were placed, whither we hasten, from what we are redeemed, what birth is, and what rebirth.

79. So long, then, they say, as the seed is yet unformed, it is the offspring of the female, but when it was formed it was changed to a man and becomes a son of the bridegroom. It is

no longer weak and subject to the cosmic forces, both visible and invisible, but having been made masculine, it becomes a male fruit.

80. He whom the mother generates is led into death and into the world, but he whom Christ regenerates is transferred to life into the Ogdoad. And they die to the world but live to God, that death may be loosed by death and corruption by resurrection. For he who has been sealed by the Father, Son, and Holy Spirit is beyond threats of every other power and by the three names has been released from the whole triad of corruption. "Having borne the image of the earthly, it then bears the image of the heavenly" [1 Cor 15:49].

81. The material element of fire lays hold of all material things, and the pure and immaterial element lays hold of immaterial things such as demons, angels of evil, and the devil himself. Thus the heavenly fire is dual in its nature, belonging partly to the mind, partly to the senses. By analogy, therefore, baptism is also dual in its nature, the sensible part works through water which extinguishes the sensible fire, but the intellectual through spirit, a defense against the intellectual fire. And the material spirit when it is little becomes food and kindling for the sensible fire, but when it has increased it has become an extinguisher, but the Spirit given us from above, since it is immaterial, rules not only over the elements, but over the powers and the evil principalities.

82. And the bread and the oil are sanctified by the power of the Name, and they are not the same as they appeared to be when they were received, but they have been transformed by power into spiritual power. Thus, the water, also, both in exorcism and baptism, not only keeps off evil, but gives sanctification as well.

83. It is fitting to go to baptism with joy, but, since unclean spirits often go down into the water with some and these spirits following and gaining the seal together with the candidate become impossible to cure for the future, fear is joined with joy, in order that only he who is pure may go down to the water.

84. Therefore let there be fastings, supplications, prayers, raising of hands, kneelings because a soul is being saved from the world and from the "mouth of lions" (Ps 21:22). Wherefore there is immediate temptation for those who long also for the things from which they have separated, and even if one has foreknowledge to endure them, yet the outward man is shaken.

85. Even the Lord after baptism was troubled like we are and was first with beasts in the desert [see Matt 4:1-11]. Then when he had prevailed over them and their ruler as if already a true king, he was already served by angels. For he who ruled over angels in the flesh was fittingly served already by angels. Therefore we must put on the Lord's armor and keep body and soul invulnerable—armor that is "able to quench the darts of the devil," as the apostle says [Eph 6:16].

86. In the case of the coin that was brought to him, the Lord did not say whose property is it, but, "whose image and superscription? Caesar's" [Matt 25:1], that it might be given to him whose it is. So likewise the faithful; he has the name of God through Christ as a superscription and the Spirit as an image. And dumb animals show by a seal whose property each is, and are claimed from the seal. Thus also the faithful soul receives the seal of truth and bears about the "marks of Christ" [Luke 11:7]. These are the children who are now resting in bed and the "wise virgins" [Matt 25:1], with whom the others, who are late, did not enter into "the goods which have been prepared on which the angels desire to gaze" [1 Cor 2:9; 1 Pet 1:12].

Clement of Alexandria

A learned pagan who found in Christianity the fulfillment of his Greco-Roman Hellenism, Clement studied under a succession of Christian teachers (see below, *Carpets*). He settled finally in Alexandria where he studied with the celebrated Christian teacher Pantaenus and subsequently became a presbyter. He succeeded Pantaenus (ca. 190) as head of one of the Christian schools that vied with the other schools in the city for adherents—it may have been the Church's catechetical school (see below, Origen). He left Alexandria in the early 200s, largely as a result of persecution under Emperor Septimius Severus. Emigrating to Antioch, he eventually found his way to Cappadocia and to his former student, Alexander, who later became bishop of Jerusalem. Clement died sometime after 215.

Clement's special appeal was to the well-to-do pagans and Christians of Alexandria. Indeed, his literary legacy, a trilogy, embodies his appeal. His first work, *Exhortation to the Greeks (Protreptikos),* written at about the time he succeeded Pantaenus, calls on pagans to give up their traditional religious practices and embrace Christianity. This first reading comprises the final appeal in the *Exhortation* to his pagan readers to abandon their worship (the "mysteries") and to accept baptism as the true initiation into the "sacred mysteries" of salvation, which yield enlightenment, fulfillment, holiness, immortality, renovation, and righteousness, making one into the image of the Word. In the process, Clement provides a window through which one can see the attractions of the mystery cults and their rites of initiation, which left their mark on Christianity. That Christ makes the appeal interlaced with allusions to, and citations from, Greek literary classics underscores a persistent Alexandrian Christian conviction that Christ is the fulfillment of whatever is best in culture.

The text is that of Claude Mondésert, SC 2 (1948) 187–193; the translation is adapted from that of A. Cleveland Coxe, ANF 2 (1926) 205–206. For a recent and valuable discussion of the mystery cults, see Everett Ferguson, *Backgrounds of Early Christianity* (Grand Rapids: Eerdmans, 1987) 197–240. For a study of Clement and the mystery of baptism, see H. A. Echle, "Sacramental Initiation as a Christian Mystery—Mystery Initiation According to Clement of Alexandria," *Vom christlichen Mysterium, Gesammelte Arbeiten Zum Gedächtnis,* ed. Odo Casels (Düsseldorf, 1951) 54–64.

Exhortation to the Greeks 12

Let us then avoid custom as we would a dangerous headland, or the threatening Charybdis, or the mystic sirens. It chokes man, turns him away from truth, leads him away from life: custom is a snare, a gulf, a pit, a mischievous winnowing fan. "Urge the ship beyond that smoke and billow" [*Odyssey* 12:219]. Let us shun, fellow-mariners, let us shun this billow; it vomits forth fire; it is a wicked island, heaped with bones and corpses, and in it sings Pleasure, a fair courtesan, delighting with music for the common ear.

"Hie you hither, far-famed Ulysses, great glory of the Achaeans;
Moor the ship, that you may hear a diviner voice" [*Odyssey* 12:184].

She praises you, mariner, and calls you illustrious; and the courtesan tries to win to herself the glory of the Greeks. Leave her to prey on the dead; a heavenly spirit comes to your help: pass by Pleasure, she beguiles.

> "Let not a woman with flowing train cheat you of your senses,
> With her flattering prattle seeking your hurt" [no source cited].

Sail past the song; it works death. Exert your will only, and you have overcome ruin; bound to the wood of the cross, be freed from destruction: the word of God will be your pilot, and the Holy Spirit will bring you to anchor in the haven of heaven. Then shall you see my God, and be initiated into the sacred mysteries, and come to the fruition of those things which are laid up in heaven reserved for me, which "ear had not heard, or have they entered into the heart of any" [1 Cor 2:9].

> "And in sooth methinks I see two suns,
> And a double Thebes" [Euripedes, *Bacchae,* 198]

said one frenzy-stricken in the worship of idols, intoxicated with mere ignorance. I would pity him in his frantic intoxication, and thus frantic I would invite him to the sobriety of salvation; for the Lord welcomes a sinner's repentance, and not his death.

Come, O madman, not leaning on the thyrsus [a wreathed shaft], not crowned with ivy; throw away the miter, throw away the fawn-skin; come to your senses. I will show you the Word, and the mysteries of the Word, expounding them after your own fashion. This is the mountain beloved of God, not the subject of tragedies like Cithaeron, but consecrated to dramas of the truth—a mount of sobriety, shaded with forests of purity; and there revel on it, not the Maenades, the sisters of Semele, who were struck by the thunderbolt, practicing in their initiatory rites unholy division of flesh, but the daughters of God, the fair lambs, who celebrate the holy rites of the Word, raising a sober choral dance. The righteous are the universe. The maidens strike the lyre, the angels praise, the prophets speak; the sound of music issues forth, they run and pursue the jubilant band; those that are called make haste, eagerly desiring to receive the Father.

Come also, O aged man, leaving Thebes and, casting away from you both divination and Bacchic frenzy, allow yourself to be led to the truth. I give the staff [of the cross] on which to lean. Haste Tiresias [the blind prophet]; believe, and you will see. Christ, by whom the eyes of the blind recover sight, will shed on you a light brighter than the sun; night will flee from you, fire will fear, death will be gone; you, old man, who did not see Thebes, shall see the heavens. O truly sacred mysteries! O stainless light! My way is lighted with torches, and I survey the heavens and God; I become holy while I am initiated. The Lord is the hierophant, and seals while illuminating him who is initiated, and presents to the Father him who believes, to be kept safe for ever. Such are the reveries of my mysteries. If it is your wish, be also initiated; and you shall join the choir along with angels around the begotten and indestructible and the only true God, the Word of God, raising the hymn with us. This Jesus, who is eternal, the one great high priest of the one God and of his Father, prays for and exhorts men.

"Hear, you myriad tribes [Christ now addresses the reader], rather whoever among men are endowed with reason, both barbarians and Greeks. I call on the whole race of men, whose Creator I am, by the will of the Father. Come to me, that you may be put in your due rank under the one God and the one Word of God; and do not only have the advantage of the irrational creatures in the possession of reason; for to you of all mortals I grant the enjoyment of immortality. For I want to impart to you this grace, bestowing on you the perfect boon of immortality; and I confer on you both the Word and knowledge of God, my complete self. This am I, this God wills, this is symphony, this the harmony of the Father, this is the Son, this is Christ, this the Word of God, the arm of the Lord, the power of the universe, the will of the Father; of which things there were images of old, but not all adequate. I desire to restore you according to the original model, that you become also like me. I anoint you with the unguent of faith, by which you throw off corruption, and show you the naked form of righteousness by which you ascend to God. 'Come to me, all you that labor and are heavy laden, and I will give you rest. Take my yoke upon you, and learn of me; for I am meek and lowly in heart: and you shall find rest to your souls. For my yoke is easy, and my burden light' " [Matt 11:28-30].

Let us haste, let us run, my fellow-men [here Clement resumes speaking]—we who are God-loving and God-like images of the Word. Let us haste, let us run, let us take his yoke, let us receive, to conduct us to immortality, the good charioteer of men. Let us love Christ. He led the colt with its parent; and having yoked the team of humanity to God, directs his chariot to immortality, hastening clearly to fulfill, by driving now into heaven, what he shadowed forth by riding into Jerusalem. A spectacle most beautiful to the Father is the eternal Son crowned with victory [Isa 63:1]. Let us aspire, then, after what is good; let us become God-loving men and obtain the greatest of all things which are incapable of being harmed—God and life. Our helper is the Word; let us put confidence in him; and never let us be visited with such a craving for silver and gold, and glory, as for the Word of truth himself. For it will not, it will not be pleasing to God himself if we value least those things which are worth most, and hold in the highest estimation the manifest enormities and the utter impiety of folly, and ignorance, and thoughtlessness, and idolatry. For not improperly the sons of the philosophers consider that the foolish are guilty of profanity and impiety in whatever they do; and describing ignorance itself as a species of madness, allege that the multitude are nothing but madmen. There is therefore no room to doubt, the Word will say, whether it is better to be sane or insane; but holding on to truth with our teeth, we must with all our might follow God, and in the exercise of wisdom regard all things to be, as they are, his; and besides, having learned that we are the most excellent of his possessions, let us commit ourselves to God, loving the Lord God, and regarding this as our business all our life long. And if what belongs to friends be reckoned common property, and man be the friend of God—for through meditation of the Word has he been made the friend of God—then accordingly all things become man's, because all things are God's, and the common property of both the friends, God and man.

It is time, then, for us to say that the pious Christian alone is rich and wise, and of noble birth, and thus call and believe him to be God's image, and also his likeness, having become righteous and holy and wise by Jesus Christ, and so far already like God. Accordingly this grace is indicated by the prophet, when he says, "I said that you are gods, and all sons of the Highest" [Ps 82:6]. For us, yes us, he has adopted, and wishes to be called the Father of us alone, not of the unbelieving. Such is then our position who are the attendants of Christ: "As are men's wishes, so are their words; as are their words, so are their deeds; and as their works, such is their life" [Matt 7:15-20]. Good is the whole life of those who have known Christ.

Enough words, though impelled by love to man, I might have gone on to pour out what I had from God, that I might exhort to what is the greatest of blessings—salvation. For discourses concerning the life which has no end are not readily brought to the end of their disclosures. To you still remains this conclusion, to choose which one will profit you most—judgment or grace. For I do not think there is even room for doubt which of these is the better; nor is it allowable to compare life with destruction.

Christ the Tutor

Clement's second work of the trilogy (ca. 190), *The Tutor (Paidagogos),* is addressed to those who heed the appeal and accept "true initiation." Primarily a manual of ethics, it is divided into three books. The first establishes his approach: Christ is the tutor *(paidagogos:* literally, "leader of children"), and the baptized are God's little ones, whom he treats by turns with severity and indulgence but always as a loving father. Books 1 and 2 deal in detail with what Clement regards as "right conduct." The critics to whom he responds are Gnostic Christians, who appear to have taxed their brethren on the subject of baptism, immaturity, and perfection as well as with questions about Christ's need for baptism. Clement is the earliest datable Christian writer to propose the baptism of Christ as the model for Christian baptism. Without doubt, however, he records a tradition that long antedated him (see General Introduction: "Baptism").

This second reading is drawn from Book 1, 6:25–28, and from Book 3, 12:101, the conclusion of the work, which contains a celebrated hymn to Christ, continuing a long tradition inaugurated in the later literature of the New Testament. Although Clementine in spirit, the hymn may have been added later, perhaps from the Alexandrian baptismal liturgy; whatever the case, it is redolent with the themes of baptismal catechesis.

The text is that of Henri Marrou and Marguerite Harl, eds., SC 70 (1960) 158–164; for the hymn, C. Mondésert, Ch. Matray, and H. I. Marrou, SC 158 (1970); the translation, Simon P. Wood, FC 23 (1954) 24–28, 275–278. See also the study of Annewies van der Brunt, "Milk and Honey in the Theology of Clement of Alexandria," in Hans Jörg Auf der Maur, and others, *Fides Sacramenti; Sacramentum Fidei: Studies in Honor of Peter Smulders* (Assen, Netherlands: van Gorcum, 1981).

Christ the Tutor 6:25–28

25. It is possible, too, for us to make a completely adequate answer to any carping critics [Gnostics]. We are children and little ones, but certainly not because the learning we acquire

is puerile or rudimentary, as those puffed up in their own knowledge falsely charged. On the contrary, when we were reborn, we straightway received the perfection for which we strive. For we were enlightened, that is, we came to the knowledge of God. Certainly, he who possesses knowledge of the perfect being is not imperfect.

But do not find fault with me for claiming that I have such knowledge of God. This claim was rightfully made by the Word, and he is outspoken. When the Lord was baptized, a voice loudly sounded from heaven, as a witness to him who was beloved: "You are my beloved Son; this day have I begotten you" [Matt 3:17; Ps 2:7, reading in Codex D].

Now let us ask the wise: on that day when Christ was reborn, was he already perfect, or—a very foolish question—was he defective? If this last, then he needed to add to his knowledge. But, since he is God, it is not likely that he learned even one thing more. No one can be greater than the Word, nor can anyone teach him who is the one only teacher. Are they unwilling, then, to admit that the Word, perfect son born of a perfect Father, was perfectly reborn, as a prefiguration of the divine plan? But if he is perfect, then why was one already perfect baptized?

It was necessary, they tell us, that the commandment given to men might be fulfilled. Very good, I reply. But was he, by that baptism conferred through John, made perfect? It is clear that he was. But not by learning anything more? No indeed.

It is then, that he was made perfect only in the sense of being washed, and that he was consecrated by the descent of the Holy Spirit? Yes, that is the true explanation.

26. This is what happens with us, whose model the Lord made himself. When we are baptized, we are enlightened; being enlightened, we become adopted sons [see Gal 4:5]; becoming adopted sons, we are made perfect; and becoming perfect, we are made divine. "I have said," it is written, "you are gods and all the sons of the most High" [Ps 81:6].

This ceremony is often called "free gift" [Rom 5:2, 15; 7:24], "enlightenment" [Heb 6:4; 10:32], "perfection" [Jas 1:7; Heb 7:11], and "cleansing" [Titus 3:5; Eph 5:26]—"cleansing," because through it we are completely purified of our sins; "free gift," because by it punishments due to our sins are remitted; "enlightenment," since by it we behold the wonderful holy light of salvation, that is, it enables us to see God clearly; finally, we call it "perfection" as needing nothing further, for what more does he need who possesses the knowledge of God? It would indeed be out of place to call something that was not fully perfect a gift of God. He is perfect; therefore, the gifts he bestows are also perfect. Just as at his command all things came into existence, so, on his mere desire to give, there immediately arises an overflowing measure of his gifts. What is yet to come, his will alone has already anticipated.

Moreover, release from evil is only the beginning of salvation.

27. Only those who have first reached the end of life, therefore, we can call already perfect. But we live, we who have even now been freed from commerce with death. Salvation is the following of Christ. "What was made in him is life" [John 1:3]. "Amen, amen," he tells us, "I say to you, he who hears my word and believes him who sent me has life everlasting and does not come to judgment, but has passed from death to life" [John 5:24]. The very fact that we believe in him and are reborn is perfection of life. For God is by no means powerless. As his will is creation, and is called the universe, so his desire is the salvation of men [see 1 Thess 4:3], and is called the church. He knows whom he has called; and whom he has called he has saved. He has called and at the same time saved [see Rom 8:30]. "Now you yourselves," the apostle says, "are taught of God" [1 Thess 4:9]. It is not right, then, for us to consider imperfect the teaching that is given by him. That teaching is the immortal salvation that comes through the immortal Savior, to whom be thanksgiving forever. Amen.

Even though a man receive nothing more than this rebirth, still, because he is by that fact enlightened, he is straightway rid of darkness, as the name itself suggests, and automatically receives light.

28. It is just like men who shake off sleep and then are wide-awake interiorly; or, better, like those suffering from some blinding eye-disease who meanwhile receive no light from the outside and have none themselves, but must first remove the impediment from their eyes before they can have clear vision. In the same way, those who are baptized are cleansed of the sins which like a mist overcloud their divine spirit and then acquire a spiritual sight which is clear and unimpeded and lightsome, the sort of sight which alone enables us to behold divinity, with the help of the Holy Spirit who is poured forth from heaven upon us. This is an admixture of eternal sunlight, giving us the power to see the eternal light. Like indeed attracts like; so it is that what is holy attracts him who is the source of holiness,

who properly speaking is called Light. "For you once were darkness, but now light in the Lord" [Eph 2:8]. That is why, I believe, the ancients once called man by a name that means light.

But, they object, man has not yet received the gift of perfection. I agree with them, except that I insist he is already in the light and that darkness does not overtake him [John 1:15]. There is nothing at all in between light and darkness. Perfection lies ahead, in the resurrection of the faithful, but it consists in obtaining the promise which has already been given to us. We say emphatically that both of these things cannot co-exist at the same time: arrival at the goal and the anticipation of that arrival by the mind. Eternity and time are not the same thing, nor are the beginning and the completion. They cannot be. But both are concerned about the same thing, and there is only one person involved in both. Faith, for example, begotten in time, is the starting point, if we may use the term, while the completion is the possession of the promise, made enduring for all eternity.

Hymn to Christ 3:12

Bridle-bit of colts untamed,
Thou Wing of birds not straying,
Firm Rudder of our ships at sea,
Thou Shepherd of God's regal sheep.

Thy simple children
Gather round Thee;
They would sing holily,
They would hymn truthfully,
With lips ne'er stained,
To Thee, O Christ, their Guide.
O Thou King of saints,
Word of Father on high,
Thou Governor of all things,
Ruling e'er wisely,
Balm for all labors,
Source of endless joy,
Jesus, Holy Savior
Of men who cry to Thee;
Thou Shepherd, Thou Husbandman,
Thou Rudder, Thou Bridle-bit,
O Wing, heaven leading
The flock of innocence;

Fisher of men
Drawn safely in
From ocean of sin;
Snaring to spotless life;
Fish unstained by
Sea of hostile foe;
O all-hallowed Shepherd,
Guide us, Thy children,
Guide Thy sheep safely, O King!

The footsteps of Christ
Are pathway to heaven,
Of ages unbounded,
Everlasting Word,
Light of eternity,
Well-spring of Mercy,
Who virtue instills
In hearts offering God
The gift of their reverence,
O Jesus, our Christ!
Milk of the bride,
Given of heaven,
Pressed from sweet breasts—
Gifts of Thy wisdom—
These Thy little ones
Draw for their nourishment;
With infancy's lips
Filling their souls
With spiritual savor
From breasts of the Word.

Let us all sing
To Christ, our King,
Songs of sweet innocence,
Hymns of bright purity,
Hallowed gratefulness
For teachings of life;
Let us praise gladsomely
So mighty a Child.

Let us, born of Christ,
Chant out in unison,
Loud chorus of peace,
We, undefiled, pure flock,
To God, Lord of peace.

Carpets

Clement's third work of the trilogy, *Stromata (Carpets)*, was composed for those who had achieved the promise of their baptism: perfection or maturity *(teleios)*. In the work he draws heavily on the Platonic and Stoic philosophy of the period and seeks to justify the study of Greek philosophy, to establish the superiority of the Bible, to refute Gnostic Christians (Theodotus), and to hand on to posterity what he considers the "secret tradition of true knowledge" *(gnosis)*.

But Clement also considers the work a memory aid for his old age. Early in the first chapter (1:10–18) he speaks about his journey to faith and baptism. His remembrance and reflections constitute this third reading. The "blessed and truly remarkable men" who preserved the apostolic tradition of "blessed doctrine" were celebrated Catholic Christian teachers who helped in his quest and in his preparation for baptism. Pantaenus appears to have been his "catechetical" master as he himself was to become for others.

The text is that of Claude Mondésert and Marcel Caster, eds., SC 30 (1951) 50–57; the translation is adapted from A. Cleveland Coxe, ANF 2 (1977 reprint) 301–303. A recent study is S. R. C. Lilla, *Clement of Alexandria: A Study in Christian Platonism and Gnosticism* (New York: Oxford University Press, 1972).

Carpets (Stromata) 1:10–18

Now Scripture kindles the living spark of the soul, and directs the eye suitably to contemplation; perhaps inserting something, as the husbandman when he engrafts, but, according to the opinion of the divine apostle, exciting what is in the soul. "For there are certainly among us many weak and sickly. . . ." This work of mine in writing is not artfully constructed for display; but my memoranda are stored up against old age, as a remedy against forgetfulness, truly an image and outline of those vigorous and animated discourses which I was privileged to hear, and of blessed and truly remarkable men.

Of these the one, in Greece, an Ionic [Tatian?]; the other in Magna Graecia: the first of these from Coele-Syria, the second from Egypt, and others in the East. The one was born in the land of Assyria, and the other a Hebrew in Palestine. When I came upon this last one (he was first in power), having tracked him down concealed in Egypt, I found rest. He [Pantaenus], the true, the Sicilian bee, gathering the spoil of the flowers from the prophetic and apostolic meadow, engendered in the souls of his hearers a deathless element of knowledge.

Preserving the tradition of the blessed doctrine derived directly from the holy apostles, Peter, James, John, and Paul—the sons receiving it from the father (but few were like the fathers)—they came by God's will to us also to deposit those ancestral and apostolic seeds. And well I know that they will rejoice; I do not mean delighted with this tribute, but solely on account of the preservation of the truth, as they delivered it. For such a sketch as this, will, I think, be agreeable to a soul desirous of preserving from escape the blessed tradition. . . .

The writing of these memoranda of mine, I well know, is weak when compared with that spirit full of grace, which I was privileged to hear. . . .

Our book will not shrink from making use of what is best in philosophy and other preparatory instruction. "For not only for the Hebrews and those that are under the law," according to the apostle, "it is right to become a Jew, but also a Greek for the sake of the Greeks, that we may gain all" [1 Cor 9:20-21]. Also in the Epistle to the Colossians he writes, "Admonishing every man, and teaching every man in all wisdom, that we may present every man perfect in Christ" [Col 1:7-8]. The nicety of speculation, too, suits the sketch presented in my commentaries. In this respect the resources of learning are like a relish mixed with the food of an athlete, who is not indulging in luxury, but entertains a noble desire for distinction.

Origen

Born toward the end of the second century in Alexandria, Origen was the eldest son in a large family. His parents were serious and well-off Christians who valued education and saw to it that their eldest son received the best that they and the empire's cultural capital had to offer. The same persecution that drove Clement from the city (203 c.e.) claimed the life of Origen's father and forever changed his own. By the time persecution struck, Origen, although quite young, was a teacher of grammar, well enough known that pagans interested in Christianity sought him out for instruction, at least now that Clement was gone. Indeed, as a result of the persecution he seems to have become the principal Christian teacher in Alexandria almost by default.

When the persecution subsided, Bishop Demetrius felt pressed to consolidate the Alexandrian Church and to bring catechetical instruction under closer control. As a result, he recognized Origen as head of the catechetical school. Serving in the post for over two decades, Origen brought to the school the form, content, and rigor of his own Hellenistic education, established the study and interpretation of the Bible as its ultimate mission, inaugurated an advanced as well as a beginner's course, and set the school on a path that brought Christianity squarely into the Greco-Roman cultural and intellectual world.

As a result of a rift with Demetrius, however, Origen left the city about 230, at the height of his career. By 233 he had settled at Caesarea in Palestine, where he was ordained a presbyter. He redesigned the catechetical school there along Alexandrian lines, including in its curriculum the study of logic, physics, geometry, astronomy, and philosophy as the necessary preparation for the study of Scripture.

In time, however, Origen found himself estranged from his friend Theoctistus, the bishop of Caesarea. He migrated to Athens, where he spent several years, returning to Caesarea in 246 or 247 only to find himself again embroiled in difficulties stemming from Alexandria. The events of imperial Roman history, however, overtook him. In 249 an Illyrian general, Decius, overthrew the emperor Philip, who was partial to Christians, and instituted the first empire-wide attempt to root out Christianity. Origen was arrested, imprisoned, and tortured. Released broken in body, he died about 253.

Origen's literary legacy touched nearly every discipline of life and thought in the Church, from asceticism to speculative theology. He wrote the first philosophically sophisticated presentation of Christian belief *(On First Principles)*, established the intellectual dominance of Catholic over Gnostic Christianity, was unrivaled as a Christian textual and literary critic, and stands as the architect of Eastern Christian theology. His distinctive legacy, however, rests on his work as an interpreter of the Bible, which in turn sprang from his contemplation of what he considered the "divine mysteries" revealed in the Bible. Indeed, he seems to have commented on all its books. As a result of the sheer volume of his work, however, coupled with the controversies that have swirled around his head in both life and death, most of his biblical legacy has been lost. Although fragments of the original Greek are extant, what remains exists largely in the Latin translations of Rufinus of Aquileia and Jerome.

Origen approached the Bible as one steeped in Alexandrian literary tradition, both Greek and Jewish, which regarded the Greek classics and the Hebrew Bible in their literal composition as suffused with "mystery." Thus understood and interpreted typologically and allegorically (see General Introduction: "The Bible and the Baptismal Liturgy"; also see vol. 5, ch. 1), they were permanently applicable to the present. In the biblical texts, therefore, Origen seeks to discover and disclose their deeper and enduringly applicable meaning. His vantage point is that the events, people, and even the words of the Hebrew Bible are lenses through which one can see God's Word (Christ, the Logos) and the Holy Spirit at work instructing the Church and the Christian about God's mysteries and summoning both to fulfillment and completion. Indeed, he regards what happened to the Israelites and to Christ as happening "today" (see below, *Joshua* 4:4). As a result, the waters of the Red Sea, the Jordan, and baptism converge. The escape from Egypt, the conquest of the Promised Land, and the struggle of Christian life are stages in a single process that endures.

Nowhere is Origen's vision of the Bible richer than in his biblical homilies, from which the readings are drawn. Although they were largely preached at Caesarea in the six-year period between 238 and 244, the city's Christian community was dominated by Alexandrian Christianity. As a result, his Caesarean work is treated for the purposes of classification as Alexandrian rather than West Syrian.

The setting of the homilies envisions two kinds of liturgical assembly. The first was daily, except for Sunday, and consisted in a chanted reading (fairly long) from a book of the Hebrew Bible, together with a homily on the text. The second setting was the Eucharist, held on Sunday morning and Wednesday and Friday evenings. The reading was from the New Testament. The homilies on the books of Exodus and Joshua (below) were preached in the non-Eucharistic assembly; and those on Luke's Gospel (below), during the Eucharist. Both the faithful and the catechumens made up the congregation, with the former often primarily in view. As for the readings, they were on a three-year cycle; doubtless, the catechumens heard the entire Bible read and commented on prior to baptism.

The richness and complexity of Origen's view of baptism can be gained only by reading him. However, one needs to keep in mind that he speaks as a pastor with both the faithful and catechumens gathered before him. Initiation and advance into the "mysteries of God" is his aim. In the readings, baptism is the indispensable first stage in the journey to God. To be sure, baptism purifies, regenerates, initiates one into Christ, and endows with the Holy Spirit. But as the *Homilies on Exodus* and the *Homilies on Joshua* make clear, baptism and its preparations are the fledgling stage of a long and dangerous journey. In the *Homilies on St. Luke*, "water" baptism opens out onto three other baptisms: (1) the baptism of the Holy Spirit, which testifies to the acquisition of the state of blessedness; (2) the baptism of fire, a remedial chastisement for those who fail to achieve blessedness by life's end (the medievals will call it "purgatory"); and (3) the baptism of blood (martyrdom), which transcends all other baptisms. Origen addresses himself to the question of infant baptism, which he justifies theologically because of the fall of humankind. Nonetheless, whenever received, he sees baptism first and foremost as a stage in the journey in search of God.

The baptismal liturgy on which he comments is difficult to reconstruct in detail because, like the text of Scripture, he treats the rites as a series of allegories about the Christian journey to saving blessedness. There is reason to believe that Caesarean baptismal custom differed little from Alexandrian. The solemn day for baptism was Easter. In addition to regular oral instruction largely on the Bible, which seems to have lasted about three years, exorcism was a prominent feature of baptismal preparation. It reached a crescendo in the renunciation of Satan, followed by the blessing of water and oil, immersion in the baptismal pool coupled with a Trinitarian baptismal formula based on the Alexandrian or Caesarean creed, postbaptismal anointing, vesting in a white garment, the use of the baptismal candle, and a procession to the Eucharist.

Suggested Reading

Blanc, Cecile. "Le baptême d'après Origêne," SP 9, 2 (1972) 113–124.

Trigg, Joseph W. *Origen: The Bible and Philosophy in the Third-Century Church,* Atlanta: John Knox, 1983.

Homilies on Exodus

The first reading is from the *Homilies on Exodus*—an excerpt from the fifth homily. The text is that of Marcel Borret, SC 321 (1985), Rufinus' Latin text; the translation (abridged) is that of Ronald E. Heine, FC 71 (1981) 275-284. The homilies were delivered about 240, probably shortly before Easter baptism. Origen here comments on Exodus 12-14, which recounts the Israelites' journey out of Egypt and which he sees as a type of the Christian journey that begins with the catechumenate. In the homily he emerges as the first Catholic Christian writer to propose the Pauline doctrine of baptism as death and resurrection with Christ (a doctrine that appears to have been a favorite of Alexandrian Gnostics). Thus, he calls baptism the "mystery of the third day."

On the Book of Exodus, Homily 5:1-2

1. The apostle Paul, "teacher of the Gentiles in faith and truth" [1 Tim 2:7] taught the church which he gathered from the Gentiles how it ought to interpret the books of the Law. These books were received from others and were formerly unknown to the Gentiles and were very strange. He feared that the church, receiving foreign instructions and not knowing the principle of the instructions, would be in a state of confusion about the foreign document. For that reason he gives some examples of interpretation that we also might note similar things in other passages. . . .

Let us see, then, what sort of rule of interpretation the apostle Paul taught us about these matters. Writing to the Corinthians he says in a certain passage, "For we know that our fathers were all under the cloud, and were all baptized in Moses in the cloud and in the sea, and all ate the same spiritual food, and all drank the same spiritual drink. And they drank the spiritual rock which followed them, and the rock was Christ" [see 1 Cor 10:1-4]. Do you see how much Paul's teaching differs from the literal meaning? What the Jews supposed to be a crossing of the sea, Paul calls a baptism; what they supposed to be a cloud, Paul asserts is the Holy Spirit. He wishes that to be understood in a similar manner to this which the Lord taught in the gospels, "Unless a man be born again of the water and the Holy Spirit he cannot enter the kingdom of heaven" [John 3:5]. And again, the manna which the Jews supposed to be food for the stomach and the satiation of the appetite, Paul calls "spiritual food" [1 Cor 10:3]. And not only Paul, but the Lord also says on the same subject in the gospel: "Your fathers ate manna in the desert and died. He, however, who eats the bread which I give him will not die forever" [John 6:49-50]. And after this he says, "I am the bread which came down from heaven" [John 6:51]. Then again Paul declares plainly of "the rock which followed them," "the rock was Christ" [1 Cor 10:4].

What then are we to do who received such instructions about interpretation from Paul, a teacher of the church? Does it not seem right that we apply this kind of rule which was delivered to us in a similar way in other passages? [Origen then proceeds to apply the rule to Exod 12-14].

2. The children of Israel "departed," the text says, "from Ramesse and came to Socoth. And they departed from Socoth and came to Etham" [Exod 12:37; 13:20]. If there is anyone who is about to depart from Egypt [i.e., a catechumen], if there is anyone who desires to forsake the dark deeds of this world and the darkness of errors, he must first of all depart "from Ramesse." "Ramesse" means "the commotion of a moth." Depart from Ramesse, therefore, if you wish to come to this that the Lord may be your leader and precede you "in the column of the cloud" [Exod 13:21] and "the rock" may follow you [1 Cor 10:3-4], which offers you "spiritual food" and "spiritual drink" no less. Nor should you store treasure "there where the moth destroys and thieves dig through and steal" [Matt 6:20]. This is what the Lord says clearly in the gospels: "If you wish to be perfect, sell all your possessions and give to the poor, and you will have treasure in heaven: and come follow me" [Matt 19:21]. This, therefore, is to depart "from Ramesse" and follow Christ [Exod 12:37]. Let us see, however, what the campsites may be to which one goes "from Ramesse."

"They came," the text says, "to Socoth." The etymologists teach that "Socoth" is understood as "tents" among the Hebrews. When, therefore, leaving Egypt, you have dispelled the moths of all corruption from yourself and have cast aside the inducements of vices, you will dwell in tents. For we dwell in tents of which "we do not wish to be unclothed but to be further clothed" [2 Cor 5:4]. Dwelling in tents, however, indicates that he who hastens to God is free and has no impediments. But departure is urged lest there be a stopping in this place. The camp must also be moved "from Socoth." One must hasten to go "to Etham."

"Etham," they say, is translated in our language as "signs for them," and rightly so, for here you will hear it said: "God was preceding them by day in a column of cloud and by night in a column of fire" [Exod 13:21]. You do not find this done at Ramesse nor at Socoth, which is called the second encampment for those departing. It is the third encampment [i.e., Etham] in which divine signs occur. Recollect what was read above when Moses said to Pharaoh, "We will go a journey of three days in the wilderness and sacrifice to the Lord our God" [Exod 5:3]. This was the three days to which Moses was hastening and Pharaoh was opposing, for he said, "You shall not go far" [Exod 8:28; LXX 8:24]. Pharaoh would not permit the children of Israel to reach the place of signs; he would not permit them to advance so far that they could enjoy fully the mysteries of the third day. Hear what the prophet says: "God will revive us after two days, and on the third day we will arise and live in his sight" [Hos 6:2]. The first day is the passion of the Savior for us. The second day on which he descended into hell. The third day is the day of the resurrection. Therefore, on the third day "God went before them, by day in a column of cloud, by night in a column of fire" [Exod 13:21]. But if according to what we said above, the apostle teaches us rightly that the mysteries of baptism are contained in these words, it is necessary that "those who are baptized in Christ are baptized in his death and are buried with him," also arise from the dead with him on the third day [Rom 6:3-4] whom also, according to what the apostle says, "He raised up together with him and at the same time made them sit in the heavenly places" [Eph 2:6]. When, therefore, you shall have undertaken the mystery of the third day, God will begin to lead you and will himself show you the way of salvation.

Homilies on Joshua

The second reading is from the *Homilies on Joshua;* the text is that of Annie Jaubert, SC 71 (1960), Rufinus' Latin text. The work also dates from about 240, and the selected homily scrutinizes baptism through the lenses of both the Exodus and crossing the Jordan. Indeed, in the first homily, Origen is at pains to show that the names Joshua and Jesus are etymologically the same and that the Jordan is identical for both events. Although

Clement (above) had already developed Christ's baptism in the Jordan as the model for Christian baptism, Origen is the first to develop the Joshua story as a type of baptism and subsequent Christian life: The Israelite journey to the Promised Land under Joshua is renewed in the Christian journey to salvation under Christ. In Origen's allegorizing hands, however, it has something of the free association of a kaleidoscope.

Crossing the Jordan, Homily 4

1. As is written about the Egyptians [see Exod 14:22-29], every creature is hostile: the land fought them, the river fought them, the very air fought them, the heavens fought them. For the just, however, these very things which seem beyond endurance are done smoothly and with ease. The just man crossed the Red Sea as though it were dry; the Egyptian, however, who wished to cross, is drowned, nor does the water become for him a wall to his right and left. But even if the just man should enter the terrifying and trackless desert, he is served with food from heaven [see Ps 77 (78):24].

And so it was at the Jordan. The Ark of the Covenant led God's people. The priests and Levites halted, and the waters, as if offering a certain reverence to God's ministers, held back their flow and banked themselves, assuring God's people a safe road across.

Do not be astonished, because these things done for your predecessors are repeated for you. Indeed, for you, O Christians, who have crossed the rushing Jordan through the mystery of baptism, the divine word promises better and higher things—a way and crossing is promised to you through the air itself. Hear what Paul says about the just: "We will be caught up in the clouds to meet Christ in the air, and so we will always be with the Lord" [1 Thess 4:17]. The just man has nothing at all to fear; all creatures serve him. Attend, then, to what God promised through the prophet: "If you walk through fire, its flame will not sear you, because I am the Lord your God" [Isa 43:2]. Every place receives the just man, and every creature shows him the proper attention.

Lest you think that the acts performed in early times have no effect on you who are just now hearing them, they are accomplished in you in mystery. For you, for instance, who have just recently left idolatry's darkness and want to draw near to hear the Law of God, you are leaving Egypt for the first time.

When you joined the company of catechumens and have begun to observe the precepts of the church, you crossed the Red Sea. And now, in place of the daily stops in the desert, you are free to hear the Law of God and to gaze at the face of Moses, through which the glory of the Lord is revealed. If you then come to the mystical font of baptism and, standing in the midst of the priests and Levites, you are initiated into those venerable and expansive mysteries, known only to those for whom it is lawful, then, on crossing the Jordan, thanks to the ministry of priests, you too will enter the Promised Land. There Jesus, in Moses' place, receives you, and he himself becomes for you the leader of the new journey.

Mindful of these things and also of the great power of God that divided the sea for you and stopped the river's flow, attend to them and ask, "Why, Sea, have you fled? And you, Jordan, why have you turned back on yourself? Mountains, why do you leap like rams, and Hills, why do you cavort like lambs?" [Ps 113 (114):5-8]. The divine word will answer you, saying, "The earth quakes before the face of the God of Jacob, who turns the rock into a pool of water and the cliff into a fountain" [ibid.].

2. What marvels have been done! The Red Sea has been crossed dryshod, manna is given from heaven, fountains have sprung up in the desert, the Law is given to Moses, many signs and wonders are performed in the desert, and yet nowhere is the "Exalted One" said to be Jesus. But where the crossing of the Jordan is described, these words are addressed to Jesus: "Today I begin to exalt you before your people" [Josh 3:7]. Jesus is not, then, exalted before baptism; rather his own exaltation and his exaltation before the people starts at the moment [of baptism]. Now, if "all, who are baptized in Christ Jesus, are baptized into his death" [Rom 6:3], and moreover, the death of Jesus is complete only by his exaltation on the cross, then it is fitting that the exaltation of Jesus for each of the faithful happen at the moment when he or she accomplishes the mystery of baptism. Thus, it is written that "God exalts him and gives him a name, which is above every name, so that every knee bends at the name of Jesus, whether in heaven or on earth or under the earth" [Phil 2:9-10].

Notwithstanding, the people are led by the priests, and the journey to the Promised Land is accomplished under the guidance of the priests. But who among the priests is of such caliber that he is worthy to be inscribed among the clergy? If there is one, the currents of the Jordan will halt for him, and even the very elements will hold him in awe. Part of the river water will spring back on itself and then hold back, but part will flee by flowing swiftly into the Salt [Dead] Sea.

Nonetheless, I judge that what is written, namely, that part of the Jordan's waters flows into the sea and runs on in bitterness, and part retains its sweetness, is not to be understood save in a mystical interpretation. For if all the baptized preserved the sweetness that comes from heavenly grace and no one turned to sin's bitterness, surely the text would not have said that part of the river emptied into the turbulent Salt Sea. The words, so it seems to me, indicate the difference among the baptized, one—I recall with sadness—we often see happen among those who attain to holy baptism. They give themselves back to worldly affairs and lawless lusts and taste the salty drink of avarice. These are those found in the part of the waters which flow into the sea and perish in the salty breakers. The part of the waters, however, which remains in place and preserves its sweetness, stands for those who have received the gift of God and have held firm. Properly speaking, these are the waters which stand as one and are saved, because one also is the bread "that came down from heaven and gave his life for this world" [John 6:33], and "one is the faith, and one the baptism, and one the Spirit" [Eph 4:4-6], of which all drink in baptism, and "one God, father of all" [ibid.].

Meanwhile, the priests and also the Levites are there, who show the way to the people that have left Egypt. They are the ones who teach the people how to flee Egypt [that is, the deceptions of this world], to journey across the trackless desert, to avoid the fangs of the serpents, to hasten past the different kinds of temptation [which are the bites of the demons], and to shun the venom of evil suggestions. If, by chance, someone in the desert is bitten by a serpent and they show him the bronze serpent suspended on the cross [Num 21:6], he who looks on him, that is, whoever believes in the one symbolized by the serpent, he will escape the diabolic venom by doing so.

The priests and Levites are there, standing by the Ark of the Covenant of the Lord, in which the Law of God is carried [Josh 3:4], doubtless, so that they may enlighten the people about God's commandments, as the prophet says, "May your word be a lamp for my feet, Lord, and a light for my paths" [Ps 118 (119):105]. This light flames up through the priests and Levites. But if, by chance, one of them "has put his lamp under a full-measure basket" and not "on a lampstand, so that it lights the way for all who are in the house" [Matt 5:15], let him beware of what must happen to him, when he begins to explain to the Lord of light why those who, deprived of light from the priests, walk in darkness and are sightless due to blinding by sins.

3. Consider, finally, the text, "Let the people stand at a distance of two thousand cubits from the Ark of the Covenant" [Josh 3:6]. But the priests and next to them the Levites stand near enough that they can carry the Ark of the Lord and the divine legislation on their shoulders. Blessed are those who are worthy to stand next to God. But remember what is written: "He who draws near me draws near the fire" [*Gospel of Thomas,* logion 82; cf. Mark 12:34]. If you are gold or silver draw near the fire, you will shine with more splendor and a deeper golden hue. But if you are guilty of having built on the foundation of your faith with "wood, hay, or stubble" [1 Cor 3:12], when you draw near the fire with such a building, you will be consumed. Blessed, therefore, are those who are near, rather, so near that the fire enlightens rather than ignites them. Nevertheless, Israel will also be saved but from afar, and makes its way not under its own power but with the support and guidance of the priests.

4. When, however, did the people cross the Jordan? I have noted that the date is not given by mere chance but to underscore time. "The tenth day," it says, "of the first month" [Josh 4:19]. This is the very day on which the people in Egypt anticipated the mystery of the lamb [see Exod 12:3]. On the tenth day of the first month they celebrated the mystery in Egypt [i.e., Passover]; on the tenth day of the first month they entered the Promised Land. What seems particularly appropriate to me is that on the very day when someone escapes deception one also enters the Promised Land—that is, while we are still living in this world. This one day stands for our whole life. And so, by the mystery [of the tenth day] we are clearly instructed not to put off until tomorrow our acts and works of justice, but "today"—that is, while we are still alive and linger in this world, let us hasten to fulfill all that pertains to perfection. And so, on the tenth day of the first month we can finally enter into the Promised Land, in short, the blessedness of perfection.

. . . For after the hardships and temptations that we have endured in the desert of this world, after crossing the Red Sea, after passing over the rushing Jordan, if we have shown ourselves worthy to enter the Promised Land, we will reach it with triumphant joy by following the priests of Christ, the Lord and our Savior, "to whom is glory and power forever and ever. Amen" [1 Pet 4:11].

Homilies on St. Luke

The third reading comprises five homilies from the *Homilies on St. Luke* (14, 21, 22, 24, and 27). They have in view primarily those catechumens considered ready for baptism (competents) and therefore able to hear the Gospels. The text is that of Henri Crouzel, and others, SC 87 (1962), Jerome's Latin text. Although from the same period, the homilies were delivered later in the Lectionary cycle.

Homily 14

On the text, "When, however, the day for his circumcision had arrived," up to the place where it says, "a pair of turtledoves and two young pigeons" [Luke 2:21-24].

[In this homily Origen sees baptism as replacing circumcision, suggests that Jesus' baptism was necessary because of the defilement inherent in flesh, and then addresses himself to the reason for infant baptism.]

1. Christ, "in his death, is dead to sin" [Rom 6:10]; it is not that he has sinned, "because he has committed no fault and no deceit has been found in his mouth" [1 Pet 2:22]; but he died that, by his dying to sin, we who are subject to death, never again need live in sin and vice. Thus it is written: "If we have died with him, we also will live with him" [Rom 6:8]. In the same place it is written: "If we have been buried with him, we will also live with him." Just as, therefore, "we have been buried with him" by his death and have also risen with him by his resurrection, so also we have been circumcised with him and, after circumcision, cleansed by solemn purification. As a result, we have no need whatsoever for physical circumcision. So that you may know how it happens that we have been circumcised, hear Paul who clearly proclaims: "In whom [Christ] dwells the entire fullness of divinity bodily," he says, "and in him you have been filled, who is head of every principality and power. In him you also have been circumcised, but not physically as in the excision of flesh. Such is Christ's circumcision. We have been buried with him in baptism, in whom we have also risen through faith in the action of God, who raised him from the dead" [Col 2:9-12]. And thus it is that his death and resurrection and circumcision have been accomplished for us.

2. "When the day for circumcising the boy had arrived," the text says, "his name was called Jesus, the name given him by the angel before he was conceived." The glorious name Jesus, most worthy of all adoration and worship—"a name which is above every name" [Phil 2:9]—was not fittingly used first by men nor by earth-bound creatures, but by certain greater and more excellent beings. Thus, the evangelist expressly added, "And his name was called Jesus, the name given him by the angel before he was conceived in the womb."

3. The text continues: "When the day for their purification had arrived, they brought him to Jerusalem, as the Mosaic Law required." The text says that it was for "their" purification. Whose? If the text read, "for her purification," that is Mary's, who had given birth, no question would come up, and we would say straight out that Mary, as a human being, needed purification after giving birth. But since the text says "the day of their purification," it does not seem to refer to one person but to two or to many. Was Jesus, therefore, in need of purification, was he unclean and polluted by some impurity? Consider what is written in the Book of Job: "No one is free from defilement, even if his life lasted for only one day" [Job 14:4]. It does not say, "No one is free from sin," but, "No one is free from defilement." For defilement is not the same thing as sin; that you may know defilements designate one thing and sin another, Isaiah clearly teaches: "The Lord will wash away the defilement of the sons and daughters of Sion, and cleanse the blood from their midst—the defilement, by the spirit of judgment and the blood, by the spirit of fire" [Isa 4:4].

4. Every soul that has put on a human body has its defilements. Moreover, so that you might know that Jesus acquired defilement by his own choice, because he assumed a human body for our salvation, attend carefully to Zacharias the prophet, when he says: "Jesus was dressed in defiled clothes" [Zach 3:3]. This saying is directed against those who [Gnostics] deny that our Lord had a human body, asserting that it was made of celestial or spiritual components. For if, they falsely assert, his body was composed of the celestial and astral and of certain other more sublime and spiritual elements, they must explain how this spiritual body can be defiled, or how to interpret the text we have cited, "Jesus was dressed in defiled clothes." Moreover, if they are constrained to accept spiritual body as the meaning of defiled clothing, they ought to say that the contents of the

promises are fulfilled, namely, "What is sown as an animal body rises as a spiritual body" [1 Cor 15:44], and that we rise polluted and defiled. To think that, however, is offensive, especially when one comes upon the following text: "What is sown in corruption will rise imperishable; what is sown in humiliation, will rise in glory; what is sown in weakness, will rise in strength" [1 Cor 15:42-44].

5. On behalf of our Lord and Savior, who was dressed in defiled clothing and had assumed an earthly body, it was necessary that there be offered those things which purify from defilements as prescribed by the Law.

At this point, I take advantage of the occasion to treat a question which our brothers frequently ask among themselves: whether infants are baptized "for the remission of sins" [Acts 2:38]. Whose sins? When did they sin? How can one defend the reason for infant baptism, if one does not accept the interpretation about which we spoke a little while ago? "No one is free from defilement, even if his life on this earth lasts only a day" [Job 14:4]. Because the defilements of birth are removed through the sacrament of baptism, even infants are baptized: For "unless you have been born again from water and the spirit, you will not enter into the kingdom of heaven" [John 3:5].

6. "When," Luke says, "the day of their purification had arrived," the words also have a mystical interpretation. The soul is not purified immediately upon an infant's birth, nor on the day of its birth can it achieve perfection. For thus is it written in the Law: "If a mother bears a male, she will sit for seven days in the unclean blood and then for thirty-three in pure blood, at the end of which she and the infant will sit in wholly purified blood" [Lev 12:2-4]. Because "the Law is spiritual" [Rom 7:14] and "the shadow of the good things to come" [Heb 10:1], we are able to understand that our true purgation happens after the passage of time. I think that even after the resurrection from the dead we will need a sacrament to wash and purify. For no one can rise free from defilements, nor can any soul be found instantly free from all vices. Thus, in baptismal rebirth a mystery is accomplished, namely, that just as Jesus is purified by an offering, according to the economy of the incarnation, so also we are purified by spiritual rebirth. . . .

[Origen continues his commentary, focusing on the significance of the Law's prescriptions for purification after birth, Jesus' virginal conception and birth, and the offering of the pair of turtle-doves and two pigeons. He concludes:]

10. Perhaps, I seem to bring to the text something new and not equal to the majesty of the subject. But if the birth of the Savior, because it was from a virgin rather than from the encounter of a man and woman, were new, then the pair of turtle-doves and the two young pigeons were not like those we see with bodily eyes. Rather, they represent the Holy Spirit, who "descended in the form of a dove and came" [Luke 3:21-22] upon the Savior during his baptism in the Jordan. So also the pair of turtle-doves: they were not those that fly through the air; but a certain divine presence [the majesty that undergirds human contemplation] appeared under the form of pigeons and turtle-doves. Thus, he who was born and had to suffer for the whole world was not purified before God by the kind of victims used to purify all men; rather, as his dispensation made all things new, so he had new victims as willed by Almighty God in Christ Jesus: "to whom is glory and rule forever and ever" [1 Pet 4:11].

Homily 21

On the text: "The fifteenth year of the reign of Tiberias," to the place where it says: "Make straight his paths" [Luke 3:1-4].

[In this homily Origen has primarily in view those catechumens actively preparing for baptism. Concentrating on the "mystical" meaning of John the Baptist's baptism, he directs himself to the preparation of the heart (the "desert") for baptism and, in the process, presents a remarkable vision of the boundless ability of the human heart. In the first two paragraphs Origen directs the hearer's attention to the fact that John the Baptist's message is addressed to Gentiles and Jews "in the desert." He then discusses the hidden meaning of "desert."]

3. At the same time note that the meaning is richer, if one takes "desert" in a mystical sense rather than literally. For he who preaches "in the desert" cries out in vain when there is no one to hear him speaking. Thus, the precursor of Christ, the "voice crying out in the desert," preaches "in the desert" of the soul, which knows no peace. Now as then, he comes first as a "lamp burning brightly" [John 5:35] and preaches "a baptism of repentance for the forgiveness of sins." After "the lamp" itself has declared: "It is necessary for him to increase and for me, however, to decrease" [John 3:30], then the "true light" [John 1:9] comes. The Word of God enters "the desert" and "makes his way around the whole region of the Jor-

dan." For besides the area around the Jordan, what place could the Baptist travel about, so that whoever wished to do penance had the washing of water at hand?

4. Further, Jordan is interpreted "descending." Implied is the river of God which "descends" with the force of strong current, namely, our Savior and Lord, in whom we are baptized with true water, the water of salvation. The Baptist preaches "a baptism for the remission of sins." Come, catechumens, do penance in order to receive the baptism "for the remission of sins." But if anyone still sinning comes to the washing, he does not receive the remission of sins. As a result, I beseech you not to approach baptism without care or diligent reflection; rather, show first "worthy fruits of repentance" [Luke 3:8]. Spend the time in profitable conversation, keep yourselves free from all defilements and vices, and then, when you have begun also to have contempt for your own sins, remission of sins will be yours. Dismiss your sins and they will be dismissed for you [cf. Luke 11:4].

5. The Old Testament passage just now presented to you comes from the prophet Isaiah. It reads, "A voice crying in the desert: prepare the way for the Lord; make his ways straight" [Isa 40:3]. The Lord wishes to find a path in you so that he can enter your souls, make his journey, and prepare his way. Thus, it says: "Make his ways straight. A voice crying out in the desert." The voice cries out: "Prepare the way." First the voice enters the ears; then, after the voice, indeed with the voice, the word, once heard, penetrates. It is in this sense that John announces Christ.

Let us, then, see what the voice announces about the Word. "Prepare," he says, "the way for the Lord." What "way for the Lord" are we to prepare? Is it physical? Can the word of God take such a journey? Or must one prepare an inner way for the Lord and dispose in our hearts ways straight and even? Such is the way on which the Word of God, who establishes in the heart the capacity to welcome him, enters.

6. Great is the human heart as well as expansive and capacious, if only it be pure. Do you wish to grasp its magnitude and extent? Consider the depth of the divine understanding the heart encompasses. It acknowledges, "He gave me true knowledge of the things that exist: to know the structure of the world and the operation of its elements; the beginning, end, and middle of the epochs; the changing seasons and succession of the

months; the cycles of the years and the position of the stars; the nature of the animals and the savagery of the beasts; the force of the winds and the thoughts of men; the varieties of plants and the powers of their roots" [Ecclus 7:17-20]. You realize that the human heart, which grasps such things, is not small. Its magnitude is not in physical size but in its ability to embrace the knowledge of such truth.

7. However, in order to get even the simple people to realize how great the human heart is, let us consider the following examples from daily life. The cities to which we have journeyed, we remember them; their characteristics, sites, walls, and buildings dwell in our heart. The route traveled, we retain in our memory by both picture and description. The sea we traversed, we embrace it by silent thought. As I said, the human heart, which is able to grasp such things, is not small. But if grasping such things is no small accomplishment, then one can prepare the way for the Lord in it and make his path straight, so that God's word and wisdom [Christ] may walk on it. Prepare the way for the Lord by good conversation and smooth the path by shining deeds, so that the Word of God may walk in you without taking offense and give you an understanding of his mysteries and of his coming: "To whom is glory and rule for ever and ever. Amen" [1 Pet 4:11].

Homily 22

On the text: "Every valley shall be filled," up to where it says, "God can make children for Abraham from these stones" [Luke 3:5-8].

[In this homily Origen again addresses himself to the preparation of the catechumens, whose lives he regards as valleys to be filled and rough paths to be made smooth (1–3). He concludes:]

4. . . . But my Lord Jesus has come, smoothed out your roughness, and set in order your disorderly life, so that the path in you may be sound, clear, and without cause for stumbling. He has done all this in order that God the Father may walk in you and that Christ the Lord may dwell in you and say, "I and my father will come and make our home with him" [John 14:23].

5. There follows, "And all flesh will see God's salvation." You were once flesh; in spite of it—I would speak of wonder— while you are still in the flesh you see "God's salvation." As

for the meaning of the words "all flesh," without which one will not see "God's salvation," I leave their comprehension to those who know how to search the mysteries and take the pulse of the Scriptures. But attend to the words which John speaks to the "people coming out" to baptism. If anyone wishes to be baptized, he comes out, for one who remains in his previous condition and does not desist from his former conduct and habits comes to baptism with thoroughly wrong dispositions. But if you would understand what to come out to baptism means, accept the testimony and listen carefully to the words which God spoke to Abraham: "Come out of your land" [Gen 12:1] and the rest.

6. To those caught in the turmoil of preparing to come out to baptism, rather than to those who have actually left, John addresses the words which follow in the text, for he would never have called those who had left "a generation of vipers." Everything he said to them, he says also to you, O Catechumens, you who have entered the ranks of those who seek baptism. Think whether, perhaps, you can be called a "generation of vipers." For if you were to have any resemblance to the vipers we see and the serpents we do not, these words are addressed to you, "generation of vipers." And according to what follows, unless you have expelled from your heart the malice and venom of the serpents, these words are also addressed to you: "Who shows you how to flee from the wrath to come?"

7. A great anger hovers over this world: the whole world will suffer the anger of God. The vast heavens, the wide world, the galaxies, the brilliant sun, the nightly comfort of the moon—all of them will the anger of God overthrow. These things will happen because of the sins of humankind. In the past God's anger fell upon the earth alone, "Because all flesh had departed from his way on earth" [Gen 6:12]; but now it will fall both on heaven and earth; "The heavens will pass away, but you will remain," it is said of God, "and like clothes everyone will grow old" [Ps 102 (101):27]. Think of the power and extent of the anger, which will consume the whole world, punish those who merit punishment, and find material on which to spend itself. In our actions each of us has prepared material for the anger: as is said to the Romans, "For because of your obstinacy and impenitent heart you are treasuring up for yourself anger on the day of wrath and of the revelation of God the just judge" [Rom 2:5].

8–9. [Origen returns, then, to the theme of preparation by repentance, concluding the homily with his customary doxology from 1 Pet 4:11: "To whom belongs glory and rule forever and ever. Amen."]

Homily 24

On the text: "I, indeed, baptize you with water," up to the place where it says, "He will baptize you with the Holy Spirit and fire."

[In this homily Origen looks beyond baptism to the passage at life's end. He sees two alternate baptisms: that of the Holy Spirit in which the perfect enter blessedness, and that of fire, in which the ordinary Christians are purified before entry into blessedness. In either case, water baptism is a necessary precondition. This is the earliest instance of the teaching which the medievals would develop into the doctrine of purgatory.]

1. The people submitted to John, who was less than Christ, thinking and pondering lest "perhaps, he was the Christ." But they did not submit to the one, greater than John, who had come. Do you wish to know why? The answer is that John's baptism was visible, but Christ's baptism was invisible. "For I baptize you in water," he says, "but he who comes after me and is greater than I, he will baptize you in the Holy Spirit and fire." When does Jesus baptize with the Holy Spirit, and again "with fire"? Is it at one and the same time that he baptizes both "with the Spirit and fire," or at clearly separate times? "You, however," the text affirms, "will be baptized by the Holy Spirit in a few days" [Acts 1:5]. The apostles were baptized "by the Holy Spirit" after Christ's ascension into heaven; whether they were baptized by fire Scripture does not record.

2. But John was waiting expectantly near the Jordan River for those coming to be baptized. Some he drove away, saying, "Generation of vipers" [and the rest], but others who confessed their faults and sins, he accepted. And so the Lord Jesus Christ will be standing in the midst of the fiery river next to the "flaming sword" [Gen 3:24]; whoever, on leaving this life, wants to go across to heaven yet stands in need of purification, Christ baptizes him in the stream and transports him to his desired goal. He however, who does not bear the prior seal of baptism, he does not baptize in the fiery path. It is necessary for one first to be baptized "in water and the Holy Spirit" [John 3:5]; so, when he comes to the river of fire, he presents himself as one baptized in the bath. Then he deserves also to receive the

baptism of fire in Christ Jesus: "To whom is glory and rule forever and ever" [1 Pet 4:11].

Homily 27

On the text: "Indeed, he announced many things, exhorting still others," up to the place where it says, "The Holy Spirit descended on him" [Luke 3:18-22].

1-4. [Origen first recounts and comments on the traditions about John the Baptist, whom he proposes as a model for the catechumen, especially because of John's belief in Jesus as the Christ coupled with his steadfastness to the point of death. These last two sections (5-6) concentrate on the descent of the Holy Spirit on Christ at baptism and, through Christ, on the candidate at baptism.]

5. When the Lord was baptized, the heavens were opened and "the Holy Spirit descended on him, and a voice from heaven sounded, saying: 'This is my beloved son, in whom I am well pleased.' " Thanks to Jesus' baptism, it should be said that heaven was unbolted for the outpouring of the remission of sins, but not on the sins of him "who committed no sin, nor was deceit found in his mouth" [1 Pet 2:22; Isa 53:9]. Rather the heavens were opened for the sins of the world and for the descent of the Holy Spirit, in order that after the Lord had "ascended into heaven, leading captivity captive" [Ps 68 (67):19; Eph 4:8], he could give us the same Spirit, who had come upon him, and whom he also gave when he had risen, saying, "Receive the Holy Spirit. Whose sins you have forgiven, they will be forgiven" [John 20:22-23]. Further, "the Holy Spirit descended on the Savior in the form of a dove," the bird of gentleness, innocence, and simplicity. And so it is that we are counseled to imitate the innocence of the dove [see Matt 10:16]. Such is the Holy Spirit—pure, swift, and soaring aloft.

6. For this reason we pray: "Who will give me the wings of a dove, and I will fly away and be at rest?" [Ps 55 (56):7]. That is, who will give me the wings of the Holy Spirit? Elsewhere the prophetic word offers this: "If you have slept within the enclosure, the wings of the dove are silvered and the pinions, gilded" [Ps 68 (67):14]. If we have taken our rest "within the enclosure" of the Old and New Testaments, the silvered wings on the dove will be given us, that is the words of God. Given also will be "pinions" gilded with "lightning" and radiant with "yellow gold," that is, our understanding is completed with

the interpretations of the Scripture suggested by the Holy Spirit. By this I mean that one's understanding is fulfilled by his coming and that we cannot say anything nor understand unless he has suggested it. For all holiness, whether in heart or in words or in deeds comes from the Holy Spirit in Christ, "to whom is glory and rule forever and ever" [1 Pet 4:11].

Serapion's Sacramentary

Serapion was bishop of Thmuis (339–360), a town in the Nile Delta about one hundred miles east of Alexandria. A friend of both Athanasius (ca. 296–373), Alexandria's bishop, and Antony (ca. 251–356), the desert hermit, Serapion had a reputation for learning and holiness. In fact, before becoming bishop he was the superior of a group of monks; in recognition of his devout life, Antony left him as his legacy one of his sheepskin cloaks (Athanasius received the other).

As part of his own legacy, Serapion left behind valuable correspondence with Athanasius. Among the letters are four from Athanasius occasioned by some Christians at Thmuis who held that the Holy Spirit is a creature, albeit an angel of the highest order. The letters constitute the first formal treatise on the divinity of the Holy Spirit. In response to Serapion's request for instruction on the status of the Spirit, Athanasius argues that, far from being a creature, the Holy Spirit proceeds from the Father and is consubstantial with both the Father and the Son. In the process, Athanasius presents the Spirit's mission as one of holiness. In a clearly baptismal context, he affirms that all creatures are renewed by the Spirit, that he gives them life, and that he is present and at work in the very chrism and seal by which candidates are anointed in baptism.

This sense of active presence is attested in an equally valuable legacy: the sacramentary composed about mid-fourth century and attributed to Serapion. Discovered in an eleventh-century manuscript at the Laura monastery of Mount Athos toward the end of the last century, it contains thirty prayers from the liturgy of Thmuis on the Eucharist (1–6), baptism (7–11), ordination (12–14), the blessing of the baptismal oils (15–17), death and dying (18), and prayers before the beginning of the Eucharist proper (19–30), including two for the catechumens.

The reading consists of prayers offered for the catechumens and the consecratory prayers over the oils as well as the baptismal prayers. Collectively, they envision a catechumenate that differs little from that attested in Origen (see above), save that Lenten preparation for Easter baptism would have been well established in Thmuis, as it was elsewhere in Egypt, by mid-fourth century. Baptism proper begins with the consecration of the baptismal water, here transformed by the descent of the Word of God rather than of the Holy Spirit. He enters into the baptismal font as he once entered into the Jordan River (7), with the result that the water can be the bearer of holiness. A prayer for their rebirth is then said over the candidates (8). There follows the solemn renunciation of Satan, coupled with a pledge of allegiance to Christ (9, 10; see below, *Canons of Hippolytus* 19), followed in turn by anointing with oil (15). Baptism is by immersion (11), after which the newly baptized are anointed with chrism in the sign of the cross together with the imposition of hands. The concluding prayer speaks explicitly of the newly baptized as established in the gifts and power of the Holy Spirit by the anointing, sealing their baptism (16), or as the medievals preferred to say, "confirming" it. Although the prayers do not suggest additional rites, their presence and position in the sacramentary point to a close connection with the Eucharist. One may also assume that the candidates were vested in white garments, received candles, prayed the Lord's Prayer, and received the kiss of peace. They may even have received crowns, as in Syriac-speaking Christianity and among the Copts (for both of which, see below).

The text is that of G. Wobbermin, TU 18, 3b (1898); the translation is that of John Wordsworth, *Bishop Sarapion's Prayerbook,* 2nd. ed. rev. (London: SPCK, 1909; rpt. Archon Books, 1964). The work contains a valuable introduction (he disagrees with the usual spelling, "Serapion"). See also G. J. Cuming, "Thmuis Revisited: Another Look at the Prayers of Bishop Sarapion," TS 41 [1980] 568–575).

The Baptismal Prayers, chapter 2:7-11

7. Sanctification of waters.

ADDRESS   King and Lord of all things and maker of the world, who gave salvation freely to all created nature by the descent of your only-begotten Jesus Christ, you who redeem the creation that

THEOLOGICAL INSIGHT

RELATIVE CLAUSE

you created by the coming of your ineffable Word: (see now [CENTRAL PETITION] from heaven and look upon these waters and fill them with holy Spirit.) Let your ineffable Word come to be in them and transform their energy and cause them to be generative, being filled with your grace, in order that the mystery which is now being celebrated may not be found in vain in those that are being regenerated, but may fill all those that descend [into them] and are baptized [herein] with the divine grace. O Loving Benefactor spare your own handiwork, save the creature that has been the toil of your right hand. Form all who are being regenerated according to your divine and ineffable form, in order that, having been formed and regenerated, they may be able to be saved and counted worthy of your kingdom. And as your only-begotten Word coming down upon the waters of the Jordan rendered them holy, so now also may he descend on these and make them holy and spiritual, to the end that those who are being baptized may be no longer flesh and blood, but spiritual and able to worship you, the uncreated Father through Jesus Christ in holy Spirit, through whom to you [is] the glory and [DOXOLOGY] the strength both now and to all the ages of the ages. Amen.

8. Prayer on behalf of those being baptized. EXORCISM PRAYER ?

We beseech you, O God of truth, on behalf of this your servant and pray that you would count him worthy of the divine mystery and of your ineffable regeneration. For to you, O loving [God], is he now offered; to you we devote him: grant him to communicate in this divine regeneration, to the end that he may no longer be led by any bad and evil one, but worship you continually and observe your ordinances as your only-begotten Word guides him: for through him to you [is] the glory and the strength in the holy Spirit both now and to all the ages of the ages. Amen.

9. After the renunciation—a prayer.

O Lord all-sovereign, seal the adhesion of this your servant that has now been made to you, and continually keep his character and his manner [of life] unchangeable, that he may no longer minister to those who are worse, but may worship in the God of truth, and serve you the maker of all things, to the end that he may be rendered perfect and your own through your only-begotten Jesus Christ, through whom to you is the glory and the strength in holy Spirit both now and to all the ages of the ages. Amen.

10. After the acceptance—a prayer.

O Loving Benefactor, savior of all those who have turned
to you for help, be gracious to this your servant. Guide him
to the regeneration with your right hand: let your only-begotten
Word guide him to the washing: let his regeneration be honored,
let it not be empty of your grace: let your holy Word accompany him, let your holy Spirit be with him scaring away and
driving off every temptation, because through your only-
begotten Jesus Christ [is] the glory and the strength both now
and to all the ages of the ages. Amen.

11. After one has been baptized and has come up—a prayer.

O God, the God of truth, the maker of all, the Lord of all
the creation, bless this your servant with your blessing: render
him clean in the regeneration, make him have fellowship with
your angelic powers, that he may be named no longer flesh but
spiritual, by partaking of your divine and profitable gift. May
he be preserved up to the end for you the maker of the world
through your only-begotten Jesus Christ, through whom [is]
to you the glory and the strength both now and to all the ages
of the ages. Amen.

Blessing of Oils, Chapter 4:15–16

15. Prayers of Sarapion, Bishop of Thmuis: a prayer in regard
to the anointing oil of those who are being baptized.

Master, Lover of men and Lover of souls, compassionate and
pitiful, O God of truth, we invoke you following out and obey-
ing the promises of your only begotten who has said, "Whosoever sins you forgive, they are forgiven them": and we anoint
with this anointing oil those who in purpose approach this divine regeneration, beseeching you that our Lord Jesus Christ
may work in them healing and strength-making power, and by
this anointing oil may reveal [himself] and heal away from their
soul, body, spirit, every mark of sin and lawlessness or satanic
fault, and by his own proper grace may afford them remission,
that dying to sin they shall live to righteousness [1 Pet 2:24],
and being re-created through this anointing, and being cleansed
through the washing, and being renewed in the spirit [Eph 4:23],
they shall be able henceforth to have victory over all the opposing energies and deceits of this world that assail them, and
thus to be bound up and united with the flock of our Lord and
Savior Jesus Christ, because through him to you [is] the glory
and the strength in holy Spirit to all the ages of the ages. Amen.

16. Prayer in regard to the chrism with which those who have been baptized are being anointed.

God of Hosts, the helper of every soul that turns to you and that comes under the mighty hand of your only-begotten, we invoke you to work in this chrism a divine and heavenly energy through the divine and unseen powers of our Lord and Savior Jesus Christ, in order that they who have been baptized, and who are being anointed with it with the impress of the sign of the saving cross of the only-begotten, by which cross Satan and every opposing power was routed and triumphed over, they also, as being regenerated and renewed through the washing of regeneration [Titus 3:5], may become partakers of the gift of the holy Spirit, and being made secure by this seal, may continue steadfast and unmovable, unhurt and inviolate, free from harsh treatment and intrigue, in the franchise of the faith and full knowledge of the truth, awaiting to the end the heavenly hopes of life and eternal promises of our Lord and Savior Jesus Christ, through whom to you [is] the glory and the strength both now and to all the ages of the ages. Amen.

Prayers for the Catechumens, Chapter 6:20-21, 28

20. After rising up from the sermon—a prayer.

God, the Savior, God of the Universe, the Lord and maker of the world, the begetter of the only-begotten, who has begotten the living and true expression of your self [Heb 1:3], who sent him for the help of the race of men, who through him called and made men your own possession, we pray you on behalf of this people. Send holy Spirit [on them], and let the Lord Jesus visit them, let him speak in the understandings of all, and predispose their hearts to faith; may he himself draw their souls to you, O God of compassions. Create a people even in this city, create a genuine flock through your only-begotten Jesus Christ in holy Spirit, through whom to you [is] the glory and the strength both now and to all the ages of the ages. Amen.

21. Prayer on behalf of the catechumens.

ADDRESS► Helper and Lord of all, deliverer of those who have been delivered, protector of the rescued, the hope of those who have come under your mighty hand: you are he who has put down RELATIVE CLAUSE lawlessness, who through your only-begotten has brought Satan to nought and has loosed his devices and released those who were bound by him; we thank you on behalf of the catechu- PRAISE mens, because you have called them through the only-begotten,

PETITION

and freely gave them your knowledge. May they be confirmed in [this] knowledge, that they may know you the only true God and him whom you sent Jesus Christ [John 17:3]. May they be continually guarded in what they have learnt and in clean wisdom, and may they advance to become worthy of the washing of regeneration [Titus 3:5], and of the holy mysteries, through the only-begotten Jesus Christ in holy Spirit, through whom to you [is] the glory and the strength both now and to all the ages of the ages. Amen.

28. Laying on of hands [benediction] of catechumens [before the offertory at the Eucharist].

We stretch out the hand, O Master, and pray that the divine and living hand may be stretched out in blessing on this people. For to you, uncreated Father, through the only-begotten they have bowed their heads. Bless this people for the blessing of knowledge and piety, for the blessing of your mysteries, through your only-begotten Jesus Christ, through whom to you [is] the glory and the strength in holy Spirit both now and to all the ages of the ages. Amen.

Didymus the Blind

Born about 313, Didymus lost his sight as a small boy. In spite of his handicap he amassed a great treasure of learning, astonishing his contemporaries. Athanasius (ca. 295–373) appointed him head of Alexandria's catechetical school—as it turned out, the last of its directors, for the celebrated institution closed its doors soon after Didymus' death. Among his best-known pupils were Jerome (ca. 347–419), Rufinus (345–410), and Gregory of Nazianzus (ca. 330–390), who extolled his learning, teaching, and ascetic life.

Didymus wrote extensively on the Bible and on the burning theological issues of the day, especially on Arianism, the Trinity, the Holy Spirit, and Christ. The fruit of his catechetical lectures, his writings provide an important window on the development of Christian thought between Athanasius on the one hand and the Cappadocian Fathers (vol. 5, ch. 1) and Cyril of Alexandria (below) on the other. He was, for instance, the first to use and promote the Trinitarian catch phrase "one nature, three persons" *(mia ousia, treis hypostaseis)*; he firmly established the conviction that the Holy Spirit is consubstantial with the Father and the Son; and he emphasized that in Christ the divine and human natures were joined without change or fusion (see below, Cyril).

As an interpreter of the Bible and a thinker, he stood, as did so many, in the tradition of Origen (above), on whose *On First Principles* he wrote a commentary as well as a defense. Unfortunately, in the subsequent controversies over Origen a cloud of suspicion overshadowed his reputation and work, and many of his writings have not survived. Among those that have, *On the Trinity* is of critical importance. Composed between 381 and 392, the first book is on the Son and the second, on the Holy Spirit; the third summarizes the first two and discusses the most important biblical passages at issue in the theological debates of the time. The reading is drawn from the second book, where, in the course of developing his teaching on the Holy Spirit, Didymus addresses himself to baptism. His principal concern is with the Holy Spirit and the remaking of the image and likeness of God lost in Adam's sin: He sees the baptismal font both as the "workshop of the Trinity" where the image and likeness are refashioned and as the virginal womb of the Church, which, while remaining a virgin, gives new life to the candidates (*On the Trinity* 2:13). Indeed, Didymus may be the first Greek-speaking author to speak of the baptismal font as the perpetual virgin-mother of the baptized, made fertile through the Holy Spirit. Doubtless his imagery was conditioned by the Alexandrian tradition that Mary, as Mother of God *(theotokos),* was perpetually a virgin, that is, before, during, and after the birth of Christ (see vol. 5, ch. 2, Ephrem and Jacob of Serugh). The liturgy to which Didymus adverts would have been much like that depicted in the next section, the *Canons of Hippolytus.*

The text of *On the Trinity* is PG 39, 269–292; the translation is Quasten 3:98; see 85–100 for his valuable study of Didymus and his works.

On the Trinity 2:12

The Holy Spirit as God renovates us in baptism, and in union with the Father and the Son, brings us back from a state of deformity to our pristine beauty and so fills us with his grace that we can no longer make room for anything that is unworthy of our love; he frees us from sin and death and from the things of the earth; makes us spiritual men, sharers in the divine glory, sons and heirs of God and of the Father. He conforms us to the image of the Son of God, makes us co-heirs and his brothers, we who are to be glorified and to reign with him; he gives us heaven in exchange for earth, and bestows paradise with a bounteous hand, and makes us more honorable than the angels; and in the divine waters of the baptismal pool extinguishes the inextinguishable fire of hell.

For when we are immersed in the baptismal pool, we are, by the goodness of God the Father and through the grace of his Holy Spirit, stripped of our sins as we lay aside the old man, are regenerated, and sealed by his own kingly power. But when we come up out of the pool, we put on Christ our Savior as an incorruptible garment, worthy of the same honor as the Holy Spirit who regenerated us and marked us with his seal. For as many of you, says holy Scripture, as have been baptized in Christ have put on Christ [see Gal 3:27]. Through the divine insufflation we had received the image and likeness of God, which the Scripture speaks of, and through sin we had lost it, but now we are found once more such as we were when we were first made: sinless and masters of ourselves.

The Canons of Hippolytus

Through the fifth century, Church orders played an important part in the liturgical life and regulation of Christian communities, especially in Egypt and Syria. They gave place thereafter to sacramentaries (see above, Serapion, and ch. 1, the *Leonine Sacramentary* and the *Gelasian Sacramentary*) and to collections of ecclesiastical rules and laws (canonical codes). Composed in the name of the apostles, the Church orders codified the rites and other traditional practices, giving structure and stability to communities—thus, the *Apostolic Tradition* of Hippolytus (ch. 1), the *Apostolic Constitutions* (vol. 5, ch. 1), the *Testament of Our Lord,* the *Egyptian Church Order,* and the *Canons of Hippolytus.*

Toward the end of the last century the *Canons of Hippolytus* was advanced as the key document underlying the others. In the early decades of this century, however, two scholars (R. H. Connolly and E. Schwartz) independently established the *Egyptian Church Order* as both the source document and none other than the *Apostolic Tradition* of Hippolytus, albeit in a much later Coptic translation.

The importance of the *Canons,* although diminished, did not recede, because the work witnesses the deep influence of the *Apostolic Tradition* and how Egyptian Christianity adapted it to fit a different time, culture, and set of historical circumstances. The original adaptation was made in an urban setting (some think Alexandria) between the councils of Nicaea (325) and Constantinople (381). A comparison with the *Apostolic Tradition* suggests that the compiler was a priest conscious of the importance of the priesthood and its doctrinal mission, devoted to Nicene theology and to the new emphasis on the divinity of the Holy Spirit (see above, Serapion and Didymus), and imbued by the holiness code of the Hebrew Bible (see vol. 5, ch. 1, *Didascalia*). Although he wrote in Greek, the document had been translated into Coptic by the early fifth century and into Arabic in the sixth, indicating the long and influential reach of the work. It is preserved only in Arabic.

The text is that of René-Georges Coquin, PO 31, 2 (1966) 340–427. The translation is from M. Coquin's French translation. For a study see his introduction. The relevant canons are 1, 10, and 11.

The *Canons of Hippolytus*

These are the canons of the church, the precepts which Hippolytus, Archbishop of Rome, wrote according to the traditions of the apostles, our Lord the Christ speaking through him.

Canon 1: On the Holy Faith

First of all, we speak of the holy authentic faith in our Lord Jesus Christ, Son of the Living God. We are content with this faith, we adhere to it with full assurance, and we say in all truth that the Trinity, equal and perfect in honor, is equal in glory. We also hold that the Word, the Son of God, has neither beginning nor end, and that he is the creator of all creatures visible and invisible. This is our settled conviction, and we embrace it fully.

As for those [the Arians] who have dared to say that it is not necessary to cling to the Word of God in compliance with what our Lord Jesus Christ has said on the subject (in the power of God we have ourselves collected the greatest possible number of his sayings), we have cut them off, because they are not in agreement with the holy books, the word of God, nor with us, the disciples of the books. For this reason we have severed them from the church and remanded their case to God, who will judge every creature with justice.

Those who do not know the faith, we, begrudging nothing, will teach them, so that they will not come to an evil death like the heretics, but be worthy of life eternal and teach their children and those who will come after them this holy faith.

[Canons 2–9 deal with rites of ordination.]

Canon 10: Concerning those who wish to become Christian

Let those who come to the church to be baptized be examined rigorously—why they have abandoned the service of their false gods—lest they enter to mock our faith. If, however, one come with authentic faith, let him be received with joy, interrogated about his profession, and be instructed by a deacon. Let him be instructed in the holy books in such a way that he renounces Satan and all his service. For the entire time that he is under instruction, he is henceforth to be counted among the faithful.

Yet if one is a slave and his master, an idolater, forbid it, let him not be baptized, for it suffices that he be [numbered among the community]—likewise, if he dies without receiving the gift—because he has not been separated from the flock.

[Canons 11–18 treat of forbidden professions. See ch. 1, *Apostolic Tradition* 16, where they were carried on by catechumens; in the *Canons,* it is Christians who took them up after baptism, suggesting that many who sought baptism were raised in Christian homes, delaying baptism for a variety of reasons. Such "professionals" were cut off from the church. For those who sought return, Lent was the solemn time for penance and reconciliation. If any were catechumens, they were not to be admitted to baptism unless they had desisted and could prove it by witnesses.]

Canon 19: Catechumens

Concerning the catechumen who is killed before baptism because of his witness: let him be buried among the martyrs. Concerning catechumens: the part which the catechumens take during baptism and exorcism; concerning the order of the liturgy of baptism: the part which the catechumens take during baptism and exorcism; concerning the order of the liturgy of baptism and of the consecratory liturgy of the Body and Blood.

When a catechumen is arrested because of his witness and killed before having been baptized, let him be buried with all the martyrs, because he has been baptized in his own blood.

Chapters on catechumens.

The catechumen, when he is to be baptized, and his sponsor gives testimony that he has been zealous for the commandments during his catechumenate, that he has visited the sick or given to the needy, that he has guarded himself from every malicious and dishonest word, that he has hated pomp and cant, that he shows contempt for pride and has chosen humility for his lot—when he confesses to the bishop that he takes his responsibilities on himself alone, in brief, let the bishop be satisfied about him and judge him worthy of the mysteries. If he has come forward truly pure, then [the bishop] places on him the [book of the] Gospel, at the same time asking him many times: "Are you hesitant, or compelled by any cause of [out of] human respect? For no one fools the kingdom of heaven, because it is given to those who love it with their whole heart."

Those who are to be baptized take a bath and eat on the fifth day of the week; let them fast on the sixth. If a woman is among them, and she has reached her menstrual period, she is not to be baptized this time; rather she waits until she is purified.

On Saturday, the bishop assembles those to be baptized; he requires them to incline their heads to the west, extends his hand over them; he prays and drives from them every malignant spirit by his exorcism, and these spirits will not return to them henceforth through their actions. When he has finished exorcising them, he breathes on their faces and signs their chest, their forehead, their ears, and their nose.

Let them keep watch the night through with prayers and the holy word. At cock-crow let someone position them near the water, a pool flowing and pure, prepared and sanctified.

Let those who will respond for the infants remove [the infants'] clothing first; then those who are capable of giving assurance for themselves; and finally the women are last of all to remove their clothes: let them take off their jewelry, whether of gold or other, and let down their hair, lest something of the alien spirits go down with them into the water of the second birth.

The bishop blesses the oil of exorcism and gives it to a priest; then he blesses the oil of anointing, that is to say, the oil of thanksgiving, giving it to another priest. He who holds the oil of exorcism takes his place to the left of the bishop, and he who holds the oil of anointing, to the right.

The one to be baptized turns his face toward the west and says: "I renounce you, Satan, and all your service." When he has said this, the priest anoints him with the oil of exorcism, which has been blessed, in order to separate from him every evil spirit. He is then sent to the priest who stands near the water by a deacon; the priest extends his right hand and makes him turn his face toward the east, toward the water. Before descending into the water, while facing the east, standing near the water, and upon being anointed with the oil of exorcism, [the candidate] says: "I believe, and I submit myself to you and to all your service, O Father, Son, and Holy Spirit."

Then he descends into the water: the priest imposes his hand on the [candidate's] head and interrogates him saying: "Do you believe in God the Father almighty?" The one who is being baptized responds: "I believe." Then he immerses him in the water for the first time, his hand on his head. He interrogates him a second time, saying: "Do you believe in Jesus Christ, the son of God, who was born of the Virgin Mary by the Holy Spirit, and who came for the salvation of humankind, who was crucified at the time of Pontius Pilate, who died and was raised from the dead on the third day, has ascended to the heavens, sits at the right of the Father, and will come to judge the living and the dead?" He responds, "I believe." Then, he immerses [the candidate] in the water a second time. He interrogates him a third time, saying: "Do you believe in the Holy Spirit, the Paraclete poured out by the Father and the Son?" When he responds, "I believe," he immerses him a third time in the water. And he says each time, "I baptize you in the name of the Father, of the Son, and of the Holy Spirit, the equal Trinity."

Then the [newly baptized] emerges from the water; the priest takes the oil of thanksgiving and signs his forehead, his mouth, his chest, and anoints his entire body, his head, and his face, saying: "I anoint you in the name of the Father, of the Son, and of the Holy Spirit." And he dries himself with a linen cloth, which he has kept specially, and he dresses and enters the church.

The bishop imposes his hand on all the baptized and prays thus: "We praise you, Lord God almighty, because you have made these [newly baptized] worthy of being born again, of having your Holy Spirit poured out on them, of being a member in the body of the church, and of not being cut off by any actions alien to it. In the same way that you have granted them pardon for their sins, grant them also the pledge of your kingdom. By our Lord Jesus Christ through whom you have glory with him and the Holy Spirit forever and ever. Amen."

Then, [the bishop] signs their forehead with the oil of anointing and gives them the kiss [of peace] saying: "The Lord be with you." And they say also, those who have been baptized: "And with your spirit."

He does the same with each of the baptized.

After this, they pray with all the faithful people, who give them the kiss [of peace], and rejoice with them in happiness. Then the deacon begins the liturgy, and the bishop celebrates the Eucharist [the prayer of thanksgiving] over the Body and Blood of the Lord. When he has finished he gives Communion to the people as he stands near the table of the Body and Blood of the Lord, while the priests carry the cups of the Blood of Christ and also the cups of milk and honey, so that those who communicate will know that they have been born again as infants, because infants receive milk and honey. If there are not enough priests to carry them [the cups], let the deacons carry them. And so the bishop gives them the Body of Christ while saying: "This is the Body of Christ." They respond, "Amen." They receive the milk and honey in memory of the age to come, and of the sweetness of its good things, namely, those who do not return to the bitter days and who do not grow old.

Thus, they have become full Christians and are nourished on the Body of Christ. They vie for wisdom, so that their life sparkles in virtues, not before each other only, but before the Gentiles also, so that they will envy them and become Christians and see that the progress of those who have been illuminated is high, indeed, out of reach of Gentile morals.

With respect to those who have been baptized and those also who have fasted with them, let them taste nothing before receiving the Body of Christ, because he would not count anything less as fasting, but as sin. He who tastes anything before receiving the Body disobeys and despises God. But when the liturgy is finished, he can eat whatever he wants.

Let all the catechumens reassemble together, and let one teacher, who can instruct them adequately, suffice for them; let them pray and bend their knees. Let them taste nothing before those who have been baptized have first received the Body and Blood.

Cyril of Alexandria

Foe to Nestorius and friend to Eutyches (see vol. 5, chs. 1, 2), Cyril followed his uncle Theophilus in the patriarchal see of Alexandria, which he held from 412 to his death in 444. Save that he was educated in the city's finest classical tradition and had Theophilus, the city's most influential figure, as his patron, little is known about Cyril's early years. But early on in his patriarchy he revealed the character traits of impetuosity and high-handedness, quite likely inherited from his uncle, which would cause controversy to plague practically every endeavor.

Withal, however, Cyril was a deeply learned and perceptive theologian. Like his forbears in the Alexandrian see, he was convinced that the root and cause of salvation was Christ, the Word of God. Along with them, he gave inadequate attention and scope to the fullness of Christ's humanity and tended to use confusing terminology. In response to the Nestorian challenge, however, he developed a Christology that, as noted above, anticipated that of Chalcedon. His underlying insight was that united in the person of the Son of God were two natures, the one fully divine and the other integrally human, including body, emotions, mind, and will. For Cyril this was what he called the "hypostatic union," which he defined as he who "in one and the same person was at the same time both God and also man" (*Homilies on Luke: Homily* 10). When he insisted that there was only "one incarnate nature of the Word," unlike Eutyches or some later adherents, he meant that Christ was one concretely existing entity in whom a divine way of being and a human way of being were intimately united in the person of the Word, without, however, any joining or mixing the two ways of being together.

Cyril's Christology shapes his understanding of baptism. Christ's integral humanity, as he says below, is the pattern of the way of salvation and life. The difference between his baptism in the Jordan and baptism of the Christian in the font is simply that those who come to the font are the descendants of a fallen Adam and bear in themselves the distorted image of God. Although they remained children of God, they had lost the status of son or daughter. Through baptism God's image is refashioned in them, and they return to the status of son or daughter. Indeed, they are conformed to Christ, even to becoming participants of the divine nature. The same Spirit who descended on Christ in the Jordan descends on the candidates in the baptismal font and accomplishes the transformation in which Christ is impressed and reproduced in them. "Christ is formed in us," we read, "in virtue of a divine form that the Holy Spirit infuses in us by justification and sanctification'' (*On Isaiah,* PG 70:936).

Cyril was a prolific writer: Ten volumes of his works have survived (PG 68–77) including letters, biblical commentaries, and doctrinal and polemical writings. His preoccupation in them is with the person of Christ, largely because his overriding concern is to assure a salvation that is at once integrally divine and human. His *Commentary on the Gospel of St. Luke,* a series of homilies preached to his congregation about 430 just before the Council of Ephesus, provides the reading.

The tenth and eleventh homilies are on baptism. In them he brings together his understanding of Nestorius' teaching, his own doctrine of the hypostatic union, and his understanding of baptism. The text on which he comments is Luke's account of the baptism of Jesus (3:15-23). In the tenth homily he argues that only the one who unites in his own person the realities of divinity and of humanity can give the Holy Spirit in baptism. In the eleventh, which constitutes the reading, he addresses himself to the question, Why, if Christ was God and man, had he to be baptized? As already noted, he responds that as the way of salvation, Christ became for humans the pattern and example for the transformation of the candidate. In the course of the homily, Cyril elaborates what he takes to be the teaching of Nestorius and its consequences; he also recapitulates what he holds to be the work of baptism. With respect to the liturgy of baptism in Cyril's Alexandria, the final reading (below, Coptic Rite) is more revealing than is Cyril.

With respect to the text, only three complete homilies of Cyril (and some fragments) exist in the original Greek. A collection of 156 homilies, however, exists in a sixth- or seventh-century version in Syriac. The Syriac text is that of J. B. Chabot, CSCO (1912); the translation is adapted from R. Payne Smith and abridged, *The Commentary on the Gospel of Saint Luke by Saint Cyril of Alexandria* (Staten Island: Studion Publishers, 1983 [rpt. of 1859 Oxford edition]). The Studion edition contains a valuable anonymous introduction as well as the translator's preface. For a recent study of Cyril's thought, see Robert L. Wilken, *Judaism and the Early Christian Mind: A Study of Cyril of Alexandria's Exegesis and Thought* (New Haven: Yale University Press, 1971).

Homily 11

"And it came to pass, that when all the people were baptized, Jesus also was baptized; and as he was praying, the heavens were opened, and the Holy Spirit descended upon him in bodily form like a dove. And there was a voice from heaven, saying, you are my beloved Son; in you I am well pleased. And Jesus himself was beginning to be about thirty years old" [Luke 3:21-23]. Again come, that, fixing our mind intently upon the evangelic Scriptures, we may behold the beauty of the truth. Come, let us direct the penetrating and accurate eyes of the mind into the mystery of Christ. . . .

[In these first few paragraphs Cyril sets out his understanding of the eternal identity of the Jesus who presented himself to John for baptism, namely, the Word made flesh (see John 1:14): "While, therefore, he immutably retains that which he was, yet as having under this condition assumed our likeness, he is said to have been made flesh. Behold him, therefore, as a man, enduring with us the things that belong to man's estate." Cyril then asks: "Was he, too, then, in need of holy baptism?" He continues:]

What is it that we gain by holy baptism? Plainly the remission of our sins. But in Jesus there was nothing of this; "For he did no sin: neither was guile found in his mouth," as the Scripture says [1 Pet 2:22]. "He was holy, harmless, undefiled, separate from sins, and made higher than the heavens," according to the words of the divine Paul [Heb 7:26].

But yes! perchance some one [i.e., Nestorius] will say, who has been ill-instructed in the faith, "Was it then God the Word that was baptized? Was he in need of being made partaker of the Holy Spirit? Not at all. Therefore we affirm that the man who was the seed of David [the Nestorian term for the man Jesus], and united to him by conjunction, was baptized and received the Spirit." The indivisible [Cyril now replies], therefore, is divided by you into two sons; and because he was baptized when thirty years old, he was made holy, as you say, by being baptized. Was he, therefore, not holy until he arrived at his thirtieth year? Who will assent to you, when thus you corrupt the right and blameless faith? For "there is one Lord Jesus Christ," as it is written [1 Cor 8:6]. But this we affirm: that he [Jesus] was not separate from him [the Word], and [thus] by himself when baptized and made partaker of the Holy Spirit; for we know, both that he is God and without stain, and holy of the holy; for we confess that "of his fullness have all we received" [John 1:16]. For the Holy Spirit indeed proceeds from God the Father, but belongs also to the Son. He is even often called the Spirit of Christ, though proceeding from God the Father. [Cyril here cites Rom 8:8; Gal 4:6; John 16:15 in support of his assertion.]

But let us retort to those who pervert the right belief with this question: "How can he who received the Spirit, if he be, according to your phrase, a man, and the Son separately and by himself, baptize with the Holy Spirit, and himself give the Holy Spirit to them who are baptized?" For to be able to impart the Spirit to men suits not any one whatsoever of things created, but, together with God's other attributes, is the distinct property of Almighty God alone. But he who gave it was man; for the wise John said, "After me comes a man, who was before me. . . . He shall baptize you with the Holy Spirit and with fire" [John 1:30]. As, therefore, it does not befit God the Word, regarded as God the Word, to draw near holy baptism, and be made partaker of the Spirit, so in like manner it is altogether incredible, or rather impossible to believe, that the ability to baptize men with the Holy Spirit is the act of a mere man with nothing in him superior to ourselves.

How then will the mystery be true? In that for our aid he assumed a kind of adaptation. The divine Word became man, even "he who was in the form of God the Father, and thought it not robbery to be equal to God" [Phil 2:6], as most wise Paul says, but took the form of a slave, being made in the likeness of men, and humbling himself to poverty. Inquire, therefore, who he was that was first in the likeness of God the Father, and could be regarded as on an equality with him, but took the form of a slave, and became then a man, and besides this made himself poor. Was it he of the "seed of David," as they argue [the Nestorian phrase for the man Jesus], whom they specially regard separately and by himself as the other son, distinct from the Word of God the Father? If so, let them show that he ever was on an equality with the Father. Let them show how he assumed the form of a slave. Or what shall we say was that form of a slave? And how did he empty himself? For what is poorer than human nature? He, therefore, who is the exact image of God the Father, the likeness, and visible expression of his person, who shines resplendent in equality with him, who by right of nature is free and the yoke of whose kingdom is put upon all creation—he it is who took the form of a slave, that is, became a man, and made himself poor by consenting to endure these human things, sin only excepted.

But how then, they object, was he baptized, and received also the Spirit? To which we reply, that he had no need of holy baptism, being wholly pure and spotless, and holy of the holy. Nor had he need of the Holy Spirit, for the Spirit that proceeds from God the Father is of him and equal to him in substance. We must now, therefore, at length hear what is the explanation of the economy.

God in his love for man provided us a way of salvation and of life. For believing in the Father, Son, and Holy Spirit, and making this confession before many witnesses, we wash away all the filth of sin, and are enriched by the communication of the Holy Spirit, and made partakers of the divine nature, and gain the grace of adoption. It was necessary, therefore, that the Word of the Father, when he humbled himself to emptiness, and deigned to assume our likeness, should become for our sakes the pattern and way of every good work. For it follows that he who in every thing is first must in this also set the example. In order, therefore, that we may learn both the power itself of holy baptism, and how much we gain by approaching so great a grace, he commences the work himself; and, having been baptized prays that you, my beloved, may learn that never-ceasing prayer is a thing most fitting for those who have once been counted worthy of holy baptism.

And the Evangelist says that the heavens were opened, as though having long been closed. For Christ said, "Forthwith shall you see the heavens opened, and the angels of God ascending and descending upon the Son of Man" [John 1:51]. For both the flock above and that below being now made one, and one chief shepherd appointed for all, the heavens were opened, and man upon earth brought near to the holy angels. And the Spirit also again came down as at a second beginning of our race, and upon Christ first, who received it not so much for his own sake as for ours; for by him and in him are we enriched with all things. Most suitably therefore to the economy of grace does he endure with us the things of man's estate: for where otherwise shall we see him emptied, who in his divine nature is the fullness? How did he become poor as we are, if he were not conformed to our poverty? How did he empty himself, if he refused to endure the measure of human littleness?

Having taken, therefore, Christ as our pattern, let us draw near to the grace of holy baptism, that so we may gain boldness to pray constantly, and lift up holy hands to God the Father, that he may open the heavens also for us, and send down upon us too the Holy Spirit, to receive us as sons. For he spoke to Christ at the time of holy baptism, as though having by him and in him accepted man upon earth to the sonship, "This is my beloved Son, in whom I am well pleased." For he who is the son by nature and in truth, and the Only-begotten, when he became like us, is specially declared to be the Son of God, not as receiving this for himself—for he was and is, as I said, true Son—but that he might ratify the glory for us. For he has been made our firstfruits, and firstborn, and second Adam; for which reason it is said, that "in him all things have become new" [2 Cor 5:17]; for having put off the oldness that was in Adam, we have gained the newness that is in Christ; by whom and with whom, to God the Father, be glory and dominion with the Holy Spirit through ages of ages. Amen.

The Coptic Rite

The term "Copt" is an Arabic word *(Qibt)* and, in its turn, a derivative of the Greek for "Egyptian" *(aigyptios)*. Coptic Christianity became a separate form of Christianity, along with so-called Nestorian Christianity, as a result of the controversy between Nestorius and Cyril of Alexandria about the humanity of Christ (see above). As noted, the dispute led to the councils of Ephesus (431) and Chalcedon (451). A third figure, however, entered the lists between the councils, Eutyches (378–454), the head of a large monastery in Antioch, who asserted that before the union of the divine and human in Christ there were two natures, divine and human, but after, only one nature. Some took him to mean either that Christ's human nature was swallowed up by the divine or that it was a hybrid of divinity and humanity. Others took him to mean what Cyril intended, namely, that after the hypostatic union there was "one incarnate nature of the Word" (*Epistle* 46:2), in a way analogous to the union that body and soul form, yet remaining conceptually distinct. For Eutyches, this "one-nature" *(monophysis)* phrase designated the Word made flesh as one concretely existing being. Unfortunately, he used the terms for nature *(physis)* and person *(prosopon/hypostasis)* equivalently, creating much subsequent confusion and controversy. In any case, the Council of Chalcedon responded to "one-nature" advocates like Eutyches by insisting that Christ, as the only-begotten Son of God, was composed of two natures *(dyophyseis)*, divine and human, united in the one person *(hypostasis)* of the Son without change, division, or separation.

The Chalcedonian "settlement" was not acceptable to a large number of Egyptian Christians. As one-nature advocates (Monophysites) they regarded the Chalcedonians, because they were two-nature advocates (Dyophysites), as unfaithful to the authentic tradition of the Fathers. The dispute was further complicated by history, culture, and politics, both ecclesiastical and imperial. The final result was a split between Monophysites (largely, but not only, Egyptians) and the Chalcedonians, sealed for good in 642 when Alexandria fell to Islam.

Coptic Christianity has retained its link with its ancient traditions and continues to express its convictions about Christ in the following Cyrillian terms: "The union of the Word of God with the flesh is as the union of the soul with the body, and as the union of fire with iron, which although they are of different natures, yet by their union they become one. Likewise, the Lord Christ is One Christ, One Lord, One Nature, and One Will" (*Arabic Jacobite Synaxary*, PO 1 [1907] 237, citing Cyril).

The liturgy, especially the baptismal liturgy, has much in common with the pre-451 rites, including (1) a catechumenate in which instruction and exorcism are prominent, (2) the consecration of the baptismal waters and Trinitarian baptism by immersion, (3) chrismation, together with imposition of hands and insufflation, and (4) vesting in white, coronation, and the Eucharist.

Naturally, time and circumstances brought modifications. The preponderance of infant baptism arising shortly after Cyril's time, for instance, required tailoring the rites accordingly. Also, as the Eucharistic liturgy came to occupy center stage in the liturgy, the rites directly connected with the act of baptism came, in time, to imitate the Eucharistic liturgy, including biblical readings, psalms, intercessory prayer, the "Lift up your hearts," a prayer modeled on the canon of the Eucharist, and the like (see below, on the consecration of the baptismal water). Nevertheless, much remains intact from Cyril's time and before.

The modern rite looks principally to infants, for whom some of the prayers and rubrics have been altered. Where the terms "children" or "infants" are used, however, they can be understood figuratively. The order has two divisions; the first has the catechumenate in view; the second, baptism proper. The Eucharist immediately follows. Crowning the newly baptized, although this has a long tradition in the Syrian rite of Mesopotamia, appears clearly here in Egypt for the first time, perhaps because of the influence of the Syrian Monophysites (called "Jacobites"). Although the order of baptism calls for inscription in the catechumenate, the renunciation, and profession of faith, space permits including only the rites in the baptistery.

The reading is based on the critical work, commentary, and translation of O. H. E. Burmester, "The Baptismal Rite of the Coptic Church: A Critical Study," *Bulletin de la societé d'archéologie Copte* 6 (1945) 27–80.

Consecration of the Baptismal Waters

The first rite in the baptistery is the consecration of the font (called "Jordan" in the ritual). The priest pours oil into the font in the form of the cross, saying: "In the name of the Father, and of the Son, and of the Holy Spirit," and prays that the candidates be made worthy of the grace of baptism, concluding, "Strip off from them the old man; beget them again for eternal life."

At this point the final remodeling of the rite calls for it to proceed in imitation of the Eucharistic liturgy, as noted above. Although it is difficult to untangle present gestures and actions from what may have earlier pertained, the prayers below are particularly redolent with ancient baptismal belief and teaching, reflecting pre-Cyril traditions.

At the sanctification of the baptismal waters the priest prostrates himself before the font and prays silently, "Send down from your holy heights your power; give me strength to perform this ministry of this great mystery which was first constituted in heaven; in your one only, holy, catholic, and apostolic church."

There follow three petitions, customary in the Eucharistic liturgy, and the creed, also customary there. In succession, oil is poured into the font, a prayer of exorcism is offered followed by a triple breathing on the waters in the form of a cross, while the priest says: "Hallow this water and this oil that they may become a laver of the new birth. Amen. Into life eternal. Amen. A garment of incorruption. Amen. A renewing of the Holy Spirit. Amen. For it was your only-begotten Son. . . . Go teach all nations, baptizing them [here the waters are signed with the cross three times] in the name of the Father and of the Son and of the Holy Spirit.''

The preface is then chanted followed by the *Sanctus,* followed in turn by a prayer recapitulating the ancient Egyptian tradition of baptismal teaching:

> Show forth yourself and look upon this your creature, this water; give it the grace of the Jordan, and the power and the strength of heaven; and by the descent of your Holy Spirit upon it, hallow it with the blessing of the Jordan. Amen. Give it power to become water of life. Amen. Holy water. Amen. Water washing away sins. Amen. Water of the bath of regeneration. Amen. Water of sonship. Amen. Grant to this water that there remain not in it, nor descend into it with him who is about to be baptized therein, any evil spirit, or any unclean spirit, or any spirit of the day, or any spirit of the noonday, or any spirit of the evening, or any spirit of the night, or any spirit of the air, or any diabolical spirit of those that are beneath the earth; but rebuke them in your power which is mighty, let them be crushed before the sign of your cross, and of your holy name which we invoke, and which is full of glory, and terrible to them that are against us. That they, who are about to be baptized therein, may put off the old man which is corruptible according to the deceitful lusts, and may put on the new man which shall be renewed again according to the image of him who created him.

The Lord's Prayer is then said, after which the priest offers three more prayers and then pours a little of the chrism into the font three times in the form of the cross.

Baptism

The ritual reads as follows:

> The deacon shall lead him who is to be baptized from the west [where they renounced Satan] and shall bring him to the east up to the Jordan [the font] to the left hand of the priest. The priest shall ask his name. Then he shall immerse him thrice, and at each immersion he shall raise him up and shall breathe upon his face, saying:
> At the first immersion: I baptize you, N., in the name of the Father.

At the second immersion: and of the Son.

At the third immersion: And of the Holy Spirit. Amen.

And when all have been baptized, the priest shall say the prayer for the de-consecration of the water.

Chrismation

The first postbaptismal rite is signing with chrism, blessed by the patriarch of Alexandria on Holy Thursday. It begins with a petition that God "bestow the Holy Spirit in the outpouring of the holy chrism." The current practice is thirty-six anointings, the last six of which are accompanied with the following form: "You, N., are anointed with holy oil in the name of the Father and of the Son and of the Holy Spirit. Amen."

The priest then imposes hands on the newly anointed, saying, "May you be blessed with the blessing of the holy ones [here he breathes on the face of the subject]. . . . Receive the Holy Spirit and be a purified vessel, through Jesus Christ our Lord."

The ritual concludes as follows:

Vesting in White

And after this, he shall clothe him that has been baptized in a white garment, and he shall say, "A garment of life eternal and incorruptible." Then the priest shall say a prayer over the crowns, and after this he shall gird the neophytes with a girdle in the form of the cross, and shall set the crown on each of them saying: "May you set, Master, Lord God, upon your servants crowns from heaven. Amen. Crowns of glory. Amen. Crowns of faith invincible and unconquerable. Amen. Crowns of strength. Amen. Crowns of righteousness. Amen."

Then he shall lay hands on them, saying the prayer, "Blessed are you, Lord God, Almighty, . . . who has made his servants worthy of the laver of regeneration, and of the forgiveness of sins . . . and the gift of your Holy Spirit . . . make them worthy of the Communion of the holy Body and of the precious Blood of your Christ."

Suggestions for Further Reading

Certain key studies are cited at the end of each chapter introduction and with the introduction of each author or work. Preference has been given to accessibility and to works in English. The following is a select general bibliography. The reader is also directed to standard reference works, especially dictionaries and encyclopedias, and in particular to Quasten, cited in the abbreviations.

Aland, Kurt. *Did the Early Church Baptize Infants?* Trans. G. Beasley-Murray. Philadelphia: Westminster Press, 1963.

Bedard, Walter M. *The Symbolism of the Baptismal Font in Early Christian Thought.* Studies in Sacred Theology 45, 2nd series. Washington: The Catholic University of America Press, 1951.

Collins, Adela Y. "The Origin of Christian Baptism," SL 19 (1989) 28–44.

Crehan, Joseph. *Early Christian Baptism and the Creed.* London: Burns & Oates, 1950.

Daniélou, Jean. *The Bible and the Liturgy.* Liturgical Studies 3. Notre Dame: Notre Dame University Press, 1956.

_____. *From Shadows to Reality: Studies in the Biblical Typology of the Fathers.* Westminster, Md.: Newman, 1960.

Davies, J. G. *The Architectural Setting of Baptism.* London: Barrie and Rockliff, 1962.

Dix, Gregory. *The Shape of the Liturgy.* New York: Seabury, 1982. First published in 1945.

Dujarier, Michael. *A History of the Catechumenate: The First Six Centuries.* Trans. Edward J. Haasl. Chicago: Sadlier, 1979.

Eliade, Mircea. *The Sacred and the Profane: The Nature of Religion.* New York: Harper & Row, 1959, reprinted 1961.

Every, George. *The Baptismal Sacrifice.* London, 1959.

Finn, Thomas M. *The Liturgy of Baptism in the Baptismal Instructions of St. John Chrysostom.* SCA 15. Washington: The Catholic University of America Press, 1967.

Fisher, John D. C. *Christian Initiation: Baptism in the Medieval West.* London: SPCK, 1965.

_____. *Confirmation Then and Now.* London: SPCK, 1978.

Gavin, Frank S. B. *The Jewish Antecedents of the Christian Sacraments.* London: SPCK, 1928; New York: Ktav, 1969.

Grant, Robert M. *Gnosticism and Early Christianity.* New York: Columbia University Press, 1959; New York: Harper & Row, Torchbook ed., 1966.

Jeremias, Joachim. *Infant Baptism in the First Four Centuries.* Trans. D. Cairns. Philadelphia: Westminster, 1962.

Kavanagh, Aidan, and others. *Initiation Theology.* Toronto: Anglican Book Centre, 1978.

_____. "The Origins and Reform of Confirmation." *St. Vladimir's Theological Quarterly* 33 (1989) 5–20.

_____. *The Shape of Baptism: The Rite of Christian Initiation.* New York: Pueblo, 1978.

Kelly, Henry Ansgar. *The Devil at Baptism: Ritual, Theology, and Drama.* Ithaca: Cornell University Press, 1985.

Lampe, G. W. H. *The Seal of the Spirit: A Study in the Doctrine of Baptism and Confirmation in the New Testament and the Fathers.* London: SPCK, 1976.

Made Not Born: New Perspectives on Christian Initiation and the Catechumenate. Notre Dame: (Murphy Center for Liturgical Research) University of Notre Dame Press, 1976.

Meyer, Martin W., ed. *The Ancient Mysteries: A Sourcebook.* San Francisco: Harper & Row, 1987.

Mitchell, Leonel L. *Baptismal Anointing.* London: SPCK, 1966.

Neunheuser, Burkhard. *Baptism and Confirmation.* Trans. John J. Hughes. New York: Herder and Herder, 1964.

Riley, Hugh M. *Christian Initiation: A Comparative Study of the Interpretation of the Baptismal Liturgy in the Mystagogical Writings of Cyril of Jerusalem, John Chrysostom, Theodore of Mopsuestia, and Ambrose of Milan.* SCA 17. Washington: The Catholic University of America Press, 1974.

Schmemann, Alexander. *Of Water and the Spirit: A Liturgical Study of Baptism.* New York: St. Vladimir's Seminary Press, 1974.

Talley, Thomas J. *The Origins of the Liturgical Year.* New York: Pueblo, 1986.

Thurian, Max, and Geoffrey Wainwright, eds., *Baptism and Eucharist: Ecumenical Convergence in Celebration.* Faith and Order Paper 117. Geneva, Switzerland/Grand Rapids, Michigan: World Council of Churches/Eerdmans, 1983.

Welles, Bradford, ed. *The Excavations at Dura-Europos: The Final Report VIII, Part I: The Christian Building.* New Haven: Dura-Europos Publications (distr. J. J. Augustin, Locust Valley, N.Y.) 1967.

Whitaker, Edward C. *The Baptismal Liturgy,* 2nd ed. London: SPCK, 1981.

_____. *Documents of the Baptismal Liturgy,* 2nd ed. London: SPCK, 1970.

Ysebaert, J. *Greek Baptismal Terminology.* Nijmegen: Dekker-van de Vegt, 1962.

Synoptic Table: The Fathers on Baptism and the Catechumenate		
Century	West Syria	East Syria
Second	*Didache* Melito of Sardis	*Odes of Solomon* *Gospel of Philip* *Acts of Judas* *Thomas*
Third	*Didascalia* *Apostolorum*	
Fourth	Cyril *Apostolic* *Constitutions* Gregory of Nyssa Chrysostom (Theodore of Mopsuestia)	Aphrahat Ephrem
Fifth	Theodore of Mopsuestia *Ordo of* *Constantinople* Dionysius the Pseudo- Areopagite	Narsai Jacob of Serugh *The Teaching* *of St. Gregory*
Sixth		
Note: A work or an author in parentheses means that work or author reflects the customs of the century even though the work or author is dated later.		

Italy	North Africa	Egypt
Shepherd of Hermas Justin Martyr Abercius *(Apostolic Tradition)*		*Excerpts of Theodotus* Clement
Apostolic Tradition Novatian	Tertullian Cyprian	Origen
Zeno Ambrose	Optatus	Serapion Didymus the Blind *Canons of Hippolytus*
Innocent I Leo the Great John the Deacon *Leonine Sacramentary*	Augustine	Cyril The Coptic Rite
(Gelasian Sacramentary)		

Index